CANADIAN–SOVIET RELATIONS BETWEEN THE WORLD WARS

Canadian–Soviet Relations between the World Wars

Aloysius Balawyder

University of Toronto Press

© University of Toronto Press 1972
Toronto and Buffalo

Printed in Canada
ISBN 0-8020-1768-1
Microfiche ISBN 0-8020-0073-8
LC 70-163802

Contents

Preface

In his bibliographical chapter, 'Selected Readings in Canadian External Policy, 1919–1959,' in *The Growth of Canadian Policies in External Affairs* (1960), Gaddis Smith remarked pointedly that 'a scholarly study of Canada's relations with Russia is sorely needed.' At the time he made this observation, Arthur Davies's *Canada and Russia, Neighbours and Friends* (1944) was the only publication available that dealt with Canadian-Russian relations. Smith referred to this work as 'slim' and 'journalistic' and 'mirroring the optimism of the wartime period.' A scholarly but equally brief treatment of Canadian-Soviet relations 1919–27 is found in Chapter VI of James Eayrs's *Northern Approaches* (1961).

The purpose of this book is to provide scholars and general readers with a long overdue reference work on Canadian-Soviet relations during the interwar years. This study shows how these relations were influenced by the following factors: the economic and foreign policies of Great Britain, the revolutionary policies of the Comintern, the economic pressures within Canada and the Soviet Union, and the political and ethnic-group pressures in Canada.

Canada's relations with Russia have been subsidiary, for the most part, to those of Great Britain with the Soviet Union. Up to 1927, when a Canadian minister was appointed to the United States, Canadian interests in other countries were represented by the British diplomatic service. During the decade beginning with World War I, Canada, as well as other British Dominions, gained wide control of her external policy. Prime Minister Robert Borden insisted during the war years that the Dominions should be consulted. The Imperial Conference of 1923 provided the Dominions with greater freedom in the negotiation, signing, and ratification of treaties. The Imperial Conference of 1926, besides amplifying and clarifying the decisions reached at the 1923 Imperial Conference, declared that all Dominions were 'equal in status' and 'in no way subordinate to one another' in respect to both domestic and external policies.

Russia also influenced Canadian-Soviet relations through the Comintern and the Communist party of Canada. Most European countries that had restored diplomatic ties with Moscow had experienced annoying interference from the Comintern in both their internal and foreign affairs. The Comintern was obviously determined to create new Soviet republics in Europe, Asia, and America by instigating revolutions, even at the time when the Soviet government was negotiating new treaties.

Canadian-Soviet relations were motivated primarily by commercial considerations. Canada, a leading trading nation, attempted to foster trade with any country that was willing to exchange goods with her, while the Soviet Union, first in the throes of the New Economic Policy and then under the five-year plans, was determined to obtain adequate credits to buy necessary industrial and agricultural equipment.

The years covered in this study correspond roughly with the interwar period. Canada's intervention in Russia during 1918–19 has been ably researched and recorded by such scholars as James Eayrs, G.W.L. Nicholson, John Swettenham, and Steuart Beattie. Chapter x on the Comintern and the Communist party of Canada does not pretend to be a history of either of these movements, but does serve to throw further light on relations between Ottawa and Moscow.

Research for this work began as a thesis, which was submitted to McGill University in partial fulfilment for a doctorate in history. Since that time the manuscript has been substantially revised and somewhat lengthened to include the years 1936–9.

The generous assistance of many people has made it possible for me to carry through this work. I am grateful to my mentor, Professor M. Mladenovic, for supervising my thesis and for encouraging me in further research. Thanks are due as well to Dean F.H. Soward, dean emeritus of the graduate school of the University of British Columbia, the late Norman Robertson, former under-secretary of state for External Affairs, 1941–6, 1958–63, and Professor William Rodney of the Royal Military College, Victoria, BC, for conscientiously reading the manuscript and for pointing out areas where revisions, deletions, and additions should be

made. I wish to record my sincere appreciation to John Holmes, director
of the Canadian Institute of International Affairs, for encouraging me to
revise the thesis for publication and for finding readers for the manuscript.

I am indebted also to Dr G. Gunn, chief librarian of the Harriet Irving
Library at the University of New Brunswick, for giving me full access
to the Bennett Papers; to G.W. Hilborn, the assistant head of the Historical Division of the Department of External Affairs, for much appreciated assistance in getting access to the governor general's numerated files
and Department of External Affairs files; to the staffs of the National
Library, Ottawa, the Redpath Library at McGill, the Columbia University Library, and the New York Public Library for their courteous and
efficient help. In my work, my wife, Marty, has been a constant source of
encouragement.

The research for this study was made possible by the Quebec Provincial
Scholarship and by Saint Francis Xavier University Council for Research
grant. This book has been published with the help of a grant from the
Social Science Research Council of Canada, using funds provided by the
Canada Council. The editing process has been made rather painless under
the able direction of R.I.K. Davidson and by the efficiency and patience
of Gertrude Stevenson, both of the University of Toronto Press.

CANADIAN–SOVIET RELATIONS BETWEEN THE WORLD WARS

CHAPTER ONE

Trade and Canada's Intervention in Northern Russia and Siberia

Relations between Canada and Russia during World War 1 were almost entirely commercial except for the military intervention which began prior to Armistice Day and continued during the first half of 1919. During the war Russia placed large orders for war materials, including rifles, ammunition, saddles, and railroad cars. Trade increased to such an extent that by the end of 1916 the Canadian government felt that a Russian trade commissioner should be appointed by Petrograd to facilitate commerce.[1]

The Russians responded favourably to this request and the Russian consul general in Montreal informed Ottawa in January 1917 that the Russian government had asked the Russian purchasing commission of the United States to investigate all means that would help to increase trade between Canada and Russia.[2] A month later Lieutenant-General A. Zaluboffsky, the president of the Russian supply committee in the United States, informed Prime Minister Borden that 'Colonel Kovaleff [had] been deputed to the Dominion of Canada for the purpose of representing the Imperial Government in all matters relating to the purchase of war material for Russia.'[3] The minister of trade and commerce, Sir George

---

1 Robert Borden to George Perley, 9 Jan. 1917, Borden Papers, oc 244(2), Public Archives of Canada [hereafter referred to as PAC], Ottawa.
2 Russian consul to Borden, 9 Jan., no. 27323, ibid.
3 A. Zaluboffsky to Borden, 6 Feb. 1917, no. 27326, ibid.

Foster, assured Zaluboffsky that the Canadian government would co-operate with Colonel Kovaleff in every possible way.[4]

Kovaleff arrived in Canada a few days before the outbreak of the February revolution in Russia, but the advent of the provisional government did not significantly alter Canadian-Russian relations. Indeed it augured an increase in commerce, for the Canadian government looked upon the provisional government with hopeful eyes. A considerable amount of credit for uninterrupted and growing trade was due to the work of the Russian commission under the leadership of Kovaleff.

In October 1917 the powers of the commission were extended to include the technical aspects of an exchange scheme. N.P. Iampolsky, the chief engineer attached to the Russian commission, approached the Canadian government for information on the mining and refining of nickel – skills for which Canada had a high reputation.[5] Reportedly, the Russian government hoped to improve the content and the production of nickel mined in the Ural Mountains, with a view to aiding the war effort. However, this project failed to materialize, for the Bolsheviks overthrew the existing provisional government under Kerensky on 6 November, and established a Soviet form of government, first in Petrograd and later in other major sections of the country.

The Bolshevik coup alarmed and bewildered the Allies who looked upon Lenin and his followers with growing distrust. The Allies knew that he planned to negotiate a separate treaty with the Germans and thus eliminate the Eastern front. In some circles he was regarded as a German agent, for his Communist activities, including his transportation to Petrograd, were rumoured to have been financed by the German government.[6]

It is not surprising, therefore, that the British Treasury asked the Canadian government to stop further shipment of goods to Russia.[7] It was feared that some of these supplies would aid the enemies' cause. Shipments of approximately 45,000 tons of material, 31,700 tons of which were railroad

4 G. Foster to A. Zaluboffsky, 10 Feb. 1917, no. 27329, ibid.
5 N.P. Iampolsky to Borden, 6 Oct. 1917, no. 27340, ibid.
6 John M. Thompson, *Russia, Bolshevism, and the Versailles Peace* (Princeton, 1966), p. 27.
7 British Treasury to Borden, 30 Nov. 1918, no. 27350, Borden Papers, oc 244(1), PAC, Ottawa.

cars from the Canadian Car Company, were to be held in abeyance until further notice.[8]

In the meantime, the British ambassador in Washington approached the United States government to discover if it had any objections to a temporary detention in Canada of American supplies en route to Russia. The United States government informed the British authorities that it did not object to the 'temporary suspension in Canada of American supplies destined for Russia provided that they [were] not involved in any expense by detention.'[9] Canada, however, was not prepared to guarantee such an arrangement. Consequently, American goods, including valuable submarine parts, were placed on board the ship *Key West*. At the same time the Canadian customs commissioner in Vancouver felt that Canadian agricultural equipment and wood-working machinery should also be placed on board ship, for they were not materials classified as 'other supplies' mentioned in a telegram of 30 November, which prohibited the shipment of railroad cars to Russia.[10] Consequently, the American submarine parts, along with the Canadian agricultural supplies, were shipped to Vladivostok six weeks after the outbreak of the Bolshevik Revolution. This equipment was exposed to the elements and was one of the main objects protected by the Canadian Expeditionary Force.

The Allies followed with anxiety the events that transpired in Russia. They realized that a relatively small group of well-disciplined Bolsheviks had gained control of Russia illegally. Admittedly, Lenin did call an election on 25 November 1917, to give an impression of democracy. Actually, of the total votes cast for the members of the Constituent Assembly, only 25 per cent were for the Bolsheviks, compared with 60 per cent for the Social Revolutionaries and 13 per cent for the Liberals and Conservatives.[11] Realizing the danger of convening such an assembly, the executive committee of the Congress of the Soviets dissolved it, and posted guards at the door of the assembly building to prevent any of the deputies from returning.

The new Soviet government attempted to rule by decree. Numerous

8 Ibid.
9 Secretary of state to British ambassador, 19 Dec. 1917, nos. 27360–61, ibid.
10 Ibid.
11 John Swettenham, *Allied Intervention in Russia, 1918–1919; and the Part Played by Canada* (Toronto, 1967), p. 26.

laws were passed uprooting social institutions, confiscating church lands, forbidding the teaching of religion in schools, and nationalizing banks. Private ownership of property was forbidden. Such drastic social changes coupled with the illegal seizure of power galvanized the opposition groups. The Don area, the Ukraine, and Finland proved to be the most vehement enemies of the Bolsheviks. Initially, Siberia, Central, and Northern Russia accepted Bolshevik rule without too much resistance. In late 1918 and early 1919 these areas became the battlegrounds of the White and Red armies, and underwent the intervention of the Allies.

By aiding the anti-Bolshevik forces the Allies hoped to re-establish an Eastern front. The signing of the Treaty of Brest-Litovsk on 15 March 1918 made it possible for Germany to withdraw more of her troops from the Eastern front and hurl them against the Allies on the Western front. Not only were the Germans in a position to increase their forces on the Western front, they were also able to obtain urgently needed raw material and food for the successful prosecution of the war.[12] Although the chaotic conditions prevented Germany from carrying out an orderly exploitation of Russian natural resources, they did not prevent the Germans from securing enough material to prolong the fighting against the Allies.[13]

Understandably, the Supreme Allied Council attempted to lessen the wholesale seizure of Russian minerals and food supplies by the Germans. To prevent such spoliation of resources, the Allies realized the importance of winning the confidence of the Russians. Consequently, they provided Russia with technical assistance and increased their trade with her. As a sign of goodwill medical supplies and food were distributed among the Russian peoples.

The Bolsheviks responded favourably to these generous tokens of friendship. They even invited the Allies to send troops and equipment to Murmansk to prevent it from falling into the hands of the Germans. Consequently, in April 1918 British marines (initially 150, but increased by 370 in May) landed in Murmansk. Furthermore, the Murmansk authorities requested the help of the British naval commander, Rear-Admiral Thomas

12 David Lloyd George, *War Memoirs of David Lloyd George* (Boston, 1933–7), vol. IV, 313–14, vol. V, 123, vol. VI, 161.
13 Erich von Ludendorff, *Ludendorff's Own Story* (New York, 1919), vol. II, 127–9.

Kemp, and placed three Russian destroyers at his disposal. Admittedly, the British were happy to strengthen the northern ports of Murmansk and Archangel, for they feared that the German army of 55,000 men stationed in Finland under General von der Goltz might seize these ports and menace allied shipping.

The threat of a German invasion and the hope of recreating the Eastern front convinced the allied ambassadors and military representatives in Russia that a larger military intervention was necessary. It was felt that some of the 35,000 members of the Czecho-Slovak Corps, who were attempting to reach France in time to participate on the Western front, might form the major portion of the Eastern front. The Supreme War Council deliberated on the recommendations of the ambassadors and the military representatives, and on 3 June 1918 sanctioned the dispatch of a military expedition to the North to bolster the forces already there.[14]

Two expeditionary forces were organized for northern Russia. The 'Syren' under Major-General C.C.M. Maynard was destined for Murmansk and the 'Elope' under the command of Major-General F.C. Poole was to be dispatched to Archangel. The British War Office inquired whether or not Canada would contribute to the 'Elope' force. Sir Edward Kemp, the Canadian overseas minister in London, informed the British authorities on 27 May that Canada was prepared to make available for overseas service five officers and eleven NCOs who were currently stationed in England.[15] The contingent sailed for Russia in June.

On 12 July 1918 Canada was asked to contribute an infantry battalion to the 'Syren' force, but declined because Canadians were needed for the Western theatre.[16] However, she did heed the demand of 30 July 1918 and contributed eighteen officers and seventy NCOs to the 'Syren' group to serve as instructors and administrators.

This was not the last request made by Great Britain, asking Canadians to serve in northern Russia. Because the United States failed to include artillery in the Archangel force, on 3 August Canada was approached about providing two batteries. Ottawa acceded to this request and agreed to

14 Leonid I. Strakhovsky, *Intervention at Archangel* (Princeton, 1944), p. 2.
15 Swettenham, *Allied Intervention*, p. 52.
16 A.E. Kemp to Borden, 1 Aug. 1918, Borden Papers, OC 518(1).

form the 67th and 68th batteries from the 16th Brigade of the Canadian Field Artillery. The two batteries, consisting of 469 men under the command of Lt.-Col. C.H.L. Sharmon, left Dundee for Archangel on 20 September.

The Supreme War Council clearly specified that the allied forces in Russia were 'to aid the Czecho-Slovaks and the patriotic elements of the Russian people' in their fight against German intrigue and 'to help reconstitute an eastern front against Germany and Austria.'[17] Significantly, the object of defeating the Bolsheviks was not mentioned by the War Council.

However, after the signing of the Treaty of Brest-Litovsk on 15 March 1918, the formal relations between the Bolsheviks and the Allies were altered. Under pressure from the German government the Soviet authorities at Petrograd demanded that the Allies leave northern Russia. A little later Trotsky, then Soviet commissar for war, cabled the Soviet council at Murmansk asking it to eject the Allies by force of arms.[18]

The Allies considered the ports of Murmansk and Archangel of strategic importance and, therefore, were ready to defend them from both German and Bolshevik attacks. But the defence of these two cities depended upon the firm control of the transportation systems south of them. The 67th Battery was detailed to the Dvina River and the 68th to Shenkursk, the most southerly of the defended towns on the Vaga River.

Hostilities ceased on the Western front on 11 November, but the Canadian artillery on the Dvina River experienced some of the most bitter fighting of the war. Although the Allied armies were outnumbered by the Bolshevik forces and the Canadian batteries outranged by the Bolshevik guns, the Allies were able to force the Bolsheviks to retreat. The Canadian artillery fought well, winning one Military Cross, three Distinguished Conduct Medals, and three Military Medals.[19] Two Canadians and ten Royal Scots were killed in this engagement.

In October 1918 Canada, along with Great Britain, France, the United

17 'Statement of the Canadian Government re Canadian Expeditionary Force,'
    18 Jan. 1919, no. 12176, ibid.
18 Major-General Sir C. Maynard, *The Murmansk Adventure* (London, 1927), p. 3.
19 Colonel G.W.L. Nicholson, *Canadian Expeditionary Force, 1914–1919*
    (Ottawa, 1962), p. 515.

States, and Japan, became involved in a Siberian intervention. Like the objectives of the Allies in northern Russia, the aims of the interventionists in Siberia included the opening of an eastern front and the safeguarding of war supplies in Vladivostok. Some military officials felt that unless an eastern front were opened soon there would be little chance for the Allies to secure a victory in 1919.[20] Even if the Allies did succeed in defeating Russia early in 1919, intervention was necessary to rehabilitate the war-torn country.[21] It was felt also that the one million German and Hungarian prisoners freed by the Treaty of Brest-Litovsk might make it exceedingly difficult for the Russians to restore order in their country.

Perhaps one of the most cogent arguments for the Allied intervention was the protection of the Czecho-Slovak Corps which was trying desperately to reach Vladivostok to obtain transport from there to the Western front. Initially the Bolsheviks had permitted the Corps to cross their country. Under pressure from the German government the Bolshevik leaders ordered the Czechs to be partially disarmed. They then were permitted only a limited number of weapons for defensive purposes. Increasing interference in their transportation occurred as the Bolsheviks planted one of their representatives on each of the trains carrying the Czech soldiers. Moreover, the Bolsheviks attempted to coerce the Czechs to join the Red Guard.[22]

The already strained relations between the Bolsheviks and the Czechs erupted into open hostility as a result of an incident which happened on 16 May. A Hungarian prisoner of war returning by train to eastern Europe severely injured a Czech soldier who was standing on a platform at Cheliabinsk. Immediately the Czechs dragged the Hungarian out of the train and killed him. Following this arbitrary act of justice, the local Soviet government arrested several Czechs who were supposedly connected with the execution of the Hungarian. In turn, a Czech delegation marched into the town demanding the release of its compatriots. When this deputation was also arrested, the Czechs convened a military council in order to decide what steps should be taken.

20 'A Detailed Military Agreement with Regard to Allied Intervention in Siberia,'
    War Office, 19 June 1918, PAC Records Centre, Ottawa.
21 Ibid.
22 Swettenham, *Allied Intervention*, p. 92.

In the meantime, upon learning of the events that had transpired at Cheliabinsk, Trotsky called upon the Czecho-Slovaks to give up their remaining arms, a proposal that they rejected. Then on 21 May he asked them to create a trade union organization and to enter the Red Army. This request also was rejected. On 25 May he demanded that they be entirely disarmed or face execution if the order was not obeyed.[23]

The Allies were concerned about the change of Bolshevik attitude towards the Czecho-Slovaks. A definite danger arose that the Czecho-Slovak Corps might be dispersed or imprisoned. The chances of using this well-disciplined unit to help create an eastern front or to fight on the Western front would be eliminated. At a meeting held in July the Supreme War Council decided that intervention was necessary to save this Corps. The council agreed that a force adequate in numbers, military in character, and allied in composition would be needed. The bulk of the force was to consist of Japanese, although American, British, and French forces were also to be represented. The Japanese were willing to send a contingent to Siberia provided the United States would do likewise.[24]

President Wilson of the United States, however, was not easily convinced that such intervention was in the best interest of America and of the Russian peoples. He felt that it was up to the Russians themselves to solve their own problems and determine their own government. At the same time he sympathized with the plight of the Czecho-Slovaks whose democratic spirit he admired. It was in order to help this stranded unit reach Vladivostok and to protect it from outside attack that he finally decided to despatch 7,000 men to Siberia. The British agreed to send an equal number, whereas the Japanese were willing to field some 71,000 soldiers. Since the Japanese force was the largest, General Kikuzo Otani of Japan was put in charge of the combined allied forces.

On 9 July, the same day the American secretary of state informed the British, French, and Italian ambassadors of his government's decision to send troops to Siberia, the War Office sought the views of Borden regarding the availability of Canadians for overseas service. British forces were sadly depleted by the continuous demands for reinforcements to bolster the Allied armies against the German offensive. From previous overtures the British

23 Ibid., p. 93.
24 'Allied Intervention in Siberia and Russia,' 2 July 1918, PAC Records Centre, Ottawa.

government was led to believe that two battalions of discharged soldiers could be raised in Canada without diverting too many troops from the Western front.[25]

The new request was given serious consideration by both Borden and General S.C. Mewburn, the minister of militia, who were in London at this time. Borden visualized the possibility of a flourishing trade if and when friendly relations were established between Ottawa and the provisional government in Siberia. The Canadian prime minister felt that the Canadian Expeditionary Force might not only protect the Czecho-Slovak Corps against attacks from German-Hungarian prisoners of war and safeguard the huge war supplies at Vladivostok, but also might help the Canadian economic mission investigate the possibility of trade in Siberia.[26]

Obviously Borden was dazzled by the economic factors when he agreed to dispatch a contingent to Siberia. Since the beginning of the war he had received promising reports from business firms and individuals regarding the potentialities of the north-east Asian market.[27] Perhaps one of the most convincing reports came from C.J. Just, the Canadian trade commissioner at Petrograd.

In his memorandum of 29 August 1918, mailed to Sir George Foster, minister of trade and commerce, Just elaborated on the decided benefits that might result from an organized economic mission to Siberia.[28] In the first place he pointed out that both the United States and Great Britain were proposing similar missions with the aim of stabilizing the political and economic conditions in Siberia. This aim might not be too difficult to achieve, for Siberia had not been as seriously affected by the Bolshevik doctrines as had other parts of Russia. At the same time Just observed that the Allies' interest in fostering trade and stabilizing the government of Siberia would not interfere with the national aspirations of the Russian people.

Then the memorandum went into considerable detail on the nature of the assistance Canada could render. Among the most important items

25 Director of military operations (Major-General P. de B. Radcliffe) to N. D. Rowell, president of the Privy Council, 9 July 1918, Borden Papers, oc 518(1).
26 Borden to S.C. Mewburn, 13 Aug. 1918, ibid.
27 Mackenzie, Mann & Co. Ltd. to Borden, 27 Jan. 1915, Borden Papers, RLB, Joseph Pope to Borden, 19 Aug. 1918, RLB, ibid.
28 'Economic Mission to Siberia,' C.J. Just to George E. Foster, 29 Aug. 1918, Foster Papers, PAC, Ottawa.

needed by the Russians were rolling stock, locomotives, river craft, tractors, dairy equipment, flour mills, grain elevators, roadmaking machinery, pulp and paper equipment, chemicals, small hardware, and lumbering equipment. Moreover, Canadian technicians could be sent to Siberia to advise the Russians on some of the new techniques in salmon canning, in lumbering, and in the mining of gold, iron, coal, and copper. Finally, illustrated manuals on methods used by Canadian industries, agriculture, and grain storage firms could be invaluable to the people of Siberia and at the same time aid in lessening the influence of German culture by replacing German scientific journals and books with Canadian ones.

The memorandum reminded the minister of trade and commerce that there were many millions of dollars worth of products accumulated at Vladivostok awaiting transportation. It suggested that the stored material, composed of hides, skins, furs, and soya beans, could be carried on ships which would bring Canadian troops to Siberia. Just intimated that the trade could be carried out by federal, provincial, or municipal governments. It could also be transacted through such reputable firms as the British Engineering Company of Russia and Siberia or by the Martens Company, an American foreign trade company with branches in Britain, France, and Russia.

R. Martens of the Martens Company also urged the minister of trade and commerce to establish an economic commission to investigate the possibilities of trade in Siberia. In a relatively long letter Martens suggested that the commission should have an agricultural expert, a mining specialist, an individual knowledgeable in financial matters, and another well-versed in the problems of transportation. Both D. Wilgress and C.J. Just were mentioned as Canadian government officials who, because of their knowledge of the problems of Russia, could advise the commission on the most suitable policy to be followed.

Martens then outlined the duties of various members of the commission. The transportation expert must have an adequate knowledge of both water and rail transportation since Siberia possessed many navigable rivers. The mining specialist should be an expert in coal mining, one of the main industries of the far eastern country. As far as agriculture was concerned, Martens suggested that the Dominion Experimental Farm in Ottawa could supply a qualified agricultural expert who would be familiar with both grain growing and animal husbandry. The financial member of the commission ought to be an authority on foreign exchange.[29]

The Canadian government did form the economic commission suggested by Just and Martens. An order-in-council of 21 October 1918 outlined the objectives of the commission as follows: (a) to make a careful study of local [Siberian] conditions, both social and economic; (b) to enquire into the facilities for transportation both by land and water, and the equipment needs of the same; (c) to ascertain the wants of the farming community in respect to agricultural machinery, tools, and equipment of all kinds; (d) to enquire into the current financial arrangements of credits; (e) to investigate the opportunities, present and prospective, for increasing commercial interchange between Russia and Canada and the particular line by which Canadian experience and industry might best contribute to the rehabilitation of Russian business activities and the development of her vast natural resources.[30]

After the order-in-council was passed the Canadian government appointed the members of the commission and detailed their duties. C.F. Just and L.D. Wilgress, members of the Department of Trade and Commerce, who opened a trade commissioner's office in Vladivostok in August 1918, were assigned the task of studying the possibility of trade markets in Siberia. R. Owen, the general agent of the Canadian Pacific Railways in Russia, and Colonel J.S. Dennis, chairman of the commission, were to serve not only as transportation directors of the Canadian Expeditionary Force, but were also to investigate the problems of future trade with Siberia. L. Kon, a Pole who spoke Russian fluently, served as secretary. A.D. Braithwaite, the former assistant general manager of the Bank of Montreal, was to examine the banking arrangements existing in Siberia. C.J. Just assisted him in this task.[31] Wilgress, Just, and Owen were in Russia at the time of their appointment, whereas Colonel Dennis and Kon arrived by the S.S. *Monteagle*, the ship that carried the second Canadian contingent of troops. Braithwaite sailed on the S.S. *Japan*, arriving at Vladivostok on 27 February 1919.

Just believed that, since most of the commissioned and non-commis-

29 R. Martens to Sir George Foster, 8 Oct. 1918, ibid.
30 'Order-in-Council, October 21, 1918,' Report of the Canadian Economic Commission (Siberia), 27 June 1919, Department of Trade and Commerce, Ottawa.
31 *Dana Wilgress Memoirs* (Toronto, 1967), pp. 52, 53.

sioned officers of the Canadian Expeditionary Force were drawn from various ranks of the commercial and industrial classes, they would be experienced and intelligent enough to aid the Economic Commission with its work. He suggested that the officers might make reports to the Canadian trade commissioner or to the Canadian Board of Enquiry on observations they might have made or on suggestions they might wish to offer regarding the districts over which they held jurisdiction.[32]

But the Canadian contingents, whose officers were to aid the Economic Commission, had difficulties of their own. The advance force of 680 officers and men under the command of General J.H. Elmsley arrived at Vladivostok on 26 October to discover that friction existed among the Allies and that general apathy prevailed among the Russians. Elmsley describes his impressions of the existing conditions in a letter to Major-General S.C. Mewburn, the Canadian minister of militia and defence:

The general situation here is an extraordinary one. At the first glance one assumes that everyone distrusts everyone else ... the Japs being distrusted *more* than anyone else. Americans and Japs don't hit it off. The French keep a very close eye on the British and the Russians as a whole appear to be indifferent to their country's needs, so long as they can keep their women, have their vodka and play cards all night until daylight. The Czechs appear to be the only honest and conscientious party among the allies.[33]

More than three thousand troops were to follow the advance force, but at the signing of the armistice there were growing demands by groups and individuals for a complete termination of Canada's involvement in Siberia. Three days after the armistice Sir Thomas White, the acting prime minister, wrote Borden who was attending the Imperial War Cabinet meeting in London, that public opinion would 'not sustain [the Government] in continuing to send troops many of whom are draftees under Military Service Act and Order-in-Council, [now] that the war is ended.'[34] In addition, White pressed for the return of the soldiers who were already in Siberia.

32 'Memorandum of Just to Sir George Foster, October 9, 1918,' Foster Papers.
33 J.H. Elmsley to S.C. Mewburn, 2 Nov. 1918, nos. 12123–24, N.W. Rowell Papers (MG 27 11), PAC, Ottawa.
34 White to Borden, 14 Nov. 1918, Borden Papers, 518.

Borden's reply on 20 November attempted to show that Great Britain did not intend to commit British or Canadian forces in an offensive campaign. He argued that the presence of Canadian forces would have an important stabilizing influence on Siberia by preventing anarchy there. Moreover, Canadians could assist the training of White armies of the anti-Bolshevik government which had been set up at Omsk under Admiral A.V. Kolchak. In summary, Borden favoured not only the retention of Canadian forces already in Siberia but also the immediate dispatch of the forces that were still in Canada.[35]

The Canadian government, on the other hand, was firmly opposed to any further transportation of soldiers to Siberia.[36] Borden, however, maintained that Canada had made definite commitments to the Allies and consequently her refusal to honour these commitments would impair her 'present position and prestige.' Furthermore, he pointed out that the draftees sent to Siberia should have much less to complain about than those sent to France, for the former would not be engaged in combat. After presenting all these arguments, he felt that it was up to the Privy Council and not up to him to decide what should be done in this situation.[37]

White emphasized that such council members as A.S. Ballantyne, T.A. Crerar, J.A. Calder, and J.F. Reid were strongly opposed to the continuation of the intervention. In addition, he argued that public opinion would not support further involvement in Russian affairs since the cessation of hostilities on the Western front made such involvement unnecessary. He observed that Britain and France were driven by selfish motives in their policy of continued intervention, for a stable government in Siberia could mean the settlement of war debts incurred by the Czarist government, but he did not see what economic benefits Canada could derive from such a government.[38]

Borden advised White that he would discuss the whole question of the Siberian expedition with the director of military operations, Major-General P. de B. Radcliffe, a former brigadier-general, general staff, of the Canadian Corps, at the War Office. Reportedly, the British were rather sympathetic to Canada's problem. They felt, however, that if it were neces-

35 Borden to White, 20 Nov. 1918, ibid.   36 White to Borden, 22 Nov. 1918, ibid.
37 Borden to White, 24 Nov. 1918, ibid.   38 White to Borden, 25 Nov. 1918, ibid.

sary to withdraw the Canadian forces, then at least Canada could contribute substantially towards the Allied cause by leaving General Elmsley and his staff, along with fifty to one hundred instructors, with the British forces to serve as instructors.[39] Curiously enough the Privy Council rejected this request for a mere handful of Canadian troops and, instead, sanctioned the dispatch of the remaining soldiers as originally planned, provided that the personnel be permitted to return to Canada within one year of the signing of the armistice.[40]

But no sooner had the council agreed to send the troops than it began to have second thoughts regarding its decision. The council was particularly concerned over the clash of interests between the Americans and the Japanese. The Americans were refusing to move farther inland towards Omsk and the Japanese, bent 'on commercial penetration,' were subsidizing insurgent elements.[41] White also pointed out that labour groups and friends of the draftees were putting pressure on the government for the return of Canadians. He wanted Borden to take up the matter with the British War Office.[42]

Understandably, both Borden and the British War Office were exasperated with the vacillation of the Canadian government. The British were already irritated by the council's refusal to permit Canadian troops to move inland. Consequently, the British War Office decided to have the two British battalions attached to the Canadian Expeditionary Force withdrawn from Omsk to Vladivostok and wired the Canadians en route to Siberia to return home.[43]

No steps were taken by Ottawa, however, to stop the Canadians and the 2700 men arrived on 5 January 1919 in Vladivostok, where the men and officers were quartered in Russian barracks some twelve miles from the harbour.[44] Except for a small staff consisting of Lieutenant-Colonel T.S. Morrisey and forty-four of all ranks who were sent to Omsk to administer the Hampshire and Middlesex battalions, the bulk of the Canadian Expeditionary Force was stationed in Vladivostok.[45]

39 Borden to White, 27 Nov. 1918, ibid.   40 White to Borden, 18 Nov. 1918, ibid.
41 White to Borden, 6 Dec. 1918, ibid.   42 White to Borden, 7 Dec. 1918, ibid.
43 Borden to White, 9 Dec. 1918, ibid.
44 Nicholson, *Canadian Expeditionary Force*, p. 522.
45 Swettenham, *Allied Intervention*, p.173.

The Canadian forces were relatively comfortable there: the climate was similar to that of eastern Canada; the soldiers were entertained by artists drawn from the refugee population; and some of them engaged themselves in voluntary auxiliary services, working for the Canadian Red Cross and the Young Men's Christian Association. Occasionally some took part in organized sports, playing baseball with the Americans and football with the crews of the British vessels.

The only other activity that promised excitement to the Canadian soldiers was their dispatch on 12 April 1919 to Shkotova, some thirty miles north of Vladivostok, where, along with detachments of Italian, French, and Japanese troops, they were to engage some Bolshevik insurgents. When the allied soldiers arrived the Bolsheviks retreated. The soldiers remained in the vicinity of Shkotova for a week and then returned, somewhat dejected, to Vladivostok. Their disappointment was tempered when the commander-in-chief, General Otani, entertained them with ninety-six bottles of wine, eighteen bottles of whisky and three casks of saké.[46]

But such entertainment did not dispel the troops' resentment of their conscription for overseas service. According to the Toronto *Globe* (28 December 1918) some 60–70 per cent of the men sent to Siberia went unwillingly, believing that Canada should not interfere in the affairs of Russia. The *Manitoba Free Press* (8 January 1919) held that there was no enthusiasm for overseas duty because the objectives of the Allies remained obscure.

Labour groups and some individuals demanded the return of the Canadian soldiers. A meeting held at the Walker Theatre in Winnipeg on 22 December 1918, under the joint auspices of the Trades and Labour Council and the Socialist party of Canada, asked for the withdrawal of troops from Russia.[47] Similarly, a meeting of workers in Morricetown, British Columbia, requested that the Canadian government withdraw the Canadian Siberian Expeditionary Force.[48] Trades and labour councils adopted resolutions demanding that 'Canadian troops now in Siberia

46 Ibid., p. 177.
47 See *Dominion Law Reports* (Toronto, 1920), vol. 51, 24.
48 Labour Hall, Morricetown, BC, to the Department of Justice, 8 Jan. 1919, *Siberian Records*, PAC, Ottawa.

and Western Russia be immediately withdrawn, also that all troops being mobilized in Canada to invade Russia be immediately demobilized.'[49]

Other influences were changing Borden's attitude towards continuing intervention in Siberia. The Economic Commission sent with the Canadian Expeditionary Force was rather pessimistic about the possibility of trade with Siberia. The transportation system there seemed to be hopelessly chaotic. Consequently, the Canadian government decided to entrust most Canadian trade interests to the Siberian Supply Company which had the backing of the British government.[50]

Among a few British members of Parliament, led by Winston Churchill, there was a strong feeling which seemed to favour military intervention in the Russian affair at the time when Borden hoped to withdraw completely from Russia. In the opinion of Churchill, the Bolsheviks under Lenin had usurped the power in Russia. He believed it was the duty of the Allies to restore democracy in that country even if it involved the use of force.[51]

Prime Minister Lloyd George did not agree with Churchill. He argued that the invasion would merely unite all dissident groups, as was the case in the French Revolution. Lloyd George supported Borden, who suggested a conference of representatives of the Red and the White Russians together with representatives from the Allied countries. The Allied leaders to the Versailles conference approved this proposal.

The proposed meeting was to take place in Prinkipo on the Sea of Marmora on 15 February. The invitation to the Bolshevik government specified that the Allies were prepared to enter into discussion regarding the Russian problem provided that all factions in Russia suspended their hostilities. The Bolsheviks in a conciliatory spirit promised to recognize the financial obligations incurred by the Czarist government but were not willing to provide assurances that all hostilities would be suspended. The leading Russian White leaders, Kolchak and Denikin, indignantly rejected the invitation on the grounds that they refused to confer on an equal basis with 'traitors, murderers and robbers.' Clearly the atmosphere

49 Quoted in the *Manitoba Free Press*, 6 Dec. 1918.
50 *Dana Wilgress Memoirs*, p. 55.
51 Michael G. Fry, 'Britain, The Allies and the Problem of Russia, 1918–1919,'
   Can. J. History, 1968, vol. II, no. 2, 72.

was too strained for an amicable meeting of the various Russian factions and the conference did not take place.[52]

Borden, who would have been the chief British delegate at the conference, acted in the spirit of its initiation by suggesting that the Canadian government withdraw her troops from Siberia and demobilize those awaiting transportation from Vancouver. The telegram notifying Great Britain of Canada's intention specified the evident lack of co-operation among the Allies and the uncertainty of their objectives as the main reasons for the Canadian government's decision to withdraw from Russia.[53]

Understandably, Churchill, the secretary of state for war and air, and Balfour, the British foreign secretary, felt that the evacuation of the Canadian forces would enable the Bolsheviks to take complete control of Russia. At the same time these British statesmen maintained that the British government had 'no option but to acquiesce' to the demands of the Canadian government, for it was 'impossible to continue to urge ... [Ottawa] to share against its will in a task of much difficulty and anxiety.'[54]

The first Canadian contingent left Vladivostok on 21 April 1919, and the last on 5 June. Following the departure of the first group Churchill made one final appeal to Borden whom he asked for volunteers to 'provide a small contingent for action both in relieving [the British] in North Russia and participating in [Britain's] mission to Admiral Kolchak.'[55] A few volunteers did remain with the British units, but these left Siberia in the fall of 1919 when Great Britain withdrew her forces.

Because the Canadians had departed from Siberia, Borden insisted that those in northern Russia also be withdrawn. In March 1919, the British War Office promised Ottawa that Canadian forces at Archangel would be withdrawn as soon as the port was open for navigation, but on 30 April Borden was informed that they could not leave until late summer or autumn. On 18 May Borden sent a strongly worded letter to

52 Robert W. Sellen, 'The British Intervention in Russia, 1917–1920,' *Dalhousie Review*, vol. 40 (1960–61), 52.
53 Governor General to the Colonial Secretary, 25 Jan. 1919, Borden Papers, OC 518(1).
54 Churchill to Borden, 17 March 1919, ibid.
55 Churchill to Borden, 1 May 1919, ibid.

Churchill emphasizing that 'the demobilization of the Canadian Corps and the withdrawal of Canadian troops from Siberia render any further continuance of [Canada's] forces at Archangel absolutely impracticable,' and pointed out that the port of Archangel was now open to navigation.[56]

The British complied with Borden's urgent request as they relieved the 16th Field Brigade by two brigades, each with a battery of howitzers. The Canadian brigade embarked for England on 11 June. On their departure General Miller inspected the brigade and distributed decorations to the men. General Ironside, the commander-in-chief, praised the Canadians for saving the Allied contingents from destruction and for maintaining at all times the highest traditions of their corps.[57]

Thus ended one of the strange events in the general history of Canadian-Soviet relations. Canadian soldiers were sent to Siberia to aid the Allies in their effort to restore order, protect the Czecho-Slovak Corps and help the anti-Bolshevik forces. In reality they did little to achieve these objectives since they were confined by government orders to the vicinity of Vladivostok. Moreover, the Economic Commission attached to the Canadian contingent had presented pessimistic reports on the possibilities of trade in Siberia.

On the other hand, some historians point out positive features of the intervention. According to C.W. Nicholson, the official historian of the Canadian Expeditionary Force of World War I, the intervention delayed for many months the ultimate Bolshevik victory in Russia and the possible occupation of Finland, the Baltic States, and Poland by the Red Army.[58] Gaddis Smith believes that the Siberian expedition gave Canada some opportunity to control her own foreign policy, insofar as the Canadian government insisted on having a Canadian officer in charge of her contingent and on employing this contingent in a manner that would best serve Canada. He also maintains that the Canadian government restrained the impetuosity of the British War Office by acting as a buffer between the United States and Great Britain.[59] Generally speaking, the Bolshevik

56 Borden to Churchill, 18 May 1919, ibid.
57 Swettenham, *Allied Intervention*, p. 221.
58 Nicholson, *Canadian Expeditionary Force*, p. 523.
59 Gaddis Smith, 'Canada and the Siberian Intervention, 1918–1919,' *Am. Hist. Rev.*, vol. LXIV (1959), 874.

regime in Moscow did not single out the Canadians as the 'innocent ones' who refused to become unduly entangled in Russian affairs. On the contrary, Canadians were placed in the British group who, along with the French, Americans, and Japanese, carried out 'predatory attack on the Soviet Republic.'[60]

60 *A Short History of the U.S.S.R.* (Moscow: Academy of Sciences of the USSR, 1965), vol. II, 62–3.

CHAPTER TWO

Adherence to the Anglo–Soviet Trade Agreement

The Canadian government's policy of non-interference in the internal affairs of the Russian people of Siberia did not mean that Ottawa favoured the teachings of the Bolsheviks or that it condoned their revolutionary activities. On the contrary, the Canadian government was perturbed by radical groups who espoused the cause of the Bolsheviks. Among these groups the Industrial Workers of the World, commonly called the IWW, appeared to have members who were openly sympathetic to the socialist experiment taking place in Russia. The IWW arose primarily out of dissatisfaction with craft unionism and the conservative policies of the American Federation of Labor. At the same time, some of the objectives of the IWW appeared very similar to those advocated by the Bolsheviks in Russia. For instance, the IWW hoped to organize the working class industrially, not only for the day-to-day struggle against the employers but also for the final overthrow of capitalism.[1]

Although it never attracted more than five per cent of all trade union members in the United States, the IWW did make itself felt effectively during its life span from 1905 to 1924. From the very beginning in 1905 this organization was 'feared as a sinister plot, hatched by foreigners, anarchists and Bolsheviks, against the American way of life.'[2] Over a hundred leading members of this organization were convicted of sabotage and subversion during the wartime hysteria in 1917–18.[3]

1 *Encyclopaedia of the Social Sciences* (New York, 1957), vol. VIII, 13–18.
2 Patrick Renshaw, *The Wobblies* (New York, 1967), p. 23.
3 Ibid.

The conviction and imprisonment of the leading members of the iww in the United States forced some of the remaining leaders to migrate to Canada, principally to British Columbia and Ontario. According to A.J. Caudon, acting chief commissioner for police, the iww was 'a very dangerous, socialistic and perhaps a murderous lot' who attempted to obtain members for the association from among such ethnic groups as Austrians, Russians, and Poles.[4] Caudon was of the opinion that much of the unrest in Canada was due to the activities of the iww.

The iww took advantage of the existing labour unrest to foster a Canadian branch. Some of the causes of this social ferment were easy to detect, whereas others required more detailed investigation. Through letters and the newspapers, members of the Canadian government were made aware of a general discontent among the Canadian people, particularly among the relatives of the wounded and dead soldiers, sailors, and airmen. These relatives and their friends were resentful of the profiteering that was going on in some war ammunition companies at the very time when civilians at home and the armed forces abroad were sacrificing their health, wealth, and even their lives for the cause of peace. In addition, some factory workers complained of the lengthening of the working day without a corresponding increase in wages.[5] Farmers objected to the conscription of their sons for overseas service, claiming that they were desperately needed at home. Both in the cities and on the farms there were bitter denunciations of the high cost of living.

The Canadian government was cognizant of the symptoms of the discontent but did not possess adequate information on its causes. Prime Minister Borden considered the unsettled conditions serious enough to ask a prominent lawyer, C.H. Cahan, to investigate the whole subject of radical activity in Canada.[6] Borden felt that this highly intellectual[7] Montreal lawyer would use his comprehensive knowledge of the nature of the unrest in other countries to discover the fundamental reasons for

4 A.J. Caudon to C.J. Doherty, minister of justice, 5 March 1918, Borden Papers, OG MG, 26 HI, PAC, Ottawa.
5 Charles Lipton, *The Trade Union Movement of Canada, 1827–1959* (Montreal, 1966), pp. 166–8.
6 Borden to C.H. Cahan, 19 May 1918, Borden Papers.
7 The *Ottawa Journal*, 17 Aug. 1944.

the Canadian unrest. Cahan accepted Borden's offer and in the autumn of 1918 he became the director of the Public Safety Branch of the Department of Justice, or simply the director of Public Safety. He was thorough in his research, spending a considerable amount of his time and energy on it. He was irritated, however, by the lack of appreciation shown him by the Department of Justice for work well done.

In his interim report to the minister of justice, Cahan outlined some of the fundamental causes of the unrest which found expression in labour agitation, strikes, and attempts to circumvent the Military Service Act. Cahan pointed out that Canada had lost her enthusiasm in the prosecution of the war. Part of this apathy was engendered by consistent rumours of war profiteering, inefficiency of government departments, and the growing resentment of conscription by farmers. He also observed that many Canadians were losing faith in the government because it failed to deal efficiently with the financial, economic, and industrial problems resulting from the war.[8]

In subsequent reports Cahan intimated that the government's efforts were jeopardized by the activities of radical groups such as the IWW, which attempted to create dissension among the generally peaceful ethnic groups of Canadians, namely, Russians, Ukrainians, and Finns. He felt that workers were saturated with socialistic doctrines disseminated by IWW pamphlets and newspapers which advocated 'the destruction of all state authority, the subversion of religion and the obliteration of all property rights.'[9]

Since the outbreak of the war, revolutionary groups of Russians, Ukrainians, and Finns had been organized into such associations as the Social Democratic party of Canada, the Ukrainian Revolutionary and the Russian Revolutionary parties. These organizations held public meetings in large cities, including Montreal, Toronto, Fort William, Winnipeg, and Edmonton. To help them become effective forces, the Third International sent several of its agents to the United States and Canada. Furthermore, Communist literature printed in the Ukrainian, Russian, and Finnish

8 C.H. Cahan to C.J. Doherty, 20 July 1918, Borden Papers.
9 Ibid., 14 Sept. 1918.

languages filtered into Canada either directly from Russia or indirectly through Spain and Finland.[10]

Cahan evidently equated the iww with the Bolsheviks, whose objectives and methods seemed similar. The iww was openly active in the mining camps of Northern Ontario, Alberta, and British Columbia. In Alberta, the majority of the miners belonged to the United Mine Workers of America, through which the iww exerted its influence.[11] In October 1918 a leftist organization associated with the iww secured control of the miners' group at the Crow's Nest coalfield, thus defying the officers of the United Mine Workers, the British Columbia Department of Mines, and the Federal Director of Mines.[12] Significantly, it was generally acknowledged that the iww encouraged the formation of the One Big Union (obu) whose main weapon was the general strike. The obu, dreaded by employers and government alike, was organized in the spring of 1919 as a protest against the craft-based union of the Trades and Labour Congress of Canada.[13]

Sympathizers of the iww were annoyingly vocal in British Columbia. J.W. Hawthornthwaite, a socialist member of the British Columbia legislature, told a labour meeting in Victoria on 23 February 1918 that 'the Bolsheviki movement is world-wide and is the hope of the workers of the world.'[14] Another socialist, Dr W.J. Curry of Vancouver, writing in a left-wing newspaper, the *Federationist* (22 February 1918), favoured the abolition of private property, whether in the form of land, banks, mills, or mines; such abolition would be a means of achieving human happiness.[15] In a speech delivered at Vancouver on 11 December, he emphasized that 'the aim and object of the workers of the world is to bring about a social revolution.'[16]

A number of drastic measures to deal with the current radicalism in Canada were suggested to the minister of justice. The chairman of the Registration Board, G.D. Robertson, urged joint action of the Departments of Justice, Labour, and Post Office. The first two departments were to have men available to collect evidence about the subversive activities of

10 Ibid.
11 *Canadian Annual Review*, 1918, p. 308 (hereafter cited as CAR).
12 Ibid., p. 313.   13 *Encyclopedia Canadiana*, 1958, vol. 8, 20.
14 CAR, 1918, p. 311.   15 Ibid., p. 313.   16 Ibid.

the IWW agents who allegedly were attempting to 'spread sedition and foment industrial unrest in British Columbia.' The postmaster general could arrest the spread of harmful literature by supervising the circulation of IWW pamphlets. Finally, Robertson advocated stern measures to prevent the immigration of IWW agents from the United States to British Columbia.[17]

The acting chief commissioner for police, A.J. Caudon, was also in favour of firm measures in dealing with IWW members. He recommended that their headquarters in Canada be raided in order to obtain more information about the activities of the members and, if possible, the main leaders be whisked away to a penitentiary.[18] Caudon also advocated that an order-in-council be passed to forbid the holding of meetings in which foreign languages were used and to prohibit the distribution of all literature financed by the IWW and the Ukrainian Socialist Democratic party.[19] On 27 September 1918 the Dominion government passed an order-in-council outlawing fourteen socialist organizations including the IWW, the Ukrainian Socialist Democratic party, and the Social Democratic party.[20]

Of the fourteen socialist groups, the Social Democratic party along with its newspaper, the *Canadian Forward*, was singled out by Cahan as the most dangerous to democratic ideals, since it spread Bolshevik doctrines and obstructed the war effort. He was in favour of banning this party which, according to him, was sponsored by German agents and advocated 'submission to German might, subversion of all constitutional government, robbery of personal property, and the accomplishment of its avowed aims of sabotage and general strikes.'[21]

Cahan's fear of the Social Democratic party was not shared by all members of the Canadian government. N.W. Rowell, the president of the Privy Council, opposed the suppression of the party because he felt that many important individuals from other countries had been associated with it. More importantly, the progressive elements in the community who insisted on freedom of speech and thought would turn against the

17 R.D. Robertson to C.J. Doherty, A.K. MacLean, acting postmaster general, N.W. Rowell, chairman of the War Committee, 20 Feb. 1918, Borden Papers.
18 A.J. Caudon to C.J. Doherty, 5 March 1918, ibid.
19 Ibid., 21 March 1918.   20 CAR, 1918, p. 388.
21 C.H. Cahan to C.J. Doherty, 5 March 1918, Borden Papers.

government if such legislation were enacted. Finally, he argued that the end of the war was not an opportune time to pass such laws.[22] Much to Rowell's delight the ban against the Social Democratic party was lifted. It remained unchanged, however, against the other socialist groups for the duration of the war.

Besides the voluminous reports of Cahan and Caudon on Bolshevik and IWW activities in Canada, Ottawa received equally disturbing reports from abroad. Early in December, Borden, who was in London, notified the acting prime minister, Sir Thomas White, that the Bolshevik regime in Russia was attempting to spread its doctrines to Germany, Switzerland, the Scandinavian countries, France, Italy, and Great Britain. He noted that there was 'reason to believe that the same effort will be extended to Canada and the United States, soon.'[23] Significantly, this rumour was subsequently substantiated by G. Zinoviev, the chairman of the Third International, who announced enthusiastically that the proletarian revolution was 'proceeding at such a terrific speed that the Communist may well forget that there was a struggle for Communism in Europe, for not only will entire Europe be [sic] Communist, but this strife will be even transferred to America, perhaps to Asia and to other parts of the world.'[24] It is not surprising that Borden exhorted White to keep 'a careful watch for Bolshevist emissaries who are exceedingly clever and skillful and are supplied with an abundance of funds.'[25]

The alarming reports of Cahan and Caudon, together with the statements of the leading Soviet leaders, created a sense of apprehension commonly called the 'Red Scare.' Canadian newspapers informed the Canadian government and the Canadian people of the existing commercial and political chaos in Russia. They continued to warn the Canadian businessmen of the dangers of negotiating deals with the Russians, be they commercial or political, for fear of encouraging subversive activities by Bolshevik agents. It is in the light of this charged atmosphere that the 'cruiser episode' and the Winnipeg General Strike should be studied.

22 N.W. Rowell to Borden, 29 Oct. 1919, ibid.
23 Borden to White, 2 Dec. 1918, ibid.
24 Quoted in M.T. Florinsky, *World Revolution and the U.S.S.R.* (New York, 1933), p. 48.
25 Borden to White, 27 March 1919, Borden Papers.

Early in 1919 Sir Frank Barnard, lieutenant-governor of British Columbia, wrote to Borden in Paris, describing the labour unrest in British Columbia and urging him to ask the British government to dispatch a cruiser to Vancouver to overawe the agitators there.[26] Borden mailed a copy of Barnard's letter to Sir Thomas White, the acting prime minister.

Obviously concerned by the reports of the progress of Bolshevism among workers and soldiers, White supported the lieutenant-governor's suggestion, claiming that the situation in Vancouver and Victoria was so serious that a show of force provided by a British cruiser would be necessary to intimidate the agitators. He argued that inactivity on the part of the government would probably lead to serious disturbances in such cities as Calgary and Winnipeg where socialism was rampant.[27]

Although Borden was sympathetic to White's suggestion, he was not too certain how a cruiser could be utilized to suppress riots and insurrections on the mainland. He recommended instead the use of the North West Mounted Police.[28] White did not agree with the prime minister, feeling that the dispatch of police would only aggravate the situation,[29] and Borden finally acquiesced. However, to avoid alarming the authorities in the United Kingdom, he suggested that the Canadian government invite several British squadrons to Halifax and Vancouver under the pretext of showing Canada's gratitude to the British navy for its service during the war.[30] The appearance of the naval squadron would provide the mayor of Vancouver and some of the members of the Canadian government with the show of force necessary to quiet the radicals, who through their propaganda were causing some concern to the government. The British squadrons, for reasons not disclosed, did not appear. In his telegram of 16 May, White reiterated the seriousness of the situation on the west coast. At the same time he notified the prime minister that some thirty thousand workers, including tramway and postal employees, had walked off their jobs in Winnipeg the day before.[31] For a period of some six weeks the events in the prairie capital overshadowed the rumours of Bolshevik-inspired disturbances in Vancouver and Victoria.

26 Roger Graham, *Arthur Meighen* (Toronto, 1960), vol. I, 230.
27 White to Borden, 1 April 1919, Borden Papers.
28 Borden to White, 18 April 1919, ibid.   29 White to Borden, 22 April 1919, ibid.
30 Borden to White, 29 April 1919, ibid.   31 White to Borden, 16 May 1919, ibid.

The stoppage of work which developed into a general strike paralyzed the city of Winnipeg and implied that a soviet was established there. The Canadian newspapers were largely responsible for giving the general public the impression that a Bolshevik regime had been initiated in the prairie capital. In its editorial of 21 May 1919 Montreal's *La Presse* claimed that 'Bolshevism has for certain planted its tent at Winnipeg.' The Toronto *Globe* (19 May 1919) maintained that the metal workers in Winnipeg were using 'Bolshevism of the most reckless sort' to obtain recognition of the principle of collective bargaining. On 15 May 1919 the *Victoria Daily Times* stated that it might not be very surprising 'to find that Bolshevik pedagogues were at the back' of the strike. Five days after the stoppage of work, the Winnipeg *Citizen*, the organ of the anti-strike movement, considered the strike 'a serious attempt to overthrow British Institutions in the Western country and supplant them by the Russian Bolshevist system of Soviet Rule.' Similarly on 24 May the *Manitoba Free Press* viewed the strike as a socialist revolution by which the Bolshevik leaders intended 'to divide the country among themselves and their following.'

The Winnipeg General Strike began with the walkout of the workers in the building and metal trades. They had been refused an increase in salary and had been denied the right of collective bargaining in negotiations with their employers. The representatives of the workers took their grievances to the Winnipeg Trades and Labour Council, which ordered a vote in all its affiliates on the question of a general strike to support the demands of the building and metal workers. The results of the vote showed that an overwhelming majority favoured a general walkout. Consequently, on 15 May about 25,000 workers walked out in sympathy with the strikers. Among these were delivery workers, bookkeepers, newspapermen, telegraph operators, and postmen.

For the greater part of the strike the workers limited themselves to demonstrations without violence. However, this calm atmosphere was shattered by the introduction of police called 'specials' who were to help the 'loyal' police maintain order in the city. Obviously the Winnipeg city council had little confidence in the existing police force. The appearance of the 'sworn-in specials' incited a riot on 10 June, at which time a Sergeant-Major Coppens was seriously injured by a missile thrown by a member of the jeering crowd. Encouraged by the Citizens' Committee, on 17 June the Royal North West Mounted Police arrested eight prominent strike leaders on the grounds that they were inciting the citizens to disobey lawful authority.

Four days after this arrest a contingent of returned soldiers decided to march to the Royal Alexandra Hotel where Senator G.D. Robertson, the federal minister of labour, was staying. The soldiers wished to show through this mass demonstration their objection to Robertson's almost exclusive association with the opponents of the strike. The parade could not be fully organized because Mayor C. Gray had asked the Royal North West Mounted Police to stop it. In the melee two bystanders were killed and twenty-four civilians and six Royal North West Mounted Police officers were injured.[32] This show of force ended the General Strike on 26 June.

The causes and events of the Winnipeg General Strike have been interpreted in many ways. An anti-strike view, originating with the Citizens' Committee, saw the strike as the beginning of the establishment of a Canadian Soviet government. Both Arthur Meighen, the federal minister of the interior, and Senator G.D. Robertson, the minister of labour, who came to Winnipeg to investigate the causes of the General Strike, let it be known authoritatively that they regarded the 'so-called strike as a cloak for something far deeper – a cloak for an effort to overthrow proper authority.'[33] In his memoirs, Prime Minister Borden wrote that the strike constituted 'a definite attempt to overthrow the existing organization of the Government and to supersede it by crude fantastic methods founded upon the absurd conception of what has been accomplished in Russia.'[34] Perhaps this observation was somewhat influenced by Colonial Secretary Milner who cabled Borden on 23 July 1919, informing him that according to trustworthy sources 'the Russian Soviet Government has a plan for resuscitating the revolutionary movement in Canada and has put two million rubles in foreign money at the disposal of the Communist sections

32 D.C. Masters, *The Winnipeg General Strike* (Toronto, 1950), p. 106.
33 The *Citizen*, Winnipeg, 24 May 1919.
34 Henry Borden (ed.), *Robert Laird Borden: His Memoirs* (Toronto, 1936), vol. II, 972.

at Ottawa, Calgary, Lethbridge, Edmonton, Regina, Victoria, Vancouver and Montreal.'[35]

Significantly, the indictment on which the leaders were tried and convicted was that they 'conspired to bring hatred and contempt of the government, laws and the constitution of the Dominion of Canada and of the province of Manitoba ... and to incite His Majesty's subjects in Canada to introduce into Canada by other than lawful means the "Soviet" form of government similar to that now in force in a portion of Russia, by unlawful means, i.e., by unlawful general strikes of all workers in Canada.'[36] The spectacular trial ended with the imposition of a two-year sentence on R.B. Russell,.the secretary of the Metal Trades Council, one-year terms on five of the leaders of the strike, and a six-month term on the sixth.[37]

Opposing views of the causes of the strike can be found in several newspapers, in government reports, in the *Debates* of the House of Commons, and in the conclusions of recent research analysts. The strikers' bulletin, *Western Labour News* (17 May 1919), continued to advocate peaceful means of demonstrating workers' grievances: 'There is great cause for congratulation during this struggle, in that until the present moment the participants are more orderly than a crowd of spectators at a baseball game ... There has evolved a weapon of great power ... orderliness.' A newspaper reporter for the Toronto *Star*, W.R. Plewman, an eye-witness observer of the strike, helped to dispel some of the prevailing views of this disturbance held outside of Winnipeg. He assured Canadians that the strike had popular support and that it was 'not Soviet,' nor was there much terrorism involved.[38]

According to H.A. Robson, KC, who was appointed by the Manitoba government to investigate the strike, the causes of this work stoppage lay in the workers' demands for an increase in salaries, for an improvement of working conditions, and for the establishment of bargaining rights.[39]

35 Milner to Borden, 23 July 1919, Borden Papers.
36 Masters, *General Strike*, p. 115.
37 Ibid., p. 102.   38 The *Star*, Toronto, 23 May 1919.
39 Manitoba, *Royal Commission on the General Strike, 1919* (Report of H.A. Robson, KC), Winnipeg, 1919.

Another Royal Commission organized by the federal government studied the causes of general unrest in Canada during the latter part of the war. It agreed with Robson's Report in that it mentioned the high cost of living, the denial of collective bargaining, unemployment, and inadequate housing as important causes of general unrest.[40] Significantly, neither report stressed Bolshevism as a major factor in the widespread discontent.

In the House of Commons, Ernest Lapointe (Liberal – Quebec East) maintained that the high cost of living and war profiteering created the upheaval in Winnipeg. He went on to blame the government for its attempt 'to mystify the public by acting a Bolshevist melodrama to cover administrative and governmental negligence.'[41] Major G.W. Andrews (Independent – Winnipeg Centre) objected to the government's labelling of the strikers as Bolshevists.[42]

One researcher on the Communist party of Canada maintains that the charge of the Soviet government's implication in the Winnipeg General Strike stemmed largely from the rumours that Moscow was subsidizing the strike. He intimates that the strikers might have received some financial assistance from Ludwig C.A.K. Martens, the so-called Bolshevik representative in New York and the head of the Russian Soviet Government Information Bureau. Evidence of the same researcher supports the allegation that the strikers were aided directly or indirectly by Russian agitators. According to a report from American officials in Chicago to British authorities in New York, some $7,000 were transmitted to the General Strike committee by a man called Fedchenko, 'a notorious Russian anarchist' of Pittsburgh. This comparatively large sum of money was originally destined to reach F. Charitonoff, a Canadian anarchist agitator, who was to use it in the publication of a radical journal, the *New Age*. When this publication failed to materialize, the money was turned over to the Winnipeg strikers who were to utilize it for propaganda purposes.[43]

40 Canada, *Royal Commission on Industrial Relations – Commission to enquire into Industrial Relations in Canada* (Report of T.G. Mathers), Ottawa, 1919.
41 Canada, House of Commons, *Debates*, 1919, p. 3010.
42 Ibid., p. 3020.
43 William Rodney, *Soldiers of the International – A History of the Communist Party of Canada, 1919–1929* (Toronto, 1968), p. 25.

A. Ross McCormack, research analyst currently with the Manitoba Department of Labour, discounts the Winnipeg General Strike as an incipient Bolshevik revolution. 'Although all the leaders were socialists,' he argues, 'there is no reason to conclude that the strike was designed to overthrow the government; in these men the British tradition was stronger than the Russian revolutionary tradition.'[44]

Although research scholars differ in their opinions regarding the causes of the strike, most agree upon its far-reaching consequences. Two of the most important results of this labour crisis were the amendments to section 41 of the Immigration Act and to section 98 of the Criminal Code. The first amendment, passed on 6 June 1919 extended the right of the government to deport even British-born subjects who were engaged in activities contrary to the law and order of Canada. This amendment was initially designed to deal with the leaders of the strike, many of whom were British born. The amendment to the Criminal Code passed in July 1919 forbade unlawful associations whose object was to bring about governmental or economic changes within Canada by the use of force, injury to person or property, or which taught or advocated these methods of securing changes. Even individuals who contributed money to the functioning of subversive associations, printed, circulated, or sold literature advocating the use of force to effect governmental or economic changes were liable to a maximum prison term of twenty years. All the property of such associations was automatically forfeited to the Crown. Individuals who rented a hall for the meeting of subversive associations were liable to a fine of $5,000.[45]

The amended Immigration Act was invoked in the summer of 1920 in an attempt to deport fifteen agitators on the grounds 'that they were members of an organization teaching disbelief in or opposition to organized government, to wit, the Union of Russian Workers, and that they belonged to prohibited or undesirable classes as prescribed by Section 41 of the Immigration Act.'[46] On 31 July 1920 Governor General the Duke of Devonshire asked Colonial Secretary Milner if Karpe Belansoff, who was

44 A. Ross McCormack, unpublished letter to A. Balawyder, 27 Sept. 1966.
45 *Statutes of Canada, 1919*, 9–10, vol. I–II (Ottawa: King's Printer), 307–11.
46 Ibid., s. 41, p. 98.

convicted of manslaughter in 1913 at Nanaimo, British Columbia, and fourteen Russian agitators could be deported to the Soviet Union.[47] Milner notified the governor general that a British agent at Reval would contact M. Litvinov, the Soviet commissar for foreign affairs, and ask him whether the information given so far on the fifteen Russians was adequate and whether his government was prepared to accept these men at the frontier.[48]

Litvinov requested further information on his fellow-countrymen. He wanted to know their full names; the places and dates of their births; their occupations; nature, date, and place of the issue of their identifications, and the dates of their emigration from Russia.[49] The Canadian Immigration Department found it difficult to obtain the requested data on four of them. This problem was resolved when the Canadian government decided to release fourteen of the agitators including Belansoff, on parole. The only one who was to be deported, Boris Zurkoff (sometimes spelled Betchier Dzukoff), was allegedly a dangerous criminal.[50]

The lenient treatment of the Russian agitators did not, however, hasten the restoration of trade between Canada and Russia. The general distrust of Russia and a suspicion of international communism as shown during the 'cruiser episode,' the Winnipeg General Strike, and the deportation of Russian agitators created an atmosphere inimical to commercial relations between Canada and Russia.

It is not too surprising, then, that the overture of Ludwig C.A.K. Martens, the Soviet envoy to the United States, regarding the resumption of trade with Canada met with little enthusiasm in Ottawa. G. Foster, the Canadian minister of trade and commerce, informed Martens, however, that there was no legislation prohibiting the establishment of trade between the two countries, provided that Russia fulfilled all the necessary stipulations governing the type of goods to be handled and the transportation of them. The minister emphasized the fact that the Canadian government did not intend to guarantee the fulfilment of contracts made between the

47 Duke of Devonshire to Viscount Milner, 31 July 1920, no. 32510, Governor General's Files (hereafter cited as GGF), G.21, file no. 34691, 1(a) (1911–24), PAC, Ottawa.
48 Milner to Devonshire, 5 Aug. 1920, no. 33278, ibid.
49 Ibid., 20 Aug. no. 33538.
50 Devonshire to Milner, 7 Dec. 1920, no. 33989, ibid.

Soviet government and individual Canadian firms, nor did it propose to arrange transportation of Canadian merchandise.[51] Such a seemingly blunt reply was, no doubt, intended to clarify any misconceptions the Soviet government might harbour about commercial transactions with a nation that favoured a free-enterprise system.

The prospects of resumption of trade between Canada and Russia were dampened when Martens was deported by the United States government for disseminating literature advocating the overthrow of that government. Martens had never been welcome in Washington; the White House continued to recognize Boris Bakhmetev, a representative of the Kerensky provisional government, as the legitimate Russian envoy to the United States.[52] As a matter of fact, the American government advised industrial and commercial firms against any dealings with Martens, disclaiming all responsibility for unfulfilled contracts.

A private request for the commencement of trade between Canada and Russia was made by General B.H. Hepburn, who served with the Canadian Forestry Corps in the war. In a cablegram to Prime Minister Meighen dated 2 September 1920 Hepburn disclosed the fact that the Russian trade delegation in London was negotiating a deal with Canadian Allis-Chalmers Limited for railway equipment worth some thirty million dollars, to be paid in gold.[53] General Hepburn asked the prime minister whether the Canadian government would act as a trustee for this gold, which was to be transferred through a bank at Reval, and whether it would authorize its fiscal agent to arrange the transaction. The net proceeds would be deposited in the Bank of Montreal. Meighen notified Hepburn that under the existing circumstances the Canadian government could not take on such a responsibility.[54]

On 28 November 1920 another request was made by the Soviet Union for the resumption of trade, this one from Leonid Krassin, an able business man who was the chairman of the Russian trade delegation in London.

51 *Dokumenty Vneshnei Politiki SSSR* (Moscow, 1958), vol. II, 500.
52 Robert Paul Browder, *The Origins of Soviet-American Diplomacy* (Princeton, 1953), p. 14.
53 General Hepburn to Arthur Meighen, 2 Sept. 1920, no. 35421, Meighen Papers, MG, 26, ser. II, file 187, PAC, Ottawa.
54 Meighen to Hepburn, 4 Sept. 1920, no. 26753, ibid.

In a letter to Sir George Perley, the high commissioner for Canada, Krassin pointed out that Martens' attempt to initiate trade between Canada and Russia could have been realized if a Russian commercial agent from London or from Moscow had been sent to Ottawa 'to handle trade matters and also to investigate the position there of the Canadian market, and the possibilities of trade with Canada.'[55] He intimated that all trade negotiations between Moscow and Ottawa would continue to prove unsuccessful unless the Canadian government permitted a Russian commercial agent to reside in her country.

Not knowing what course to take, Meighen asked the British Foreign Office for advice. The Foreign Office informed Meighen through Milner, the colonial secretary, that it had no objections to the presence of a Russian commercial representative in Canada if Ottawa agreed.[56] At the same time it reminded Meighen that negotiations between Great Britain and Russia regarding a trade agreement were going on in London. If Canada did not wish to wait until the trade agreement was concluded, she was free to make a separate arrangement with Moscow provided that she informed the Kremlin leaders 'that if Russia wants to do business with Canada, she must first desist from hostile action against any part of the British Empire.'[57] In this manner Canada would join with the United Kingdom in presenting a united front against Communist infiltration. After careful consideration Meighen notified Perley that the Canadian government did not deem it advisable to enter into commercial relations with Russia before the Anglo-Soviet Trade Agreement was drawn up.[58]

The preliminary Anglo-Soviet discussion, however, reached an impasse as each side accused the other of disloyalty to the agreed principles of procedure. The two countries disagreed on the means of repatriating their respective nationals and on an adequate means of compensating citizens who had suffered damage or loss of property during and immediately after World War I. In addition, the British claimed that the Executive Committee of the Third International was subsidizing the British newspaper, the *Daily Herald*.

While England and Russia were encountering difficulties in negotiating

55 Leonid Krassin to Sir George Perley, 28 Nov. 1920, no. 026756, ibid.
56 Milner to Meighen, 26 Dec. 1920, no. 026775, ibid.
57 Ibid., no. 016776.   58 Ibid., 4 Jan. 1921, no. 026772.

a satisfactory trade agreement, the executive of the Trades and Labour Council of London, Ontario, was urging Meighen to adhere to the treaty as soon as it was concluded. In the opinion of this executive, resumption of trade with Russia would partially solve the existing acute unemployment problem by having the workers gainfully employed in the manufacture of urgently needed railway equipment and farm machinery.[59] G.D. Robertson, federal minister of labour, to whom the letter from the Trades and Labour Council was finally referred, remarked that Russia had vast quantities of unused railway equipment lying idle in Vladivostok.[60] Furthermore, he added, Russian currency was worthless abroad and practically valueless at home. The universally recognized Czarist and Kerensky money was being hoarded by the Russian peasants as security for their future.

When the Anglo-Soviet Trade Agreement was finally signed on 16 March 1921, increased pressure was exerted on Meighen's government to adhere to it. The Trades and Labour Council of Fort William suggested that the deteriorating unemployment conditions in the Lakehead city could be alleviated by government-sponsored sale of automobiles to the Soviet Union.[61] A more detailed request for trade was made by the Independent Labour party of Ontario. In a resolution drafted at Welland, Ontario, this organization put forward convincing arguments for trade with Russia:

Whereas Russia constitutes an almost unlimited market for manufactured commodities of all kinds and whereas Canada is at present experiencing a crisis through over-production resulting in unemployment and economic depression causing great suffering to the masses of our people. Be it therefore resolved: That we urgently request our Dominion Government to arrange and enter into Trade Agreement with the Russian Government and that a copy of this resolution be sent to the Prime Minister of Canada.[62]

Requests for a trade agreement with Russia also came from manufacturers and a bank president. Alex Marshall, manager of the Commercial Intel-

59 F. Burk to Meighen, 7 Feb. 1921, no. 026783, **ibid.**
60 G.D. Robertson to Meighen, 11 Feb. 1821, no. 026785, ibid.
61 Trades and Labour Council of Fort William to Meighen, 26 March 1921, no. 026808, ibid.
62 Independent Labour party of Ontario to Meighen, 31 March 1921, no. 026808, ibid.

ligence Department of the Canadian Manufacturers Association, held that although the possibility of a flourishing commerce with Moscow might never be realized, he was, nevertheless, interested 'in seeing that no possible prospects of increasing Canadian trade are neglected.'[63] At the same time he was curious to know whether the Canadian government was contemplating adherence to the Anglo-Soviet Trade Agreement.

Major H.J. Daly, president of the Toronto Home Bank, informed Meighen that he had held several interviews with L. Krassin, the chairman of the Russian trade delegation in London, and was convinced that the Soviet representative was utterly confused about the Canadian commercial policy. With an air of self-confidence, Major Daly declared that he had spent eighteen months investigating the possibility of trade with Moscow and would 'probably have a better grasp of the situation than most Canadian business men.'[64] For that reason he asked the Canadian prime minister to leave further discussions in abeyance until he had an opportunity to detail the entire problem to him. Meighen invited Major Daly for an interview, but bluntly reminded him that the Canadian government alone had the right to negotiate with foreign countries.[65]

Major Daly's conversation with Meighen no doubt centred around Krassin's proposal to purchase Canadian agricultural machinery, railway materials, and metallic goods, and to pay for this merchandise in gold. But, as in the request of 28 November 1920, Krassin emphasized that resumption of trade was not possible unless the Canadian government granted the Soviet government 'the right of having in Canada one or more trade representatives for conducting negotiations with firms, placing orders and organizing inspection and shipment of machinery and goods manufactured in the Canadian works and factories.'[66] In addition, the Soviet representative asked the Canadian government to guarantee against possible loss and to extend diplomatic immunity to all the property belonging to the Soviet representatives.

Following his interview with Major Daly, Meighen informed Sir Henry Drayton, the Canadian minister of finance, that there was a good possibility

63 Alex Marshall to Meighen, 2 April 1921, no. 026810, ibid.
64 Major H.J. Daly to Meighen, 23 March 1921, no. 026788, ibid.
65 Meighen to Daly, 24 March 1921, no. 026972, ibid.
66 Leonid Krassin to Daly, 11 March 1921, no. 026797, ibid.

of Krassin's coming on a business trip to Canada. Drayton, however, viewed such a visit with suspicion, claiming that the Soviet trade delegate was not sincerely interested in developing trade with Canada, and that his chief concern lay in using this country as a base for future negotiations with the United States.[67]

Meighen also corresponded with Foster, minister of trade and commerce. In a letter to him, the prime minister suggested that it would be practical to have a Canadian representative attached to the British Trade Mission to Moscow in order 'to investigate and report to us in Ottawa on conditions generally and on the advisability of appointing a permanent trade representative.'[68] He added, however, that no such appointment could be justified before Canada officially agreed to the terms of the Anglo-Soviet Trade Agreement, for otherwise it would appear that Ottawa was seeking favours from Moscow. Although Meighen did not see any objections to such an adherence, he felt that the decision rested with the cabinet. He therefore asked Foster to consider carefully in council the 'question of adhering to the Agreement and of attaching a Canadian representative to the British Trade Mission.'[69] The prime minister even mentioned Colonel H.J. Mackie, member of Parliament for South Renfrew, who was also in England, as a possible Canadian representative to Russia.

About five months later, C.H. Payne, Foster's private secretary, cabled Meighen informing him that the committee of the Privy Council sanctioned Canada's adherence to the Anglo-Soviet Trade Agreement. The minutes of the committee of the Privy Council read in part as follows:

The Committee of the Privy Council have had before them a report dated 17th December, 1921, from the Right Honourable Secretary of State for External Affairs, to whom was referred a dispatch from the Right Honourable the Secretary of State for the Colonies, dated 15th October, 1921, regarding the desire of the Canadian Government to participate in the arrangement for the resumption of trade with Russia, proposing a formula to be embodied in notes to be exchanged between the Foreign Office and the Russian Trade

67 Sir Henry Drayton to Meighen, 5 July 1921, no. 026825, ibid.
68 Meighen to George Foster, 21 July 1921, no. 026835, ibid.
69 Ibid.

Delegation with the object of making applicable to Canada the provisions of the Trade Agreement between the United Kingdom and the Russian Soviet Government, and enquiring whether Your Excellency's Ministers would concur in the terms of such formula.

The Minister, with the concurrence of the Minister of Trade and Commerce, states that the proposed formula is approved by the Canadian Government.[70]

The committee of the Privy Council, however, strongly urged that L.D. Wilgress, who possessed a thorough knowledge of the Russian language and who had five years of experience as a Canadian trade commissioner to Russia, be selected as the Canadian representative to Moscow, rather than Colonel Mackie.[71] Apparently disappointed with the council's decision, Meighen asked Foster whether the council would object to the addition of Colonel Mackie as an assistant to Wilgress. Much to the delight of the prime minister the council found no objection to this suggestion provided it be temporary.[72]

The decision of the Privy Council was forwarded to the Soviet government through the British Foreign Office, since Canada lacked diplomatic representatives abroad. Ordinarily, dispatches from the Canadian government would be forwarded by the governor general to the colonial secretary, who in turn would pass them on to the British Foreign Office and then to the Soviet Foreign Ministry. After slightly altering Canada's original request for adherence to the Anglo-Soviet Trade Agreement, Churchill, the colonial secretary, communicated the modified version to J. Berzin, the head of the Russian trade delegation in Britain, through Lord Balfour, the British foreign secretary. The original request specified that the Canadian government wanted the terms of the Anglo-Soviet Trade Agreement of 16 March 1921 to be applied also to 'Canada, and to merchandise, the produce and manufacture of Canada.'[73]

The Soviet government responded warmly to the Canadian wish. Through J. Berzin, G. Chicherin, the Soviet commissar for foreign

70 Minutes of a meeting of the Privy Council, 26 Dec. 1921, *Sessional Paper*, no. 274, Journal Section of the House of Commons, Ottawa.
71 C.H. Payne to Buskard, 26 July 1921, no. 026842, Meighen Papers.
72 Ibid., 29 July 1921, no. 026849.
73 Esmond Ovey to Berzin, 3 July 1922, no. 40793, ibid.

affairs, informed the Canadian government that his government agreed to the arrangement suggested by the note forwarded by Ottawa through the British Foreign Office.[74] Moscow found L.D. Wilgress and H.J. Mackie acceptable as representatives to be attached to the British Trade Mission, even though the negotiations between Russia and Canada were still in the preliminary stage.

While negotiations between Ottawa and Moscow were proceeding through the British Foreign Office, a general election in Canada, held on 6 December 1921 turned out the Conservatives under Meighen and brought in the Liberals, with Mackenzie King as their leader. In a letter to Chicherin dated 26 August 1921 Berzin made reference to the elections, but intimated that, even though the Liberals would most likely form the new government, there would be, in his opinion, no change in the policy regarding the resumption of trade with Russia. Berzin's prognosis turned out to be correct; the negotiations continued despite the change of government in Ottawa.

Most of the terms of the Anglo-Soviet Trade Agreement dealt with such items as obstacles to normal trade and arrangements for postal and telegraphic correspondence. Of special interest to Canada were the Preamble of the treaty, sections 4, 5, 6, and 13, and the declaration of property claims. The Preamble contained two important stipulations on which the entire trade agreement was based and whose violations by Russia in 1927 brought about the severance of diplomatic relations between Moscow and Ottawa:

(a) That each party refrains from hostile action or undertakings against the other, and from conducting outside of its own borders any official propaganda, direct or indirect, against the institutions of the British Empire or the Russian Soviet Republic respectively, and more particularly that the Russian Soviet Government refrains from any attempt by military or diplomatic or any other form of action or propaganda to encourage any of the peoples of Asia in any form of hostile action against the British interests or the British Empire especially in India and in the independence of Afghanistan.

74 Chicherin to Berzin, 3 July 1922, ibid. This reference is also found in *Dokumenty Vneshnei Politiki SSSR*, vol. v (Moscow, 1961), 478.

The British Government gives a similar particular undertaking to the Russian Soviet Government in respect to the countries which formed part of the former Russian Empire and which have now become independent.

(b) That all British subjects in Russia are immediately permitted to return home, and that all Russian citizens in Great Britain or other parts of the British Empire who desire to return to Russia are similarly released.[75]

Article IV detailed the extent of immunity to be enjoyed by the members of the trade delegations. Some of the more important privileges included the exemption of nationals from civil, naval, and military training; the exemption from taxation and the free use of post and telegraph services. Article V extended these privileges to semi-official agents who might even 'receive and dispatch couriers with sealed bags subject to a limitation of three kilograms per week, which shall be exempt from examination.'[76] The Soviet delegation, which arrived in Montreal in March 1924 maintained that, according to article V, the members of the delegation had the right to receive any type of literature Moscow sent, even though it was Communistic in nature. Article VI simply stated that 'each party undertakes generally to ensure that persons admitted into its territories under the two preceding articles shall enjoy all protection, rights and facilities which are necessary to enable them to carry on trade, but subject always to any legislation generally applicable to the respective countries.'[77] Article XIII stipulated that the trade agreement bound the signatories only if the first two articles were faithfully observed by both sides.

Of particular interest to some individual Canadians was article XIV, which dealt with the recognition of claims of nationals whose property was either confiscated or destroyed before, during, or immediately after World War I. Even before Canada agreed to the terms of the Anglo-Soviet Trade Agreement, a number of Canadians asked the British Foreign Office to register their claims with the proper authorities. Edward Barker of Vancouver requested an adequate compensation for 44,889.08 roubles ($4,243.49) which were allegedly deposited with the Russian Government

75 'Trade Agreement between His Britannic Majesty's Government and the Government of the Russian Socialist Federal Soviet Republic,' *League of Nations Treaty Series,* 1921, pp. 128–9.
76 Ibid., p. 132.   77 Ibid., pp. 132–3.

Bank at Nikolayevsk but looted by the Red Army in January 1920.[78] A shotgun valued at sixty dollars was also stolen on the same occasion. The Department of Militia and Defence placed a claim amounting to $55,571.82, which the Imperial Russian government had failed to pay for Canadian-made horse saddles.[79] Churchill, the colonial secretary, reassured both parties that their claims would be duly registered with the Russian Claims Department of the Board of Trade, which replaced the former Russian Section of the Foreign Claims Office.[80]

Unfortunately, article xiv did not provide workable machinery for an effective settlement of the claims. It merely stated that 'The Russian Soviet Government declares that it recognizes in principle that it is liable to pay compensation to private persons who have supplied goods or services to Russia for which they have not been paid. The detailed mode of discharging this liability shall be regulated by the treaty referred to in the preamble.'[81] The lack of satisfactory methods of settling war debts and claims continued to plague Anglo-Soviet relations.

Approximately two years had expired between Canada's adherence to the Anglo-Soviet Trade Agreement on 3 July 1922 and the arrival of the Soviet trade delegation in Montreal. Part of this delay was caused by the difficulty of selecting members of the delegation who would be acceptable to the Canadian government. The British Foreign Office permitted Canada to use its available services to screen undesirable Soviet delegates. At the same time, Foreign Minister Curzon reassured Ottawa that his ministry did not want 'to hamper the discretion of the Canadian Department concerned either as to the character of any Russians whom they admitted to Canada, or as to any particular trading transactions which may be contemplated.'[82]

As a general rule, however, any Soviet delegate who was considered acceptable to the British Foreign Office was also deemed suitable by Ottawa. Each Russian delegate applying for a Canadian visa was carefully

78 L.H. Davies to Winston Churchill, 28 April 1921, no. 35679, GGF, 1(a) 1911–24.
79 Byng of Vimy to Churchill, 7 Sept. 1921, no. 37335, ibid.
80 Churchill to Byng of Vimy, 22 Oct. 1921, no. 37863, ibid.
81 *League of Nations Treaty Series*, 1921, p. 135.
82 Lord Curzon to P.C. Larkin, 22 Nov. 1923, nos. 75419–20, W.L.M. King Papers, MG 26, PAC, Ottawa.

evaluated as to his suitability by the British Foreign Office under the following headings: (a) political interest, (b) trade interest, and (c) desirability or otherwise of the individual.

The Soviet government's original slate of delegates to Canada met with unusual difficulties in gaining acceptance by Ottawa. Both Gregory Weinstein and Peter Voikov were rejected outright by the British Foreign Office, and hence by the Canadian government. Voikov, the proposed head of the trade delegation, had experience in diplomatic service as a president of the delegation to the Far East, and at the time of the new appointment acted as the assistant director at the Commissariat of Ways and Means at Moscow.[83] Samuel Kahan and Maxim Divilkovsky were first denied entry to Canada but eventually were cleared.[84] Kahan was subsequently dropped by the Soviets themselves as a prospective member of the trade delegation.

Moscow was unusually bitter over Canada's refusal to accept the proposed delegates. Prompted by Chicherin, the Soviet commissar for foreign affairs, H.N. Klishko, the official representative of Russia in Britain, protested that Ottawa arbitrarily rejected the Soviet delegates, G. Weinstein and Peter Voikov, whereas Russia unconditionally accepted L.D. Wilgress and Colonel Mackie as Canadian representatives to Moscow.[85] He further accused Ottawa of violating the first part of section v of the Anglo-Soviet Trade Agreement, to whose terms she had agreed on 3 July 1922.

In response to the Soviet allegation, Sir Joseph Pope, the Canadian under-secretary of state for external affairs, explained that Ottawa's refusal to admit the two members of the delegation was based on the personal unsuitability of these representatives rather than on the principle of having a Soviet mission in Canada.[86] J.A. Robb, minister of trade and commerce, elaborated on Pope's statement by disclosing that the two rejected Russian delegates, Weinstein and Voikov, possessed records of revolutionary activities, thus making them undesirable as members of the trade delegation.[87]

83 Duke of Devonshire to Byng of Vimy, 17 Oct. 1923, no. 45466, GGF.
84 Esmond Ovey to George Berzin, 25 July 1923, no. 44736, ibid.
85 *Dokumenty Vneshnei Politiki SSSR* (Moscow, 1963), vol. VI, 142.
86 Ibid.
87 Canada, House of Commons, *Debates*, 1923, p. 987.

Satisfied with the Canadian explanation that the original refusal by Ottawa to issue visas to the two Soviet citizens was not directed at the basic principles of establishing a trade delegation in Canada, Moscow selected Alexander Alesandrovich Yazikov to replace Peter Voikov as the head of the trade mission. Following the formal Canadian acceptance of Yazikov as the new Russian head, Chicherin begged Ottawa to co-operate with him in the fulfilment of duties.[88] Because of sudden illness, Yazikov did not reach Montreal, where the Soviet trade delegation was to be located, until early in March. He was welcomed to his new office at 212 Drummond Street by the members of his staff: Ivan Kulik, Maxim Divilkovsky, Dimitri Pavlovich Pavlov, and Nikolai Nikolaevich Kostritsin. The Drummond Street office continued to be the headquarters of the Russian delegation until May 1927, when it was officially closed following the severance of diplomatic relations with Moscow by Ottawa.

88 *Dokumenty Vneshnei Politiki, SSSR* (Moscow, 1963), vol. VII, 17.

CHAPTER THREE

Help for the Famine-stricken Peoples

Fourteen months prior to Canada's adherence to the Anglo-Soviet Trade Agreement on 3 July 1922, Lenin asked his representative in London, Leonid Krassin, to ascertain whether Moscow would be permitted to buy 72,000,000 pounds of bread and preserved foods from Canada.[1] Several days later, Krassin informed the Soviet leader that Prime Minister Meighen was ready for discussions on the purchase of Canadian food and the method of payment for it.

Evidently Lenin was attempting to alleviate the sufferings of his people caused by a shortage of food in certain regions of Russia. At the very time when the Volga district and the Ukraine were beginning to feel the effects of the famine, other parts of Russia were plagued with acute economic crises. Nearly all factories were closed; many trains had ceased to run; peasants had grown increasingly discontented, and an army detachment was ordered to quell a revolt at Kronstadt.[2] The fact that Soviet Russia was still considered an outcast by other nations did not help her internal problems.

The plight of the people of Russia was brought to the attention of the League of Nations by Dr Nansen of Norway. Speaking to the General Assembly, he described the pathetic situation: 'But when I tell you that mothers kill and eat their children and have bodies hanging in their larders,

1 *Dokumenty Vneshnei Politiki SSSR* (Moscow, 1960), vol. IV, 112.
2 Maxime Mourin, *Histoire des Grandes Puissances, 1919–1947* (Paris, 1947), p. 342.

and that salted human flesh is sold in the market places, the extreme poverty and starvation to which Russia has been reduced will be realized.'[3]

The causes of this appalling disaster have not been determined precisely by historians and economists. Lenin considered the famine 'a serious legacy of Russia's backwardness and seven years of war, first imperialist, then civil, which were imposed upon the workers and peasants by the pomieschiks and capitalists of all countries.'[4] Many Western observers did not accept the explanation; they agreed that the revolution, the Allied intervention, and the civil war had disrupted Russia's economy, but they also pointed out that the Communists' insistence on the introduction of 'pure socialism' had created chaos in industries and in the transportation systems. All agreed that the unprecedented drought in the Ukraine and Volga regions was the immediate cause. In his book, *The Famine in Soviet Russia, 1919–1923*, Harold Fisher claimed that there was a lack of evidence to justify the allegation of some historians that the Russian government deliberately ignored the plight of such avowed enemies as the Ukrainians in order to decimate, or at least subdue, the rebellious factions.[5]

One of the most humiliating tasks of the new Communist regime was to acknowledge publicly its failure to provide the Russian people with the social and economic utopia it promised, and to beg help from the capitalist countries it so often condemned. Chicherin sent a circular letter to the European governments and to the United States urging them not to place any obstacles in the path of citizens of their countries who wished to help the Russians.[6] Maxim Gorky, the eminent Russian writer, asked the admirers of Tolstoy, Dostoyevsky, Mendeleyev, and Pavlov for bread and medicine for his stricken countrymen.[7] Lenin appealed to the International Proletariat, intimating that 'the Soviet republic of workers and peasants expects that help from the toilers, from the industrial workers

3 Address of Dr Nansen of Norway to the League of Nations Assembly, *League of Nations – Records of the Third Assembly Plenary Meetings*, vol. 1 (Geneva, 1922), 59.
4 Quoted in X.J. Eudin and H.H. Fisher, *Soviet Russia and the West* (Stanford, 1957), p. 76.
5 H.H. Fisher, *The Famine in Soviet Russia, 1919–1923* (New York, 1927), p. 235.
6 Quoted in Eudin and Fisher, *Soviet Russia and the West*, p. 74.
7 Ibid.

and from small farmers' will not only alleviate the sufferings of his peoples but also repulse further capitalist 'intervention and counter-revolutionary conspiracies.'[8]

The causes and effects of the famine were fully discussed in the League of Nations. Lord Cecil, representing South Africa, regretted the undue delay of the League in providing some assistance to the unfortunate peoples of Russia. In his view, a timely intervention would not only have 'mitigated the horrors of the terrible affliction, but it might have opened the door for the renewal of the world without raising those very difficult political questions ... of economic theory.'[9] Dr Nansen, who was elected the high commissioner of relief to Russia by the assembly, reminded Lord Cecil that the unfortunate delay was caused by the lack of proper and effective machinery for collecting and distributing food and supplies. He hoped that the aid would come 'not in the form of charity but in the direction of reconstruction and self-help,' and only after a thorough study had been made of the causes, the extent, and the consequences of the famine.[10]

Lord Balfour, of England, sympathized with the peoples of Russia and claimed that his own country, despite a coal strike, had contributed £250,000 worth of goods and cash to this humanitarian cause. At the same time he emphasized the difficulty encountered in helping Soviet Russia because of her consistent refusal to permit visits from economic experts from other countries on the ground that such a concession would violate her national independence. He cautiously added that there were well-founded suspicions that the donations were not used in the precise manner designated by the donors.[11] Furthermore, he charged that the Moscow regime had refused to use its own gold reserve for the relief of its inhabitants.

The American Relief Administration, under the able leadership of Herbert Hoover, partly solved the problem of distribution by obtaining a written statement from the Soviet government to the effect that none of the supplies sent by the organization would be diverted to aid the

8 Ibid., p. 76.
9 Lord Cecil's address at the League of Nations, *League of Nations Records of the Third Assembly Plenary Meetings.*
10 Dr Nansen of Norway, ibid., p. 57.   11 Lord Balfour of England, ibid., p. 68.

Bolshevik forces or official institutions, except railway and transport workers. The Americans had also insisted that they themselves choose officials to distribute their relief supplies, although the Soviets were permitted to send observers along with the American officials to the afflicted areas.

The Nansen Convention, signed by Chicherin for Russia and Dr Nansen for the League of Nations, left the distribution problem unsolved. It did, however, propose two men to administer the relief fund; one was to be chosen by Moscow and the other by Dr Nansen.[12] Furthermore, O.D. Kaneva, chairman of the Famine Commission, did relieve some of the anxiety when he promised that the supplies would be distributed according to the wishes of the donors.[13] If the donors failed to provide directives on the manner of distribution, then the funds and supplies would be used for agricultural reconstruction or apportioned among children and invalids.

Dr Nansen faced difficulties which Hoover and the American Relief Administration avoided. Unlike the Americans, who confined their work of mercy to the helping of children and invalids, the league representative extended his relief to the parents as well in the stricken areas.[14] In the administration of this larger objective Dr Nansen was assisted by the Secretariat of the League which collected, arranged, and tabulated all the available information on various organizations and charitable agencies to which countries could appeal effectively.[15]

Besides the League of Nations, the Red Cross, and the American Relief Administration, private organizations and individuals expressed their desire to help the Russian victims. Among the prominent humanitarians to volunteer was James Roll, the lord mayor of London, who on 25 August 1921 asked the Canadian government if it would like to contribute to the Famine Relief Fund which had been launched in London.[16] Even though

12 C.E. Bechofer, 'Starving Russia and the Nansen Scheme,' *New Statesman*, vol. 17, 1921, 688.
13 O.D. Kaneva, 'Disposal of Russian Relief Funds,' *Russian Review*, vol. I, 1923, 67.
14 Bechofer, 'Starving Russia and the Nansen Scheme.'
15 For further details on Dr Nansen's plea for help in the Russian famine, see
   A. Balawyder, 'Canada and the Famine in Soviet Russia and the Ukraine (1921–1923),' *New Review*, vol. IV, no. 4, Dec. 1964, 3.
16 James Roll to Byng of Vimy, 11 Feb. 1921 [GGF], G. 21, no. 34691, vol. I(B) (1910–39), PAC, Ottawa.

the purpose of this drive was to unify the differing methods used by the various Imperial charitable organizations, the Canadian government felt that it was inadvisable to send donations through London at that particular time.

John Lewis, one of the editors of the Toronto *Globe*, was startled by Canada's indifference to the agony of millions of people, including children. He blamed the government's unreasonable prejudice against anything connected with Communism for the refusal to contribute. 'The matter,' he wrote, 'must be dealt with by the Government ... small private contributions are of little value. Canada could easily spare a few millions, and if Canadian grain and other food was sent, some benefit would come to our farmers.'[17] Similar representations were made to the prime minister by Methodist congregations and so-called Independent Labour party groups.[18]

J.S. Ohsol, acting representative of the Russian Red Cross in America, expressed his awareness of the 'great interest' of the Canadian people in the plight of the famine-stricken population, and thought that much could be done for them if 'through legislative action properly initiated a few million dollars could be appropriated by the Parliament of Canada for relief of the Volga farmers in Russia.'[19] He went on to suggest that if such a gift were not feasible, possibly an interest-free loan payable after five years or more could be arranged. The under-secretary of state for External Affairs, Sir Joseph Pope, informed Ohsol that, although the Canadian government was sympathetic to such a suggestion, it could not subscribe to it under present circumstances.[20] As a matter of fact, Canada was having some difficulty in honouring her commitments for outstanding loans to other countries which were on a priority list.

On 11 January 1922 a direct request for a Canadian governmental contribution came from Leonid Krassin, the chairman of the Russian trade delegation in London. On behalf of the governments of Soviet

17 John Lewis to Mackenzie King, 7 December 1921, no. 54282, W.L.M. King Papers, MG 26, PAC, Ottawa.
18 Although these groups professed to be independent, they were obviously sympathetic to the Soviet Union.
19 J.S. Ohsol to Mackenzie King, 6 Jan. 1922, no. 67000, vol. 82, King Papers.
20 Sir Joseph Pope to J.S. Ohsol, 31 Jan. 1922, no. 67004, ibid.

Russia and the Ukraine, Krassin outlined the valuable but inadequate assistance obtained from the United States government. The American aid, in the form of seed grain, amounted to $1,600,000, out of which the governments of the Soviet Union and the Ukraine were to pay about $100,000 in cash, with the balance of payments to be spread over a period of two or three years. He suggested that a similar arrangement perhaps could be made with the Canadian government: 'On behalf of the government and the people of Russia and the Ukraine, I ask assistance of your Government to come to a corresponding arrangement with Canadian farmers. If agreeable in principle we will send over representatives immediately to conclude negotiations.'[21]

Canada turned down the Russian proposal, for she was anxious to receive immediate cash for her grain rather than sell it on long-term arrangement. This attitude stemmed from Ottawa's desire to bolster the sagging Canadian economy, not from a callous indifference to the misfortunes of others. In a letter to Prime Minister King, dated 24 January 1922, James Robb, the minister of trade and commerce, explained his policy towards the Soviet request:

However much Canadians may desire to contribute to the relief of the famine-stricken peoples of Russia I submit that the Canadian Government would not be justified in guaranteeing credit on sale of seed wheat. The superior qualities of strength and colour of the Canadian wheat is world renowned. The quantity desired is available on a cash basis at current market prices. If a representative of the Russian Trade Delegation should visit Canada and advise us of the date of his arrival, this Department will place him in communication with the best Canadian wheat exporters.[22]

Petitions from individuals and private Canadian groups, as well as a request from Soviet officials, finally forced the Canadian government to study the famine seriously with a view to forming a definite policy consistent with that of the League of Nations and of the British government. The cabinet examined the deplorable conditions in the famine-stricken

21 Leonid Krassin to Mackenzie King, 11 Jan. 1922, no. 64098, vol. 78, ibid.
22 James Robb to Mackenzie King, 24 Jan. 1922, no. 67780, vol. 83, ibid.

areas and concluded that the causes of the famine were drought, a lack of proper means of transportation, the havoc created by World War I, the Allied blockade, and the civil war. Then it reviewed the means used by Great Britain, the United States, and the League of Nations in helping the distressed peoples. The cabinet discussions ended on 2 February 1922 with the following observation:

The Committee of the Privy Council do not feel that the Government would be justified in attempting to meet (*sic*) Russian famine relief by an appropriation of public money unaccompanied by contributions from private sources and organized effort on the part of the Canadian people. The Government is prepared, however, to consider means of co-operating with voluntary agencies, should they succeed in effecting some responsible relief organization of which the Government could approve, e.g., the Save the Children Fund.[23]

On the question of aid to the distressed peoples of Russia, Canada sought advice, and followed some of the suggestions made by the government of the United Kingdom. The British Foreign Office informed the governor general that it would be inadvisable for Canada to confine her contributions to the Save the Children Fund. It strongly recommended that financial and material help be apportioned, according to Ottawa's wishes, between the Save the Children Fund and the Russian Famine Fund, the latter being administered by the British Red Cross and the Society of Friends.[24] It also suggested that all collected relief money be earmarked before being forwarded to the distribution agencies.

Anxious to keep Ottawa thoroughly informed about British plans for aiding the hapless peoples, the colonial secretary again notified the governor general that such organizations as the Russian Famine Relief Fund, the Save the Children Fund, and the Society of Friends had combined under the chairmanship of Sir Benjamin Robertson.[25] At the same time a liaison was maintained with the Nansen committee and the International Red Cross committee in Geneva. To facilitate the co-ordination of these several efforts, Professor M. Atkinson, representative of the British Appeal

23 Minutes of the Governor General-in-Council, 2 Feb. 1922, GGF.
24 Winston Churchill to Byng of Vimy, 11 Feb. 1922, no. 68275, King Papers.
25 Churchill to Byng of Vimy, 31 March 1922, ibid.

for the Russian Famine Relief, visited Canada early in the spring of 1922.

Presumably unaware of the government's plan to help the Russians, J.B. McLachlan, a member of the Communist party of Canada, cabled Lenin, asking him whether or not the Soviet government would guarantee the repayment of a possible fifteen million dollar distress loan which was to be spent on the purchase of wheat and food for the Volga region.[26] Lenin heartily agreed to the terms suggested by McLachlan, but intimated that some of this money would, most likely, be used on the reconstruction of rural industry and agriculture.[27] When Prime Minister King heard of this unusual offer by a Canadian citizen, he immediately informed Moscow, through the British Foreign Office, that Canada disclaimed all responsibility for McLachlan's overture.[28]

Nevertheless, King and a number of the members of his cabinet, as well as some members of the Opposition, were willing to co-operate with voluntary agencies in the collection of money and supplies for the unfortunate peoples. King accepted the position of an honorary president of the Save the Children Fund, while Arthur Meighen, the leader of the Conservative party, Thomas C.A. Crerar, leader of the Progressive party, and Rudolphe Lemieux, a prominent French-Canadian Liberal, agreed to act as honorary vice-presidents. Two other leading Canadians on the Save the Children Fund committee were Louis Davies, chief justice of the Supreme Court of Canada and W.S. Fielding, minister of finance in King's cabinet.

Despite the moving oratory of Colonel H.J. Mackie, who was the chief organizer of Canadian aid to Russia, and the sympathetic editorials of the Canadian newspapers, Canadians in general remained apathetic. The sparsely attended public meetings and rallies demonstrated a lack of understanding of the scope and intensity of the tragedy as well as increasing prejudice against the Soviet regime.

This attitude was particularly evident in the Canadian newspapers. After urging Canadians not to spare themselves in contributing to the worthy cause, the *Financial Post* (8 February 1923) in the same editorial pictured Mackie as 'a big, good-natured, kind-hearted man,' who was

26 CAR, 1922, p. 54.
27 Ibid.
28 Byng of Vimy to Churchill, 9 June 1922, GGF.

obviously brainwashed by the Soviet propaganda machine. In like manner, the *Manitoba Free Press* (14 April 1922) encouraged Canadians to be generous in their support of the humanitarian cause, but concluded with a stinging attack on the Communist leaders and their revolutionary policy: '... if the Soviet Apostles had devoted their time and money to the industrial and agricultural rehabilitation of the country with as much zeal as they turned them to propagating the nonsense of world revolution, the lot of the Russian people might be easier to-day.' The *Ottawa Journal* (31 January 1922), following the same line, intimated that, although Russia might be paying the penalty for her political debauchery, the innocent Russian people ought to be helped in this time of need.

A more conciliatory attitude towards the Moscow government and particularly towards the tragedy was shown, however, by a number of well-known newspapers. After outlining the existing machinery for aiding the victims, the *Hamilton Spectator* (15 February 1922) 'hoped that the response will measure up to Canada's reputation as a generous-hearted compassionate country.' Similarly, the Halifax *Morning Chronicle* (9 February 1922), quoting Lieutenant-Governor MacCallum Grant's appeal, begged all men of good will to assist the peoples of the Volga and the Ukraine regions, particularly the innocent children.

The *Catholic Register* of Toronto on 23 March 1922 launched a scathing attack on the apparent apathy of the Western nations. The editorial reminded the Allies that without Russian assistance, they would not have stemmed the powerful German war machine during World War I. 'In those days,' it concluded, 'all was praise and enthusiasm for the Russian people. The Russian people are the same to-day, but the face of the Allies is turned away from them.'

No official statistics are available to show how much Canadians contributed to the Russian Relief Fund. Reportedly, after several weeks of effort by the Canadian committee of the Save the Children Fund for Russian Relief, enough money and food was collected to feed some 18,500 children.[29] During its five years of operation, the Famine Relief Committee organized in 1921 by Toronto Communist sympathizers, and assisted by the Canadian Friends of Soviet Russia, delivered about one

29 The *Morning Chronicle*, 9 Feb. 1922, Halifax.

million dollars worth of goods to Russia.[30] The latter group under the leadership of F. Custance organized local committees in almost every section of Canada with the purpose of collecting money, clothing, food, and medical supplies for the Russian victims.

Apart from this sporadic show of generosity, Canadians in general remained indifferent towards the famine. True, they were undergoing an economic depression at home, but it is difficult to support this argument as the main reason for their lack of response to a misfortune of such proportions, since they willingly helped other nations in distress during the same period of economic disorganization. The Montreal *Gazette* (5 April 1922) held that although Canadians generally did not lack 'in sympathy either sentimental or practical,' they did not dare send money or food to a country which they could not trust and whose name 'stinks in the nostrils.' The editorial concluded with a rather strange solution for the existing Canadian apathy by suggesting that a humble acknowledgment on the part of Lenin and Trotsky of their dismal failures as social innovators would somehow magically inspire Canadians with a new spirit of generosity.

The solution to the problem of general apathy was not as simple as the Montreal *Gazette* suggested. The causes were complex indeed. The Soviet government appeared to be 'consistently ungrateful' for the aid given them by foreign countries. Moscow lost no opportunity to decry the efforts of relief organizations and to create suspicions as to the motives that inspired the contributions of the people of the world.[31] Everywhere agents of relief societies were obstructed by officials sent to the famine areas by the Soviet government and were forced to overcome insistent propaganda which gave all credit to the Soviet administration and little or none to the Allies. Furthermore, Moscow continued to beg for assistance from foreign powers and at the same time discouraged such aid by boasting how efficient the Soviet economic system was and by imposing restrictions on relief organizations.[32]

30 Tim Buck, *Thirty Years, 1922–52: The Story of the Communist Movement in Canada* (Toronto, 1952), p. 32.
31 Hodgson to Curzon of Kedleston, 14 Aug. 1922, W.L.M. King Papers, MG J.4, vol. 142, PAC, Ottawa.
32 William Peters to Curzon of Kedleston, 24 Oct. 1922, ibid.

Finally, Dr Nansen of Norway was regarded in some quarters with distrust and suspicion. Reportedly, individuals in charge of the distribution of food collected by the Nansen organization were badly selected and, generally speaking, inefficient. Lack of unity and harmony plagued this organization from its inception. There was a rumour to the effect that Nansen hoped to use his agency for the purpose of reconstructing the economy of Russia so that he could subsequently exploit her vast natural resources.[33] Obviously, the atmosphere was far from being conducive to unstinted generosity.

33 Hodgson to Curzon of Kedleston, 14 Aug. 1922, ibid.

CHAPTER FOUR

De Jure Recognition

On 3 July 1922 Canada finally adhered to the Anglo-Soviet Trade Agreement. Ottawa favoured a rehabilitated Soviet Russia, not only for commercial reasons, but also for the preservation of peace in Europe. To support her views, Canada sent Sir George Gordon, president of the Bank of Montreal and Dr E. Montpetit, director of the School of Social, Economic, and Political Science of the University of Montreal, to represent her at the Genoa Conference which had opened on 10 April 1922.[1] Lloyd George, the British prime minister, convened the conference for the purpose of removing obstacles to the admission of the Soviet Union into the family of nations and for the settlement of the problem of German reparations.

Several factors seemingly contributed to the success of this conference. The New Economic Policy introduced by Lenin advocated a more liberal trading policy with the non-Communist countries. The principal European countries, too, encouraged more friendly relations with Moscow by accepting the socialist system of government of Russia in the Cannes resolution drawn by the Allied Supreme Council in January 1922.

However, Georgii V. Chicherin, the Soviet commissar for foreign affairs, made it clear to the Allies that neither the new trade concessions nor the Communists' willingness to attend the Genoa Conference should be construed as a sign of weakness on Moscow's part. On the contrary, he argued that the Soviet government felt strong enough to negotiate with the capitalist countries on an equal basis.[2] Such a determined stand on the part of the Soviets was bound to conflict with the interests of France, an equally inflexible nation.

---

1 The Montreal *Gazette*, 10 April 1922.
2 Chicherin to British, French, and Italian governments, 15 March 1922, Jane Degras (ed.), *Soviet Documents on Foreign Policy*, vol. 1 (Toronto, 1951), 295.

In his initial address to the plenary session of the Conference on 10 April 1922, Chicherin dwelt on the necessity of disarmament, proposed a world economic conference on the internationalization of all great waterways, and demanded a just redistribution of world gold stocks.[3] Chicherin's speech antagonized the French delegates since they were primarily interested in reaching some type of workable formula whereby the Soviets could compensate France for her generous contributions to the Czarist government. Much to the consternation of the Russian and German delegates, the French and British representatives decided to study the problem of war reparations thoroughly at Lloyd George's temporary residence at Villa Alberti.

In the meantime, the Russians and Germans decided to play a diplomatic game of their own. After several preliminary meetings, they concluded the Rapallo Treaty on 16 April. The terms of this treaty called for mutual cancellation of prewar debts and war damage claims, as well as for an immediate resumption of diplomatic relations between the two countries.

These agreements stunned the Allied representatives. To their annoyance, Chicherin referred to the Rapallo Treaty as a model which the Western nations could well afford to imitate. Obviously flushed with victory, he accused the French and the English of ignoring the original purpose of the conference, reminding them that no positive reconstruction of Europe was possible without a rehabilitated Russia. He added that adequate credits from non-Communist countries could help accomplish this objective.[4]

The Canadian editorial writers' reaction to the failure of the Genoa Conference varied.[5] The *Ottawa Journal* (17 May 1922), which originally had hailed Lloyd George as a creator or an architect of a new world order, placed the blame for this diplomatic fiasco on the glaring absence of Americans from the international parley and the evident lack of co-

3 Statement of Chicherin at the First Plenary Session of Genoa Conference, ibid., pp. 298–301.
4 Ibid., pp. 308–18.
5 Because of mutual suspicion between the Allies and the Russians and Germans, the Genoa Conference failed in its objectives. At The Hague Conference, where the discussions continued, the hostile climate persisted, with the Allies demanding compensation for prewar debts and the Soviets insisting on the necessity of foreign credits for the rehabilitation of Russia.

operation between the Russians and the French. The Montreal *Gazette* (10 April 1922) unhesitatingly singled out the Kremlin's reluctance to co-operate with other nations for the permanent rehabilitation of Europe as an important cause of the failure of the meeting. The French-Canadian daily, Montreal's *La Presse* (26 May 1922), found the Communists' behaviour singularly baffling in that they continued to insist on getting credits from capitalist countries without providing guarantees of repayment. Agreeing with the general policy of Russian rehabilitation, the Halifax *Morning Chronicle* (21 May 1922), however, continued to maintain that no nation could effectively help the Russians until they themselves replaced the Communist regime by one that was sincerely interested in the welfare of the people.

Lloyd George lost the general election of 1922 and was succeeded by the Conservative leader, Bonar Law. During Law's brief ministry and following his untimely death, Britain's relations with the Soviet Union grew progressively worse. Moscow blamed the Conservative administration for this deterioration, claiming that it deliberately organized an anti-Soviet propaganda campaign.[6] The British Foreign Office dismissed such charges as unfounded, pointed to the Russian violation of the Anglo-Soviet Trade Agreement of 1921, and demanded adequate compensation for the material damages and the loss of prestige caused by the Soviets.

The deterioration of relations came to a head in a British ultimatum of May 1923. The British foreign minister, Lord Curzon, recounted the illegal seizure of the steam trawlers *Magenta, St. Hubert,* and *James Johnson,* which were engaged in fishing off the coast of Murmansk.[7] According to this ultimatum, ten British fishermen from the *Magenta* were drowned because of neglect on the part of the Russians, and the captain of the *James Johnson* was sentenced to forced labour. In all cases, the crewmen were unduly detained. The British Foreign Office demanded satisfactory compensation for damage to property, and for the lives lost. The Curzon ultimatum also pressed for adequate compensation for Russia's execution of C.F. Davison, an alleged British spy, and for the arbitrary arrest of

6 Litvinov's reply to Lord Curzon's note of 2 May 1923 on 'Violations of the Anglo-Russian Agreement,' Degras, *Soviet Documents,* p. 385.
7 Curzon to Krassin, 3 May 1923 (Great Britain, HMSO, *Accounts and Papers*), vol. xxv, cmd. 1869, Russia no. 2, 10–11.

Mrs Stan Harding, a journalist. Moreover, Moscow was to cease interfering with the peoples of India, Persia, and Afghanistan. And finally the
ultimatum demanded an apology for an insulting Soviet reply to a British
protest against religious persecution in Russia. The Soviet Union was
given ten days to provide an adequate answer to these charges; failure
to comply with the suggested terms would free the United Kingdom from
the obligations of the Anglo-Soviet Agreement of 1921.

Moscow's response to the ultimatum was remarkably conciliatory. In
the 'interest of peace' the Soviet government agreed to conclude a convention with the British government, 'granting to English citizens the right
of fishing outside the three-mile limit, pending the settlement of this
question, in the shortest possible time, at an international conference, and
to pay compensation for the case in point.'[8] Dropping its original demand
for British restitution for the death of twenty-six Azerbaijani nationalist
insurgents in Baku and for the imprisonment of three others,[9] the Soviet
government expressed its willingness to pay compensation for the execution of C.F. Davison, and for the arbitrary arrest of Mrs Harding. It
stipulated, however, that 'this willingness in no way signifies that the
Russian Government recognizes that there was any irregularity in the
repressive measures it took against these spies.'[10] Furthermore, the note
denied all charges of anti-British propaganda in the Middle East, and
apologized for the two insulting letters dealing with religious persecution
in Russia.

Following the Soviet reply, tensions eased between London and Moscow. Both governments reiterated the pledges contained in the Anglo-
Soviet Agreement of 16 March 1921, whereby the two parties agreed to
desist from all hostile propaganda aimed at each other.[11] Without men-
tioning the Comintern, Great Britain asked the Soviet Union to refrain
from supporting those bodies or institutions which fomented rebellions
in various parts of the British Empire. It was exceedingly difficult for
Soviet Russia to maintain such strict neutrality since her foreign policy
continued to be controlled by a combination of the Commissariat for

8 Krassin to Curzon, 23 May 1923, cmd. 1890, no. 4, ibid., p. 3.
9 Twenty-six Azerbaijani nationalists were supposedly killed with the approval of
   Great Britain.
10 Krassin to Curzon, 23 May 1923, cmd. 1890 (HMSO).
11 Curzon to Krassin, 29 May 1923, ibid.

Foreign Affairs, which transacted official business in matters of external interest, and the Comintern, whose chief aim was to encourage socialist revolutions in foreign countries.

Undoubtedly, the concessions of the Soviet government in response to the Curzon ultimatum salvaged the Anglo-Soviet Trade Agreement to which Canada adhered. Of great significance, they helped to create a friendlier atmosphere which resulted in the British and Canadian *de jure* recognition of the Soviet Union in 1924.

As early as 1921 a number of smaller nations accorded the Soviet government the official status of an acceptable nation. Among these, Estonia, Lithuania, Latvia, Finland, Persia, Afghanistan, and Turkey signed peace treaties with the Soviet regime. That same year Austria gave the Moscow government *de jure* recognition and England signed a trade agreement with Russia.[12]

With the formation of the new minority Labour government under the leadership of Ramsay MacDonald the restoration of full diplomatic relations with the Soviet Union was taken for granted. In their election promises both the Labourites and the Liberals pledged themselves to recognize the Soviet Union. 'Labour's vision of an ordered world,' read the Labour party's election manifesto of November 1923, 'embraces the nations torn with enmity and strife. It stands, therefore, for the resumption of free economic and diplomatic relations with Russia.'[13] The Liberals, too, in their pre-election campaign, favoured 'the re-opening of full relations with Russia.'[14]

Although the Labour party hoped that Russia would enter the family of nations, it refrained from giving the British Communists public support. As a matter of fact, it rejected three offers by the British Communist party to become an integral part of the Labour party: at the Annual Labour Conference at Brighton in June 1921; at the Annual Executive Conference at Edinburgh in June 1922; and again at the Annual Labour Conference of June 1923.[15]

---

12 Michael T. Florinsky, 'Soviet Foreign Policy,' *Slavonic Review*, vol. 1, 1934, 540.
13 W.P. and Zelda K. Coates, *A History of the Anglo-Soviet Relations* (London, 1943), p. 129.
14 Ibid.
15 Carl F. Brand, *British Labour's Rise to Power, Eight Studies* (Stanford, 1941), pp. 245-58.

These rejections of the overtures by the Communist party of Great Britain proposing amalgamation with the Labour party did not prevent MacDonald's minority government from legally recognizing the Soviet regime. On 2 February 1924 Great Britain forwarded the following note to the Soviet government:

His Majesty's Government recognizes the Union of the Soviet Socialist Republics as *de jure* rulers of those territories of the old Russian Empire which they now administer. Recognition will not itself suffice to create normal conditions, complete friendly relations and full commercial intercourse, which it is the earnest desire of His Majesty's Government to see restored at the earliest possible moment. For this purpose it will be necessary to conclude a definite practical agreement on a variety of matters, some of which are not directly connected with *de jure* recognition.[16]

Naturally, the Soviets interpreted this recognition in the light of Marxian ideology. Chicherin maintained that the *de jure* recognition was brought about by 'the unanimous demand of the working class ... which, in the form of unemployment, feels bitterly the present disruption of the world's economic system, and with the whole strength of its just instincts, strives for the only real remedy – namely, the drawing of Soviet Russia into completely normal intercourse with Great Britain.'[17]

The question of Canada's *de jure* recognition of the Soviet Union came up for the first time at the Anglo-Soviet discussions when the Russian representative asked the British representative whether British recognition bound the whole British Empire. Great Britain had accepted the Soviet Union into the family of nations without consulting the British Dominions and contrary to the recommendations of the Imperial Conference of 1923, which advocated mutual consultation in foreign affairs. After an exchange of a series of cablegrams between Ottawa and the British Dominion Office, the Canadian government agreed to accept most of the proposed clauses of the Anglo-Soviet Trade Agreement, whose stipulation providing the liberty to renounce 'the most favoured nation' clause within six to

16 L.S. Amery to Byng of Vimy, 30 January 1924, no. 46481, [GGF], G. 21, no. 34691, vol. 1(b) (1911–24) [PAC], Ottawa.
17 Interview by Chicherin on British Recognition, 4 Feb. 1924, Jane Degras, *Soviet Documents*, p. 424.

twelve months was of vital concern to Canada. In other words the trade agreement of 1921 to which Canada adhered in 1922 was to continue in force. However, Canada took the position that it was not desirable for her to adhere to the new commercial treaty until complete studies by the Departments of Trade, Finance, and Immigration were made. Upon the completion of such studies Canada could express her decision regarding the commercial treaty by an exchange of notes with the Soviet Union.[18]

The Labour member of Parliament for Winnipeg Centre, J.S. Woodsworth, raised the question of Canadian-Soviet relations in the House of Commons by asking George Graham, the acting prime minister, whether Britain's recognition of the Soviet government automatically included the same type of official acceptance by Canada. Graham told the House that he did not know the answer to the question, but he was certain that trade between the two countries would not be appreciably affected by such a diplomatic move.

When Prime Minister King returned to the House, William Irvine (Labour – East Calgary) asked him to enlighten the members of Parliament on whether Canada had already accorded Soviet Russia the official status of a sovereign nation by the very fact that the United Kingdom had restored diplomatic relations with Moscow, or whether this was to be done separately. King, who also held the portfolio of the secretary of state for external affairs, responded ambiguously that the 'Canadian Government will take its own position in regard to the Soviet republics, just as we would take our position in regards to anything else.' Then in reply to J.S. Woodsworth he added that 'when Great Britain takes a certain position in an international matter, the Dominion Government may, for the same reason, take a similar position.'[19]

That King agreed to endorse the British decision is patently evident from his answer to A. Yazikov, the head of the Russian trade delegation in Canada, who sought to clarify his own status by ascertaining whether Ottawa had given the Soviet government *de jure* recognition.[20] In diplomatic but vague phraseology, King notified the Soviet representative on

18 O.D. Skelton to J.A. Russel, tariff commissioner of the Department of Finance, 1 Aug. 1924, and W.L.M. King to the Dominion Office, 1 Aug. 1924, Department of External Affairs, no. 598, vol. 95, PAC, Ottawa.
19 Canada, House of Commons, *Debates*, 23 June 1924, p. 3503.
20 *Dokumenty Vneshnei Politiki SSSR* (Moscow, 1963), vol. VII, 158.

24 March that he had the honour to say 'that Canada is ready to recognize the u.s.s.r.'[21] Three months after sending this notification, the Canadian prime minister informed the House of Commons that Canada had accorded the Soviet Union formal diplomatic recognition.[22]

The British Foreign Office was upset by King's letter of recognition. One senior official of the Office felt that recognition of the government of the ussr by Great Britain bound the entire British Empire, even though details of commercial relations were to be negotiated by each dominion.[23] This opinion was upheld by the Treaty Department of the Foreign Office.[24] The position adopted by the British government was presented to the Canadian prime minister who was advised that the *de jure* recognition of any country, according to international law, could only be conveyed through diplomatic channels and by the British government on behalf of the whole Empire.[25]

According to British advisers and some Canadian constitutional experts, King's gesture to Yazikov and his statements in the House of Commons were superfluous and meaningless. A.B. Keith held that the British recognition 'clearly bound the whole Empire' and that King's letter to the Russian trade delegation chairman was 'neither necessary nor effective.'[26] Robert MacGregor Dawson interpreted King's separate formal recognition as a gesture against Great Britain's neglect to consult the Dominions before acting in the matter.[27] Finally, R.A. MacKay and E.B. Rogers maintained that King was 'simply clearing up the doubt that had arisen' in the minds of some Canadians and some Russian officials.[28]

There appears to be another explanation for King's display of independent decision. In order to retain the support of French Canadians and

---

21 Ibid.
22 Canada, House of Commons, *Debates*, 23 June 1924, p. 3503.
23 Minutes of the Foreign Office, 10 May 1924, signed by W.F. Adams, FO 371/2456/380, Public Record Office, England.
24 Minutes of the Treaty Department of the Foreign Office, signed by P.M. Roberts, 18 June 1924, ibid.
25 George Mounsey of the British Foreign Office to the under-secretary of state for Colonial Affairs, 1 April 1924, ibid.
26 A.B. Keith, 'Notes on Imperial Constitutional Law,' *Journal of Comparative Legislation*, vol. vii, 985, ser. 3, 106.
27 Robert MacGregor Dawson, *The Development of Dominion Status* (Toronto, 1938), pp. 86–7.
28 R.A. MacKay and E.G. Rogers, *Canada Looks Abroad* (Toronto, 1938), p. 173.

of many English-speaking Canadians, he wished to give Canada the semblance of an autonomous nation which could and would make her own decisions rather than follow in the footsteps of the mother country.[29]

Although King informed Yazikov that Canada was prepared to recognize Soviet Russia, he, according to the chief Soviet trade delegate in London, denied the latter the right 'to fulfill consular functions or even to communicate with the Soviet nationals in Canada, but at the same time ... recognized the old Ukrainian consul ...'[30] These allegations were reiterated by M. Litvinov, the Soviet commissar for foreign affairs, in his talk with G. Mounsey of the British Foreign Office.[31] Litvinov intimated that the matter was so serious that Yazikov was contemplating leaving Canada.

The Foreign Office, perturbed by these accusations, attempted to discover their validity. Although King maintained that the chief function of the Trade Mission was to sponsor commercial relations, he was prepared to honour the terms of the Anglo-Soviet Trade Agreement which authorized the trade delegation to grant diplomatic visas.[32] As to the question of contacting Russian nationals, the reference probably applies to King's insistence on non-interference of the Soviet delegates with the lives of Ukrainian and Russian Canadians. The last allegation, that referring to the Ukrainian consul, was denied by the prime minister in answer to a question asked by a member of the House of Commons. He disclosed that Canada's recognition of the USSR did include the Ukrainian Soviet Socialist Republic but not the Ukrainian People's Republic.[33]

---

29 Escott Reid, 'Mr. Mackenzie King's Foreign Policy, 1935–36,' *Canadian Journal of Economics and Political Science*, vol. III, February, 1937, 88.

30 M. Rakovsky to the British Foreign Office, 16 June 1924, FO 371/N7343/38, PRO.
  A group of Ukrainian emigré nationalists attempted to keep the idea of a Ukrainian Republic alive by engaging a Montreal businessman, M.M. Campbell, to act as their agent in Canada. Campbell, accordingly, issued Ukrainian Republican passports and visas to Russia and to Ukraine to anyone who was willing to pay five dollars. The arrival of the Soviet trade delegation forced the issue to the public for Yazikov argued that his agency was the only authority having the right to issue visas to Russia. The under-secretary of state, Sir Joseph Pope, was upset with Campbell's assumed authority and notified him that Canada did not recognize the Ukrainian Republic. See J. Pope to Campbell, 13 June 1924, Dept. of External Affairs.

31 Memorandum of G. Mounsey, 18 June 1924, ibid.

32 Memorandum of an Interview of A. Yazikov by the Prime Minister, Dept. of External Affairs [PAC Record Centre], Ottawa, box 265183, file 1110.

33 Canada, House of Commons, *Debates*, 1924, p. 3503.

Formal recognition was an important step towards the drafting of detailed terms of the treaties dealing with such items as prewar debts and agreements, claims of British and Russian nationals, propaganda, and fishing rights. The colonial secretary continued to inform Canada of the progress of the negotiations going on in London. Furthermore, in the spirit of the Imperial Conference of 1923, the British Foreign Office asked Ottawa for advice whenever Canada's interests were involved. Consequently, Canada was requested to forward a list of private and federal prewar claims to the British Foreign Office. She was also consulted on the advisability of contesting the ownership of Wrangel Island. Finally, she was approached on the reassessment of the terms of the Fur Seals Treaty concluded in 1911.

In a dispatch dated 8 March 1924 the Canadian government informed the British foreign secretary of four groups of claims.[34] The first consisted of prewar state and municipal loans amounting to $3,000. Then there were twenty-two claims totalling $119,255.49, resulting from debts incurred by the Czarist government in the purchase of saddlery and in the seizure of patents. The third group involved some 528 claims registered against the Imperial Russian Bank which became indebted to Canada in 1916 for a 5½ per cent bond issue valued at $23,400. The last group, comprising ten claims, amounted to $1,520 and was filed against several Russian companies.

When the Anglo-Soviet Treaty was signed on 8 August 1924 the question of claims and counterclaims was shelved until a later date. Evidently, more detailed information was necessary regarding Russian state and municipal bonds before a satisfactory solution could be reached. In the meantime, negotiations were to be carried on with bondholders, and in case of dispute recourse was to be made to the Arbitration Tribunal.

In preliminary discussions the Soviet delegation did not object to the inclusion of British colonies and protectorates in the impending treaties, but insisted that self-governing Dominions such as Canada and Australia arrange individual trade agreements with the Soviet Union. After consulting with the Dominions, the British delegates inserted the following clauses, to which the Russians agreed:

34 Byng of Vimy to L.S. Amery, 8 March 1924, no. 4894 [GGF].

Stipulations of the present Treaty shall not apply to any of His Britannic Majesty's Self-Governing Dominions but, subject to any modifications mutually agreed, may be extended thereto by an exchange of notes to be effected between the Government of the Union and the Government of the Dominion concerned.

In the event of the Treaty not being extended to any particular Dominion, goods produced or manufactured in such Dominion shall enjoy in the territory of the Union complete and unconditional most favoured nation treatment, so long as the goods, manufactured or produced in the territory of the Union are accorded, in such Dominion, treatment as favourable as that accorded to goods manufactured or produced in any other Foreign country, but liberty is reserved to the Government of the Union to denounce this paragraph at any time in respect to any particular Dominion.[35]

The Canadian government fully agreed with the greater portion of the stipulations. However, it hoped that the liberty of denunciation of the most favoured nation would be made reciprocal and open to the Dominions as well as to the Soviet Union.[36] In addition, Canada suggested that a period of six to twelve months' notice be given for any such denunciation.

One of the most contentious claims involving Canada was the ownership of Wrangel Island, located in the Arctic Sea eighty-five miles northeast of Cape Billings, eastern Siberia. Anticipating a dispute over this island, the British Foreign Office asked Canada whether she wished to contest its legal proprietorship. Canada's claim to the controversial piece of land was based on the occupancy of the island from 12 March 1914 to 17 September 1914 by the survivors of the brigantine *Karluk*, the property of the Canadian government.[37]

However, the United States and the Soviet Union also had legal claims to the island. In 1881, Captain Calvin L. Hooper had taken formal possession of it in the name of the United States.[38] The Russian claim was based primarily on priority of time, for the Soviet foreign minister maintained that the Isle of Wrangel was officially incorporated into Imperial Russia, and a Russian flag had been raised on it by members of an expedi-

35 Ibid., 14 July 1924, no. 48573.
36 Byng of Vimy to L.S. Amery, 4 Aug. 1924, no. 48903, ibid.
37 The Montreal *Gazette*, 15 April 1922.   38 Ibid.

tion organized by the Czarist government in the years 1822 to 1824, under the command of Baron F. Wrangel.[39]

The Russian claim to the ownership of Wrangel Island conflicts with the accounts of the Arctic explorer, V. Stefansson, and with an article presumably written by one of the editors of a periodical published by the Royal Geographical Society of London.[40] According to this periodical Baron F. Wrangel failed in 1824 to reach the island which he learned about from the natives of Eastern Siberia. On 6 August 1849 a British seaman, Captain H. Kellett, landed on Herald Island and took possession of it in the name of Queen Victoria, but did not visit Wrangel Island. Eighteen years later an American whaler, Captain Thomas Long, sailed along the south part of Wrangel Island and named it after the Russian lieutenant. In 1881 another American, Captain C.L. Hooper, landed on the island.

There seems to be no record of any Russian ship having reached the island until 1911 when the crews of the Russian icebreakers, *Taimur* and *Vaigach*, erected a thirty-five foot beacon between Blossom Point and Cape Thomas. In the summer of 1914 the same icebreakers tried to rescue the crew of *Karluk*, but were unable to get within thirty miles of the island. Significantly, the crew of this Canadian expedition under the leadership of the Arctic explorer, Stefansson, remained on Wrangel Island for a period of about six months – a period of occupation supposedly long enough to establish ownership of it. However, in 1916 the Russian government notified the British government that it had incorporated the island, along with numerous others, into the Russian Empire.

Stefansson insisted that the Russian claims to Wrangel were third in rank, coming after those of Great Britain and the United States. Therefore, in 1921, he organized with the Canadian government's approval, a small expeditionary group and placed it under the command of Allan Crawford of Toronto. Crawford and four other members, Milton Galle, Fred Maurer, Lorne Knight, and an Eskimo woman, Ada Blackjack, the cook, took enough food and other supplies to last them for six months, with the understanding that a relief ship would be sent in 1922. While on the

39 A note from Chicherin to the British agent in Moscow, 22 Aug. 1923, *Russian Review*, 1923, vol. 1, 25.
40 'Wrangel Island,' the *Geographical Journal*, vol. 62 (London, 1923), 441–4.
   V. Stefansson, *The Adventure of Wrangel Island* (New York, 1925).

island this Arctic expeditionary group was to carry out some scientific investigations aimed at discovering whether the island could be used in transpolar aerial trade routes. In addition, they were to assert the British claims to Wrangel by hoisting the Union Jack.

Unfortunately, the group did not receive the much needed food and supplies in 1922. Financial difficulties delayed the sending of the supply ship until August 1922, a month after the close of favourable navigation. Consequently, the ship failed to reach the island. In the summer of 1923, another ship, the *Donaldson*, under the command of Harold Noice, set sail for Wrangel Island. Before his departure, Noice was commanded by the Soviet authorities of East Cape, Siberia, to call at Petropavlovsk for proper clearance papers and to take a detachment of Red Guards to the island, or risk the penalty of confiscation of the vessel and its contents.[41] Noice cabled this ultimatum to Stefansson who advised him to ignore the Russian demands and proceed as planned.

When the *Donaldson* finally reached the island, the crew discovered that tragedy had struck the expeditionary party. The lone survivor, the Eskimo cook, related how Knight had died, presumably from scurvy, on 22 June 1923. The other three, Crawford, Galle and Maurer, perished in an attempt to reach the Siberian coast in order to get provisions. Although the exact fate of the party is not known, it is presumed that the trio broke through the ice.

The *Donaldson* had brought from Nome, Alaska, a trapper, Charles Wells, and thirteen Eskimos, all American citizens, who would continue occupying the island and recording the weather conditions in its vicinity. Apparently, the decision to take American colonists to Wrangel was reached by Stefansson when he was unable to get financial assistance for his Arctic project from the Canadian or British governments. Therefore, he planned to sell his rights to an American group which, in his opinion, would be delighted with the presence of American colonists on the island. The Soviet government called Stefansson 'an agent of imperialism' who seized property that belonged to others, namely Russia.[42]

41 A note from Chicherin to the British agent in Moscow, 22 Aug. 1923, *Russian Review*, vol. 1, 25.
42 William Peters to Curzon, 16 July 1923, no. 79825, W.L.M. King Papers, MG 26, vol. 93, PAC, Ottawa.

In a note to the British representative in Moscow, Chicherin enquired whether the expedition led by Stefansson was authorized by the British government. Then he attempted to furnish proof that the island legally belonged to the Soviet Union. Using such English publications as the *Arctic Pilot* and *Philip's New General Atlas*, he pointed out that even English scholars admitted that the island was discovered by the Russians. Furthermore, he emphasized the fact that in 1910 the Russian Hydrographic Arctic Expedition, under the command of B.A. Vilkitsky, measured the length and the width of the island and erected an iron navigation pyramid for the guidance of ships seeking entrance to the southeast section of it. Finally, he argued that in 1916 the Russian Imperial government had received no objections from the major powers of Europe when it announced that the Isle of Wrangel, together with other islands and territories adjoining the coast of Siberia, constituted an integral part of Russia.[43]

The British allayed the fears of the Soviet government by informing Moscow that the first expedition was strictly a scientific one without any aim of occupying the island. The second expedition, also organized by Stefansson, was primarily concerned with bringing help to Allan Crawford of Toronto and his four associates, who had been engaged in scientific investigations on the island. Since no attempts were being made to claim this piece of land, the British Foreign Office considered any undue interference with this mission of mercy 'an extremely serious matter.'[44]

The Soviet government, in turn, reassured the British and Canadian governments that it did not intend 'to place any obstacles to any salvaging or scientific expeditions to this Island.' However, it reminded the two governments that 'such expeditions to the Wrangel Island and to any Russian territory in general should be made with the consent of the corresponding organs of the State Administration of the U.S.S.R.'[45]

Stefansson did not agree with the Russian claims to the island. He urged the British government 'to stand on her rights' and press for the recognition of British ownership. If the Soviet government continued to insist that the territory belonged to Russia, he suggested that the dispute should be submitted to the League of Nations or to some court. He argued that if the

43 Chicherin to the British agent in Moscow, 22 Aug. 1923, *Russian Review*, 1923, vol. 1, 25.
44 British agent to Chicherin, 23 Sept. 1923, ibid.
45 Chicherin to the British agent in Moscow, 5 Sept. 1923, ibid.

work of his company, Stefansson Arctic Exploration and Development, were forced to terminate for financial reasons, he would be in favour of selling his interests to an American company, for in his opinion the United States had more rights to the island than did Russia.[46]

In an effort to assert her sovereignty over Wrangel Island, the Soviet government, in July 1924, dispatched its icebreaker, *Krassny Oktiabr*, to the island. Upon their arrival, the Russians solemnly hoisted their own flag, with the obvious purpose of demonstrating to Charles Wells and his thirteen Eskimos that the island belonged to the Soviet Union. Then a representative of the Russian Commissariat for Foreign Affairs interrogated Wells in order to discover the specific role of the group, and to ascertain the purpose of the Union Jack which was found in the group's possession.

Wells explained that he and his thirteen Eskimos were employed by the Stefansson Arctic Exploration and Development Company. In his contract with the company, Wells agreed to keep a record of weather conditions on and around the island as well as to supervise the Eskimos. In return for their services, the American group was granted the right to trap. As far as the presence of the Union Jack was concerned, Wells assured the Soviet representative that it was intended merely to show the nationality of the company for which they worked.

The Soviet representative reminded Wells that he and his group had violated the sovereign rights of the Russian government by occupying the island without Moscow's authorization. At the same time he agreed that the Americans were evidently not aware of the Russian claim to the island. He implied that the Soviet government would make arrangements for their repatriation. Subsequently they were transported to Vladivostok where they were housed and fed as guests of the Soviet government.[47] Wells and two of the Eskimos did not see their homeland again; they died before they were repatriated. The remaining eleven Eskimos were taken to Seattle by a Japanese steamer.

The question of the ownership of Wrangel Island arose again at the time

---

46 V. Stefansson to the Foreign Office, 2 June 1924, no. 92256, King Papers, vol. 93. For detailed account of Stefansson's attempt to secure Canada's claims to it, see Richard J. Diubaldo, 'Wrangling over Wrangel Island,' *Canadian Historial Review*, vol. XLVIII, Sept. 1967, 201–26.
47 J.C. Hill, acting assistant agent in Vladivostok to P.H. Hodgson, British chargé d'affaires in Moscow, 31 Oct. 1924, no. 92729, ibid.

of the Anglo-Soviet negotiations. The British delegation asked the opinion of the experts of the three armed forces on the strategic value of the island in order to decide whether to press claims of ownership to it. The Army Council expressed the view that Wrangel was of no military significance. The Air Council also concluded that the island was not of 'sufficient potential importance' to warrant pressing for it, and the Admiralty found the barren rocky land of little immediate value either strategically or commercially. But since this island was the only territory in the vast area to which Great Britain had claim, the Admiralty considered 'it would be a short-sighted policy to surrender ... claims to it.'[48] Having received the opinions of the three armed forces, the British government decided to renounce all claims to the island, and immediately forwarded the information of the military experts, as well as the decision of the government, to the Canadian government, which was to feel free to make its own judgment on the advisability of pressing for the right of ownership.

One of the main supporters of the claim to Wrangel Island was Stefansson. Both by correspondence and by interviews he attempted to impress upon the Department of External Affairs the importance of retention of this land not only as a possible air base but also as a territory from which walrus hunting could be carried out and on which fur-bearing animals could be trapped.[49] Loring Christie, the legal adviser for the Department of External Affairs, disagreed with Stefansson, arguing that the British Empire already had the burden of developing backward countries and therefore could not sustain further expenses. Moreover, he held that it was not necessary for Canada to own the island in order to use it commercially. Furthermore, insistence on the acquisition of this land might lessen Canada's claim to the ownership of territory of greater value to her ... the Arctic Archipelago directly north of Canada.[50] Finally, he pointed out that neither the Air Board, nor the Naval Service Department, nor the Department of Commerce had shown any interest in acquiring it. This view coincided with that held by the British Air Ministry and Admiralty.[51]

48 L.S. Amery to Byng of Vimy, 18 June 1924, no. 4856, GGF.
49 V. Stefansson to L.C. Christie, 25 Sept. 1920, Loring Christie Papers, MG 30, E15, vol. 3, PAC, Ottawa.
50 Memorandum of L.C. Christie for O.D. Skelton, 17 Feb. 1921, ibid.
51 Memorandum of L.C. Christie, for the prime minister, 9 Aug. 1922, ibid.

Perhaps Canada's most convincing reasons for not claiming Wrangel Island involved the international implications. The Soviet government protested against Stefansson's ventures of 1921 and challenged his position. In any dispute over this island it seemed probable that the United States government would not press its own claim but would support Russian sovereignty over it. This American attitude seems to stem from the suspicion that Great Britain and Japan intended to co-operate against the United States. Allegedly, a British air base established on Wrangel Island would threaten American bases and wireless stations in Alaska and the Aleutian Islands as well as the American fleet in the North Pacific.[52]

In light of the conclusions of the British military experts and in view of the arguments of the Department of External Affairs, the Privy Council agreed to follow the example of England and drop all claims to the island:

The Committee of the Privy Council on the recommendation of the Secretary of State for External Affairs, with the concurrence of the Minister of the Interior, advocates that your Excellency Governor-General may be pleased to inform the Right Honourable the Secretary of State for the Colonies, by telegraph, for the information of His Majesty's Government, that the view taken by the Imperial authorities as to the undesirability of laying claims to Wrangel Island is shared by the Government of Canada.[53]

Another official statement of ownership of the island was made by Moscow on 15 April 1926, when Rakovsky, the Soviet chargé d'affaires in England, notified the British government of a Soviet decree which laid claim to all polar islands, including Wrangel, and considered any attempt by the citizens of the Dominions to occupy them a violation of the sovereignty of the USSR.[54] To make its decree effective the Moscow government transported some fifty Chukchee families, with a number of officials, including a doctor, to form an embryonic colony on the island.[55] Amply supplied with provisions for three years, the settlers landed on the coast of Rogers

52 H.G. Chilton, of the British Embassy in Washington, to the under-secretary of state for the colonies, 21 Sept. 1923, CO/532/252, PRO, England.
53 Byng of Vimy to L.S. Amery, 19 July 1924, no. 48662, GGF.
54 L.S. Amery to Lord Willingdon, 28 Nov. 1926, no. 50590, ibid.
55 Ibid., 18 Nov. 1926, no. 59764.

Bay and travelled towards the interior. They immediately began to construct huts for themselves and a special building for their officials.

To avoid further misunderstandings with the Soviet Union, Canada was asked whether she was satisfied with the existing terms of the 1911 convention, which dealt with the protection of fur seals in the north Pacific. The British Foreign Office thought that the Canadian government might wish some alteration in the terms of the treaty. However, the committee of the Privy Council studied the convention and notified the British delegation that Canada saw no necessity for any modification of the treaty, provided that the other original signatories, Japan and the United States, were also satisfied. The minutes of the Privy Council summarized the conclusion of the deliberations: 'The [Prime] Minister represents that, as has already been intimated to His Majesty's Government, it is the desire of the Government of Canada that the Fur Seal Treaty of July 7, 1911, referred to, which is at present being fully respected by Canada, the U.S.A. and Japan should be maintained, and he considers the arrangement proposed in the Colonial Office telegram a satisfactory one.'[56]

For the purpose of inquiring into possible counterclaims, the Canadian government was also requested to investigate the amount of property owned by the Imperial Russian consuls. The Russian consul-general for Canada, S.A. Likatscheff and the vice-consul, H.B. Zaniewsky, were the central Canadian representatives with their headquarters in Montreal; Constantine Ragosine, residing in Vancouver, was the far western representative and I.H. Mathers, a representative for several European countries including Russia, resided in Halifax. Cursory inquiry showed that C. Ragosine carried out his diplomatic mission in Vancouver from his private home, which he rented and H.B. Zaniewsky held no personal or real property.[57]

The problem of ascertaining the extent of property owned and administered by Likatscheff was complicated by the fact that he and his staff were accepted in May 1918 as employees of the Canadian Department of Immigration. Because of unsettled conditions in Russia, Likatscheff was

56 Byng of Vimy to L.S. Amery, 'Minutes of a Meeting of the Committee of the Privy Council,' 9 Aug. 1924, no. 49096, ibid.
57 Sir Joseph Pope to the Commissioner of the RCMP, 17 Nov. 1920, Department of External Affairs, PAC, Records Centre, Ottawa, box 240997, file no. 439.

not able to obtain financial support from the Russian government at Omsk to carry out his duties. Therefore, the Russian consul-general asked the Canadian government whether he could continue servicing some 200,000 Russian and other Slavic people whose language and tradition were familiar to him. The Canadian government was favourably disposed towards him and felt that 'such assistance' would indeed help create contentment among the Canadians of Slavic origin thus enabling them to become good citizens. However, Likatscheff and his staff were no longer to be considered as members of the Russian consular services but rather as employees of the Canadian government.[58] The Foreign Office sanctioned this arrangement.[59]

Reportedly, Likatscheff continued his consular duties until 1920 when he took an extended leave of absence. He was replaced by C. Ragosine, the Russian consul in Vancouver, who was ordered by Likatscheff to close his office and take over consular duties in Montreal.[60] Evidently Likatscheff considered himself and was considered by the Department of External Affairs to be a representative of the Russian government at Omsk. At the same time he was an employee of the Canadian Department of Immigration and as such did not have the authority to appoint his successor while he was on leave of absence. The secretary of state for the colonies, Lord Milner, alluded to this irregular procedure in his letter to the governor general but did consent to have Ragosine continue consular services in Montreal in an official capacity.[61]

The problem was finally resolved when the Canadian government followed the British government's policy of ceasing to recognize non-Bolshevik diplomatic and consular officials on the ground that they no longer represented the existing government.[62] In accordance with this policy I.H. Mathers, who in reality had ceased to act as Russian consul in

58 Governor General Devonshire to Lord Milner, secretary of state for the colonies, 3 May 1918, co42/1007, Public Record Office, London.
59 Foreign Office to the under-secretary of state for the colonies, 17 May 1918, co/42/1008, ibid.
60 C. Ragosine to Joseph Pope, 22 Sept. 1920, box 265143, file no. 1209, Department of External Affairs.
61 Lord Milner to the governor general, 13 Nov. 1920, ibid.
62 W.S. Churchill, secretary of the colonies, to Governor General Byng of Vimy, 19 Sept. 1921, box 265164, file no. 1486, ibid.

1920, resigned officially as representative of the Russian Imperial government on 7 April 1922.[63] Ragosine closed the Russian consulate in Montreal on 20 June 1922.

There is some mystery surrounding the disposal of the property, particularly the archives of the general-consulate in Montreal. According to the chief Russian representative in Canada, the archives were in the hands of the Canadian government.[64] The under-secretary of state for External Affairs denied that the Canadian government had the archives or possessed any information as to their whereabouts, stating firmly that it was never concerned about their disposition.[65] The Soviet government claims to the property of the Russian consuls came after the conclusion of the Anglo-Soviet Treaty of 1924.

Since the problem of claims was deferred to a later date, Canadian and British citizens, as well as the Soviet government, received little comfort from the newly concluded treaty. The British members of the Parliamentary Opposition expressed their dissatisfaction with the treaty, claiming that it offered practically nothing of substantial value to the people of Great Britain. Lloyd George, irked by the extreme vagueness of its terms, observed that 'in the proposed Treaty every point in dispute has been left unsettled, and it is a very remarkable document to be called a treaty.'[66] Sir Robert Horne, a former Conservative cabinet minister who signed the Anglo-Russian Trade Agreement of 1921, referred to the treaty as a 'hurriedly patched up document' which would satisfy only a small portion of the electorate. 'But,' he continued, 'when the document is read one can only come to the conclusion that there is no agreement which is of any advantage to anyone.'[67]

The Canadian press was rather critical of the *de jure* recognition in general and of the concluded treaties in particular. The *Ottawa Journal* (7 October 1924) remained extremely critical of Russian promises to satisfy bondholders and claimants: 'That the Russians had any means or any intention of paying these claims was not suggested: nevertheless, Mr. MacDonald and his lieutenants plunged hopefully into negotiations with

63 I.H. Mathers to Sir Joseph Pope, 7 April 1922, ibid.
64 A. Yazikov to O.D. Skelton, 18 Nov. 1925, box 265269, file no. 1312, ibid.
65 O.D. Skelton to A. Yazikov, 20 Nov. 1925, ibid.
66 Quoted in the Montreal *Daily Star*, 7 Aug. 1924.   67 Ibid.

them.' The *Montreal Star* (7 August 1924) called the agreement 'The Ghost Treaty': 'What a farce to call such an arrangement a Treaty! What a victory for the friends of Soviet Russia in Glasgow and elsewhere! To talk of this arrangement by which secrecy and diplomatic privilege is granted to an army of propagandists under the guise of trading as a Treaty is absurd.'

Although reservedly favouring *de jure* recognition as a necessary step towards the formal admission of the Soviet Union into the family of nations, the *Manitoba Free Press* (9 August 1924) termed the treaty of 8 August a Russian victory over British negotiators. Montreal's *La Presse* (13 August 1924) denounced the treaty as a 'diplomatic comedy' and the strangest, the most disconcerting and demoralizing thing that ever happened in the annals of history.' The French-Canadian newspaper objected to the lump sum proposed by the Soviets as restitution payments to satisfy Canadian claimants. Inspired by Canadian nationalism, the editorial attacked the Canadian government for being a dormant partner to such a treaty: 'Since we are theoretically partners of the treaty made by England and since we are members of the Commonwealth, how come did we allow ourselves to be forced to adhere to this treaty without our consent – even after Lausanne?'

On the other hand, the *Victoria Daily Times* (9 August 1924) complimented Ramsay MacDonald for negotiating the treaty despite constant opposition. According to the editor, the British prime minister placed Russia on her honour with regard to commerce. Still dwelling on trade, the editorial envisioned no difficulty in initiating a flourishing commerce between London and Moscow, for it claimed that British traders are traditionally business like and refuse to take unnecessary risks. In a similar vein, the Montreal *Gazette* (6 February 1924) optimistically expressed the hope that full diplomatic relations 'with the land of the bear' might initiate 'a bright future for Canadian trade in Russia,' provided, of course, that financial confidence were restored and the Moscow government were stabilized.

The Soviet government lauded the newly concluded treaty as a positive step towards the maintenance of world peace. In his report to the Central Executive Committee on Foreign Relations, G. Chicherin disclosed that the purchase of machines and machine parts from England would not only help rehabilitate Russia, but would also boost the stagnant economy of Europe.[68] He stressed the fact that the capitalist countries had finally realized the absolute need of the Soviet Union for the proper economic restoration of Europe.

Despite Soviet Russia's declaration of desire to trade with the capitalist countries, and despite the *de jure* recognition of the Communist regime by many major European countries, the United States remained cool towards extending full diplomatic status to the Moscow government. The Americans insisted that they could not conscientiously restore full diplomatic relations with a government that repudiated legal debts incurred by the Czarist government and that insisted on trying to overthrow the lawfully consti-tuted government of the United States. In his first Message to the Congress delivered on 6 December 1923, President Coolidge expressed his willing-ness to welcome Soviet Russia into the accepted family of nations provided that she demonstrate good-will in fulfilling her obligations as a respectable state:

Whenever there appears any disposition to compensate our citizens who were despoiled and to recognize the debts contracted with our government, not by the Czar, but by the newly formed Republic of Russia; whenever the active spirit of enmity to our institutions is abated; whenever there appear works meet for repentance, our country ought to be first to go to the economic and moral rescue of Russia. Our country does not propose, however, to enter into relations with another regime which refuses to recognize the sanctity of international obligations.[69]

Even up to 1930, three years prior to President F.D. Roosevelt's recogni-tion of the Soviet government, there still remained in the United States opposition to such a diplomatic move. One American observer maintained that *de jure* recognition of the Communist regime would definitely en-

---

68 Jane Degras, *Soviet Documents*, p. 466.
69 N.D. Houghton, 'Policy of the U.S.A. and other Nations with Respect to the Recognition of the Russian Soviet Government, 1917–1929,' *Documents of the American Association for International Conciliation* (New York, 1929), p. 9.

courage Moscow's aggressive attacks on democratic countries.[70] Other Americans held that little or no advantage would be gained by such a diplomatic move, for the United States enjoyed a flourishing trade with Russia without entering into formal ties with her.

Although the Anglo-Soviet Treaty to which Canada adhered was signed by Ramsay MacDonald, it remained unratified by the British Parliament because of the defeat of the Labour party on 29 October 1924. The incident that forced an election was the so-called Campbell Case. Allegedly, R.J. Campbell, an editor of the *Workers' Weekly*, an official organ of the British Communist party, exhorted British soldiers, sailors, and airmen to desist from serving in British armed forces in case a national or class war broke out. The attorney general, backed by MacDonald, decided to drop all charges of conspiracy with which the Communist editor was accused and even refused to permit the organization of a parliamentary committee to investigate the allegation. Consequently, some Labour and Liberal members supported the non-confidence motion which brought the downfall of the Coalition government.

Whereas the 'Campbell Case' was the cause of the new elections, the 'Zinoviev Letter' was largely responsible for the defeat of the Labour party. The general handling of the negotiations with Russia, the failure to solve the unemployment situation, and the lack of an effective housing policy, however, proved to be the underlying causes of MacDonald's fall from power.[71] They provided the fuel for the conflagration set off by the 'Zinoviev Letter.'

G. Zinoviev, the president of the Executive Committee of the Communist Third International, supposedly sent a letter on 15 September to A. McManus, head of the British Communist party, urging him to do his utmost to have the Anglo-Soviet Treaty ratified since such a diplomatic achievement would 'assist in the revolutionizing of the international and British proletariat,' not only in England, but also in the colonies.[72] The letter encouraged the formation of revolutionary cells in all branches of the military forces and 'particularly among those quartered in the large

70 Paul Scheffer, 'American Recognition of Russia; What it would mean to Europe,' *Foreign Affairs*, vol. IX, 1930, 37.

71 CAR, 1925, p. 21.   72 Jane Degras, *Soviet Documents*, p. 472.

cities of the country,' and among factory workers employed in munitions plants and military storage depots. It concluded with a detailed description of the methods to be used in penetrating the armed forces. The letter advocated the indoctrination of energetic, capable men, preferably specialists, who had left the armed services and who held strong socialist views. After a short investigation, the Foreign Office released the letter to the public along with a protest to the Soviet government, claiming that it was forced to do so by the *Daily Mail,* whose editor threatened to publish the letter if the government refused to disclose its contents.

The Soviet government repeatedly branded the letter a forgery, indicating that both the heading of the letter and the signature were works of ignorant conspirators. In a note to MacDonald, Rakovsky, the Russian chargé d'affaires in London, pointed out that the letterhead, 'Third Communist International,' was obviously incorrect, because there had never been first or second internationals. In addition, Zinoviev's signature designated him 'President of the Presidium of the Executive Committee of the Communist International,' whereas he had consistently signed himself 'President of the Executive Committee.'[73] The Soviet historian, Vygodskii, dismisses the Campbell case and the Zinoviev letter as deliberate attempts by the Conservative party and the British imperialists to wreck the Anglo-Soviet Treaty of 8 August 1924.[74]

The authenticity of the letter continued to be disputed as members of the House of Commons, research students, trade unions, and the Soviet government each secured new evidence to support its case.[75] It is doubtful

73 Ibid.
74 Semenivlevich Vygodskii; *Vneshniaia Politika SSSR, 1924–29* (Moscow, 1963), pp. 49–50.
75 Sir Eyre Crowe, permanent head of the Foreign Office, said that the Foreign Office received proof that Zinoviev himself had admitted to the Soviet government sending the letter on 15 Sept. The Conservative Cabinet Committee set up in 1924 to investigate the genuineness of the letter also agreed on its authenticity. A recent article by R.D. Warth found in the *South Atlantic Quarterly* (1950), vol. 49, 441–53, confirms the genuineness of the letter, but does not disclose the source of its information.

On the other hand, the British Trade Union Congress studied the incoming and outgoing correspondence of the Comintern and concluded that no 'Red Letter' ever left the offices of the Comintern. This conclusion was bolstered by statements of three defendants, two in Germany and one in the Soviet Union, who testified that the Zinoviev letter was a forgery committed by White Russian émigrés.

whether this historical problem will ever be resolved. However, regardless of the opinions on the genuineness of the letter, it did help to defeat the Labour government and to usher in the Conservative party.

Upon coming to office, the Conservative administration notified the Soviet government that it could not recommend the treaties for parliamentary ratification. As Austen Chamberlain, the British foreign minister, writing to Rakovsky, declared: 'I have the honour to inform you that, after due deliberation, His Majesty's Government find themselves unable to recommend the treaties in question to the consideration of Parliament or to submit them to the King and His Majesty's ratification.'[76] The note elaborated on the reasons for the decision of the British government and informed Moscow that the Zinoviev letter was but a specimen of the whole body of revolutionary propaganda to which Great Britain was continuously subjected. This, it added, was inconsistent with the solemn promises made by the Soviet Union in both 1921 and 1923.

Rakovsky regretted the fact that the British government felt unable to ratify the treaties, which, according to him, constituted an important step towards peace. He claimed that the Soviet government did its utmost to help the working classes by having the treaties ratified. 'Therefore my Government,' he concluded, 'cannot take any of the responsibility for the feeling of discontent which the decision of the British Government will cause in both countries.'[77] Thus, the treaties remained unratified until 1929 when, after some modification, they were taken up by the Labour government and at last approved by Parliament.

A new aspect of the 'émigrés' version of the origin of the 'Red Letter' is found in the 18 Dec. 1966 issue of the London *Sunday Times*. According to this newspaper, a certain Mrs Bellegrade, who had been living in England since 1945, disclosed that her husband, Alexis, and his close friend, Gumanski, along with several accomplices, forged this letter. A Soviet agent named Driezelovski supplied the two émigrés with an official letterhead; a Lithuanian, Edward Friede, copied the signature from Communist International circulars, and a British Army official, Conrad Donald -m-Thurn, helped the Conservative party to exploit the letter during the election campaign of 1924. Reportedly Thurn received £5,000 from the Conservative Central Office for his contribution to the Conservative victory.

76 Duke of Devonshire to Byng of Vimy, November (n.d.) 1924 [GGF].
77 Jane Degras, *Soviet Documents*, p. 477.

CHAPTER FIVE

Diplomatic Rupture

Most countries that resumed diplomatic relations with the Soviet Union discovered, to their utter dismay, that the Soviet foreign policy was formulated and executed by an unacknowledged, but nonetheless real, combination of the Narkomindel, the Foreign Office, and the Comintern. Paradoxical as it may seem, even while the Narkomindel laboured strenuously to regularize diplomatic relations with capitalist states, the Comintern, in order to gain concessions from the countries with which Moscow was negotiating, seemingly employed every means to undermine their international prestige so as to place them at the mercy of Soviet negotiators.[1] If a country complained of such underhand methods, the Soviet government would unhesitatingly announce that it was not responsible for the policy of the Comintern. Since newspapers and the radio were controlled by Moscow, the Russian people would not be aware of the negotiation problems caused by the Narkomindel-Comintern union.[2] Even the Soviet diplomats possessed little flexibility in negotiating treaty terms, as they, too, were forced to follow the dictates of the Kremlin.[3]

Early in her relations with the Soviet government, Canada experienced the effects of the unusual Soviet diplomacy. She was shocked by the incident of the importation of Communist literature into Canada and by the forged money scheme. Although relations with Moscow were unduly strained by these two occurrences, Ottawa did not sever her ties with Russia until 1927, when the 'Arcos Raid' took place.

After Canada's adherence to the Anglo-Soviet Trade Agreement in 1922, Russia agreed to send a trade delegation to Canada to foster trade.

1 Bruce C. Hopper, 'Narkomindel and Comintern – Instruments of World Revolution,' *Foreign Affairs*, vol. XIX, 1941, 736.
2 Richard E. Pipes, 'Domestic Politics and Foreign Affairs,' in I.J. Lederer (ed.), *Russian Foreign Policy* (New Haven, 1962), pp. 163–4.
3 Gordon A. Craig, 'Techniques of Negotiations,' ibid., p. 365.

Delayed somewhat by sudden illness, the Russian official agent, Alexander Yazikov, finally arrived in Montreal, the headquarters of the delegation, in March 1924. On 27 February 1924 J.S. Dennis, chief commissioner of the Department of Colonization and Development of the Canadian Pacific Railways, informed T.A. Low, minister of trade and commerce, that his company representatives in the Soviet Union had advised him that some twenty cases of literature had been shipped to Canada on consignment to the Soviet trade mission in Montreal. He was rather puzzled at the size of the reference library and expressed the view that it might be advisable to examine its contents in case subversive materials were contained therein.[4] Low agreed that such a large number of books for a trade delegation seemed irregular and he therefore notified the prime minister the next day of this shipment, suggesting at the same time that 'a close scrutiny on the movements and activities' of the Soviet trade delegation group should be kept.[5] Low further informed King on 31 March 1924 that the Russian material would arrive at Saint John, NB, on 3 April and enquired whether he would like the contents to be examined in this city by Mr Ter-Assatouroff, a member of the former Imperial Russian embassy in Washington, but now residing in Canada.[6]

In the meantime, Yazikov, prompted by F.H. Clergue, a prominent Montreal industrialist, arranged his first interview with Prime Minister King on 7 August 1924.[7] During the discussion the Russian official agent maintained that 'the only material of which he had knowledge or for which he had any responsibility' was the collection sent by the Russian government in twenty boxes which comprised his official library and contained publications of the Russian Academy intended for exchange with Canadian universities or learned societies. He did admit, however, that some of these works were written from the Communistic point of view, but he vigorously denied that they were designed for propaganda purposes. As to the other material which arrived by post, he disclaimed any knowledge of it. He asked the prime minister if this literature could not be released

4 J.S. Dennis to T.A. Low, 27 Feb. 1924, no. 87949, W.L.M. King Papers (hereafter cited as King Papers), MG 26, PAC, Ottawa.
5 T.A. Low to King, 28 Feb. 1924, ibid.   6 Ibid., 31 March 1924, no. 97968.
7 Memorandum of an interview between Prime Minister King and A.A. Yazikov, 7 Aug. 1924, no. C104091, ibid.

immediately for he wanted the president of the Russian Academy of Sciences, who was presently in Canada attending an international mathematical congress, to distribute some of the collections to various institutions.

At this interview with the prime minister, Yazikov alleged that the mail of the trade delegation was being opened and examined. King promised to investigate this claim. Investigation showed that several letters addressed to the Soviet agency had found their way to the offices of the Canadian Pacific Railway because of inaccurate addresses.[8] D. Ter-Assatouroff, currently employed by the Colonization Department of the Canadian Pacific Railway, had the agency's mail opened after obtaining the authorization of the minister of customs, Jacques Bureau.[9] The letters were then crudely resealed and returned to the post office. The government expressed its regret that such a procedure was necessary to determine the destination of the mail and assured that steps would be taken to prevent the reoccurrence of any seeming tampering with Soviet mail.[10]

Despite the attempt of Yazikov to expedite matters, the size of the library delayed the procedure. However, on 10 September 1924 Yazikov was informed that sixteen of the twenty boxes would be released by Customs, but the remaining four, which allegedly contained objectionable literature, would be detained indefinitely.[11] Since Yazikov refused to

---

8 Memorandum for the postmaster general re: mail matter addressed to the Soviet agency, Montreal, 9 Aug. 1924, Department of External Affairs, file, 599, PAC Record Centre, Ottawa.

9 Ibid.

10 However, the problem reoccurred in about one year's time when Yazikov complained about tampering with the agency's mail. In a letter to O.D. Skelton, he claimed that someone had opened two of the envelopes which were mailed to the agency by the USSR embassy in France. Along with this letter he enclosed two envelopes which were allegedly opened and then crudely glued together (see A. Yazikov to O.D. Skelton, 29 April 1925, file 637, Department of External Affairs Files, ibid.). Skelton reassured Yazikov that he did not know any grounds 'for the assumption that the responsibility for the tampering' rested with the Postal Department. At the same time he promised to have the matter investigated (O.D. Skelton to A. Yazikov, 30 April 1925, ibid.).

The investigation by the postal authorities was unable to unearth any reason for this postal irregularity. The general superintendent of Postal Services, P.T. Collican, argued that, in his opinion, letters sent from France in a thin delicate paper would inevitably suffer damage in transit. Furthermore, the enclosed envelopes showed that they were sealed by a margin paper taken from a sheet of French postage stamps not available in Canada (P.T. Collican to O.D. Skelton, 24 June 1925, ibid.).

11 Memorandum on detention of the library, 20 March 1925, King Papers.

accept the consignment unless the four boxes were included, the minister of Customs called for a re-examination of the contents of these containers.

Pending the results of this second investigation, Yazikov paid King another visit on 18 December 1924. In this interview he argued that, although some of the detained books were anti-religious, most were not.[12] According to his article published in *Izvestia* on 5 August 1925, the boxes contained such innocuous literature as Pushkin's dictionary and the writings of S. Witte. During the course of his discussion with King, Yazikov intimated that under the terms of the Trade Agreement of 1921, as an official agent he was as immune from search as are consuls. King retorted that even consuls were not permitted to bring into the country they entered any materials which violated the general laws of that country.

The re-examination of the detained baggage was duly carried out from 16–18 March by D. Ter-Assatouroff, G.W. Woodhouse, acting on behalf of the government, and O.D. Skelton, under-secretary of state for External Affairs. About 50 per cent of the literature was classified as inoffensive; 24–40 per cent as probably dangerous and undesirable; 10–15 per cent as absolutely dangerous. In the last category belonged literature which urged workers in capitalistic countries to overthrow their governments by force and to establish Soviet regimes. Some of this literature denied the existence of God and derided all religions, particularly Christianity.[13] Some fifty books and pamphlets removed from these boxes were forwarded to the Canadian high commissioner in London.

Naturally both Russia and Canada were concerned about the events and consequences of the 'importation episode.' G. Rakovsky, the chief of the Soviet delegation in Britain, termed the seizure of the Russian literature 'a grievous national indignity,' maintaining that Yazikov, as an official agent, was entitled to a reference library containing material published in Russia. At the same time he did not condone the practice of importing contraband literature for propaganda purposes.[14]

Prime Minister King pondered the best procedure to be followed in resolving this dilemma. In order to ascertain if he were following the

12 Memorandum on an interview between King and Yazikov, 18 Dec. 1924, ibid.
13 Memorandum on the detention of the library, 20 March 1925, ibid.
14 F.H. Clergue to King, 25 July 1924, ibid.

accepted method in dealing with the imported literature, he consulted the colonial secretary about the legality of searching the belongings of the Soviet officials, who insisted that they were immune from such an investigation according to the terms of the Trade Agreement of 1921.[15] The colonial secretary informed King that although, strictly speaking, a trade agent such as Yazikov did not enjoy diplomatic status comparable to that of a consul, since his position was entirely governed by articles IV and V of the Trade Agreement, nevertheless, he and his staff were immune from arrest and search. At the same time, the cablegram added that the British officials themselves occasionally examined the contents of the mail sent to the Soviet agency, except for that contained in sealed bags.[16]

Satisfied with the legality of the government's search of Soviet literature, King awaited recommendations from O.D. Skelton, the under-secretary of state for External Affairs, before taking further action against the Soviet delegation. Skelton felt that, although the importation of objectionable literature by a foreign diplomat was somewhat irregular, nevertheless it was not altogether alarming. In the first place, he maintained that the books contained in the consignment for the Soviet mission could be found in most Canadian university and public libraries. He noted that many of these books had been translated into French, English, and German. Secondly, he argued that the difficulty of communicating with Russia made the importation of a large reference library imperative. Finally, he agreed with Yazikov, who contended that these books could not be designed for propaganda purposes since they were in single copies.[17]

Another person who had a moderating influence on King's policy toward the Soviet delegation was F.H. Clergue, an influential industrialist. With potential deals with Russia for railway equipment pending, Clergue attempted to dissuade King from any decision that would jeopardize his chances for a profitable trade transaction. In a letter to King dated 14 July 1924 he argued that Yazikov was innocent of the charges of alleged implication with the objectionable literature. He intimated that the Soviet agent received instructions from his government to close the mission and

15 Byng of Vimy to L.S. Amery, 23 March 1925, no. 51540, GGF, MG 21, PAC, Ottawa.
16 Ibid.
17 Relationship between Canada and the Soviet Union, July 1925, no. C104159, King
    Papers.

return to Russia 'as soon as he is convinced that his usefulness here has come to an end ...'[18] Clergue predicted that such an action would regrettably eliminate all possible trade with the Soviet Union in the future.

There is some evidence to show that Moscow retaliated against Canada's policy of retaining some of the Russian books and pamphlets and particularly against D. Ter-Assatouroff, who was appointed by the Canadian government to censor these books and who reportedly opened some of the envelopes destined for the Soviet agency. According to Ter-Assatouroff, the Soviet government refused to grant an exit visa to his mother, Madame Barbe Ter-Assatouroff.[19] After five months of painful negotiations, she was finally granted the long-awaited visa to visit her daughter in France.

But no sooner had the Canadian government accepted the opinion of the under-secretary of state and of some of the industrialists not to overreact to the literature question than another issue of a more serious nature appeared on the horizon. The Canadian government was informed by the Imperial Bank of Canada that extensive forgeries of one-hundred dollar Imperial Bank notes were emanating from the Soviet Union.

The events of this affair began to unfold in apparently harmless fashion when in November 1924 Yazikov received instructions from the State Bank of the USSR asking him to obtain specimen sets of the Canadian bank notes.[20] Such a request was not unusual since governments frequently ask for specimens of foreign currency to protect themselves against forgery. Yazikov did request twenty sets, but was informed by the manager of the Royal Bank that the cost would be $100,000 rather than the usual $50,000 charge for currency in circulation.[21]

In the meantime Yazikov received an Imperial Bank of Canada one-hundred dollar note from the State Bank of the USSR, which requested that he ascertain from the appropriate officials its genuineness. Reportedly, forged Canadian one-hundred dollar notes were circulating in Russia.

Officials of the Imperial Bank apparently did not consider the Soviet

18 F.H. Clergue to King, 14 July 1924, no. 83582–3, ibid.
19 Byng of Vimy to L.S. Amery, 9 May 1925, no. 52140, GGF.
20 Yazikov later provided a résumé of the correspondence for King, King Papers, no. C104140.
21 Royal Bank of Canada to A. Yazikov, 11 Dec. 1924, King Papers, J4 series, no. C104150.

request seriously, for they neglected to report this information to the RCMP. However, on 9 March, the Toronto-Dominion Bank received a shipment of one-hundred dollar notes from its clearing house in London and turned these in to the head office of the Imperial Bank in Toronto for redemption. A close examination of these bills revealed a highly sophisticated level of forgery. Although eight hundred and twenty bills were checked in this shipment, some $20,000 worth of bogus notes had been redeemed in October 1924 from the Bank of Montreal.[22] Following this discovery the general manager of the Imperial Bank called in the RCMP and asked Scotland Yard to investigate this forgery in England. The Canadian government was also duly informed. The Department of Finance decided to appoint one of its employees, Walter Duncan, as special investigator. At the same time, the RCMP commissioner, Cortlandt Starnes, ordered his detachments to carry out a quiet and a careful investigation of the sources of these bogus notes. Within a relatively short period of time some interesting data were gathered.

One of the first persons to be questioned by police for passing Imperial hundred dollar bills was Charles Hannah, the federal member of Parliament for Belleville, Ontario.[23] Hannah was visibly disturbed by such unexpected investigation and offered the explanation that this money could have been given to him for election purposes. Another bill turned up in the hands of a Montreal porter and several others appeared in a Saskatchewan post office. Police did trace these bills to the local banks.

Duncan also discovered some startling facts. In the course of interviewing people he learned that Yazikov had requested specimen sets of Canadian bank notes during the previous December. Duncan took it upon himself to call on the Soviet agency in Montreal in order to obtain further details. However, his request to see the files in the agency was turned down by Yazikov who insisted that Duncan leave the premises at once.[24]

Duncan immediately informed the prime minister of the new development in the case, stressing the rude reception he received at the office of the Soviet agent. Painfully aware of the unsolved puzzle of the importation

22 Supt. H.M. Newson to Cortlandt Starnes, 9 March 1925, RCMP Records, file 1925, HQ-761-Q-1 (vol. 2).
23 D. Const. P.H. Miller to Supt. T.S. Belcher, 16 March 1925, ibid.
24 Duncan's actions related in an interview, 16 April 1925, King Papers.

of literature by the agency, King decided to act at once in the case of alleged forgeries. Accordingly, he summoned to a secret meeting on 20 March Commissioner Cortlandt Starnes, Minister of Justice Ernest Lapoint, Acting Minister of Finance J.A. Robb, and Walter Duncan. After a considerable amount of discussion it was decided to raid the Soviet agency in three days' time in an attempt to discover incriminating evidence on the wholesale forgery which appeared to be emanating therefrom.[25]

Fortunately for the Canadian government, the planned raid was not carried out. Skelton, who was absent from the meeting but who subsequently learned about the impending raid, dissuaded King from taking such action. In Skelton's opinion an investigation of this nature would only strain the relations between Ottawa and Moscow and interfere with the prospective trade arrangements. Secondly, he felt that all action should be delayed until the government could inquire about the legality of a raid from the Colonial Office, since it did appear that the Soviet agency and its members were immune from search according to the Anglo-Soviet Trade Agreement of 1921 to which Canada adhered. King agreed to make the necessary inquiries and sent off two coded telegrams to London.[26]

In the meantime the Soviet trade delegation appeared to be a hive of activity. Early in the afternoon of 25 March, General Sir Arthur Currie, the president of McGill University, whose office was located near the Soviet agency, telephoned the RCMP chief-inspector, J.W. Phillips, informing him about the unusual movement of people and boxes from the agency. Phillips immediately had the agency under twenty-four hour surveillance which continued for some four months without producing any worthwhile clues on the problem of the forgeries.[27]

The details of this sensational news reached the public on 4 April 1925, when the Montreal *Standard* came out with a glaring front-page headline – 'Attempts to Debauch Canadian Currency.' Sir John Aird, president of the Canadian Bankers' Association, was quoted in the article as saying that the forgeries were a deliberate attempt 'on the part of Soviet Russia to swamp the world with counterfeit money and so precipitate a condition of universal chaos.' Although there was no conclusive proof that Russia

25 Memorandum of Cortlandt Starnes, 26 March 1925, RCMP Records.
26 W.L.M. King to secretary of state for the colonies, 23 March 1925 [GGF], file 34691, vol. 2(a).
27 Confidential memorandum of Cortlandt Starnes, 26 March 1925, RCMP Records.

was responsible for the forgeries, nevertheless the article argued that 'the apparent magnitude of the crime and the consummate skill with which it has been carried out are taken as indications pointing away from the ordinary gang of counterfeiters and in the direction of Russia.'

Two days after the appearance of this article in the Montreal newspaper, King received his reply from the Colonial Office. The colonial secretary, L.S. Amery, fully agreed with King about the gravity of the situation. 'It would appear,' he told King, 'to be intolerable that so flagrant an abuse of the immunity conferred by the 1921 Agreement ... should be allowed to prevent not only the punishment of the criminals but the cessation of a nefarious practice.'[28] The cablegram suggested that a thorough search be made of the Soviet delegation premises, located at 212 Drummond Street, provided that convincing evidence could be obtained.

The same cablegram detailed the procedure to be followed in the search of the premises. If the Canadian government possessed sufficient information that the Soviets were guilty of forgery, then a search warrant should be issued to enable the police to examine the offices and the private houses of the Soviet delegation and to seize all incriminating evidence. If the official agent were found guilty, he would be required to leave Canada in accordance with the provisions of article v of the Trade Agreement, but no legal proceedings could be taken against him. The dispatch warned the Canadian authorities to be prepared to apologize to the Soviet government should the police raid fail to uncover adequate proof of criminal activity.

With this cautious advice from the Colonial Office, King proceeded to secure all possible information on this unfortunate incident by an interview with Yazikov before taking any further steps. In his discussion with the Soviet agent on 16 April 1925, King told him that he was informed by the Imperial Bank of Canada, which in turn was tipped off by its correspondent in London's Lloyds Bank, that the Imperial Bank of Persia had received large amounts of Canadian one-hundred dollar bank notes. Reportedly these bank notes came to Persia from Russia, where they were received as donations for the Save the Children famine fund.[29]

28 L.S. Amery to Byng of Vimy, 6 April 1925, no. 54724, GGF.
29 Memorandum of an interview between King and Yazikov, 16 April 1925, King Papers.

Yazikov denied having any knowledge of the alleged forgeries but he did repeat some of the information already known to the bank and government authorities. He mentioned that on 16 November 1924 the State Bank of the USSR asked him to secure specimens of Canadian bank notes of various denominations for verification purposes. On 29 December of the same year the Imperial Bank of Canada, upon request from Yazikov, forwarded several issues of Canadian bank notes to Moscow and charged the Soviet trade delegation in Montreal with the expenses involved. Yazikov agreed to show King any of the correspondence he had had with his government in connection with the bank issues and reassured the prime minister that he would ask his government to help trace the sources of the forgeries.[30]

True to his word Yazikov returned to Ottawa on 21 April 1925 to present King with the correspondence between himself and the State Bank of the USSR. One of King's interpreters during the discussion, Ter-Assatouroff, felt that the letters presented by the Soviet official were 'genuine and perfectly in order.' He also observed that while 'it was improbable that the State Bank had any knowledge of the forgery, it was quite possible that the agencies of the Soviet authorities or unofficial Communists had made use of the notable facilities which exist in Russia for issuing paper money.'[31]

Yazikov's presentation of the Soviet trade delegation involvement was complicated by the account of the counterfeit story found in a Soviet subsidized periodical published in New York. According to this article, one of the State Bank's representatives received an offer of some 5,000 Canadian one-hundred-dollar bank notes on the Stock Exchange. Upon close examination of the bills by experts, the money was declared to be counterfeit. The seller was promptly arrested, and when questioned by the police, named one Chaichi, a Persian, as the individual who had supplied him with the notes. A thorough search of Chaichi's premises uncovered some 15,000 notes. Similar forged Canadian hundred-dollar bills appeared in Baku, Kanentz, and Podalsh. In order to confirm their suspicion that the money was counterfeit, the State Bank officials forwarded

30 Ibid.
31 Memorandum of an interview between King and Yazikov, 21 April 1925, ibid.

one-hundred-dollar notes to London, where an expert agreed with their conclusion. Neither the Russians nor the English ventured to conjecture as to the source of the money. Chaichi, in turn, named another Persian by the name of Sadyk-Emin-Zadu as the culprit responsible for this illegal currency.[32]

Further light on the counterfeit story was provided by Scotland Yard. Reportedly, a large quantity of Canadian notes had been used as payment for goods bought by Soviet merchants in the Persian coastal town of Rasht. The counterfeit bills were forwarded by the Rasht branch of the Imperial Bank of Persia to its head offices in London and eventually found their way back to the Imperial Bank of Canada. Sets of bills also originated in the town of Hamadan, a town on the main road from Teheran to Baghdad. At the same time many of the bank notes were forwarded to the head office in London from such cities as Peking, Hong Kong, Harbin, Hamburg, San Francisco, Strasbourg, Berlin, and Paris.[33]

The inconclusive evidence provided by the RCMP and Scotland Yard convinced King that it would be better not to raid the Soviet delegation. On the other hand, the Soviet government announced that no Canadian paper money would be accepted in any of the branches of the State Bank, a seemingly retaliatory move which was considered by Skelton as unnecessary and spiteful.[34]

Although Canadian-Soviet relations were strained by the Russian delegation's importation of Bolshevik literature and by the alleged Soviet forging of Canadian bank notes, it was not until 1927 that Canada severed diplomatic ties with Russia. This rupture resulted from diplomatic irregularities in England rather than in Canada. As a partner to the Anglo-Soviet Trade Agreement of 16 March 1921, Canada was naturally affected by the tension between the original signatories.

Since the controversial Zinoviev letter incident, relations between London and Moscow had remained cool. Early in June of 1926, however, the situation seemed to deteriorate, as the Soviet Commissariat of

---

32 Yazikov to Skelton, 28 April 1925, no. 108021, King Papers, and "Counterfeit Canadian Bank Notes," *Russian Review*, vol. III, 1925, 284.
33 Captain H.M. Miller (New Scotland Yard) to Cortlandt Starnes, 25 Aug. 1926, Department of External Affairs.
34 O.D. Skelton to King, 28 April 1925, King Papers, J4 series, no. C104138–9.

Finance was allegedly supporting the nine-day British general strike.[35] The walkout began on 3 May 1926 as a protest against the threatened closing of certain coal mines and an unusual reduction of workers' wages. Five days after the commencement of the strike, *Izvestia* enthusiastically announced that 'the whole world's proletariat watches with the greatest delight the British working classes' gigantic struggle.' Furthermore, the Soviet trade unions, virtual branches of the Soviet government, contributed £226,427 to the success of the strike.[36] Prime Minister Baldwin strenuously objected to the use of funds for the purpose of fomenting unrest in his country, but at the same time he welcomed donations from any sources destined to help the miners and their families.

The British foreign secretary, Austen Chamberlain, continued to complain to Moscow about her interference in Britain's domestic affairs. Chicherin, on the other hand, insisted that the funds remitted to the General Council of the British Trade Unions were forwarded by the Central Council of the All-Russian Trade Unions and not by the Soviet government.[37] The controversy finally ended with the unexpected rejection of the Russian donations by the British trade unions.

At the time of the general strike, the secretary of state for Dominion Affairs, L.S. Amery, notified Ottawa that the British government was watching carefully further developments in the involvement of Russia in the strike, and had even given some thought to a complete break with Moscow. However, it decided against such a measure, at least for the time being, convinced that such a severance would not result in any cessation of Communist propaganda, and would probably create undesirable repercussion in Europe and Asia.[38] Almost a year later, the impending bomb exploded with the controversial Arcos raid.

With the authorization of the British prime minister and the foreign secretary, on 12 May 1927 a large force of policemen accompanied by plain clothesmen conducted a search of the Arcos building and the Soviet trade delegation premises at 49 Moorgate, London. The object of the

35 L.S. Amery to Byng of Vimy, 11 June 1926, no. 56954, GGF.
36 Arnold J. Toynbee, *Survey of International Affairs*, 1927 (London, 1929), p. 259.
37 Chicherin to Austen Chamberlain, 15 June 1926, Jane Degras (ed.), *Soviet Documents*, vol. II (Toronto, 1952), 259.
38 L.S. Amery to Byng of Vimy, 18 June 1926, no. 57037, GGF.

intensive search was an important document relating to the British armed forces and allegedly stolen by Soviet agents. Although the document was not found, several suspicions about the activities of the members of the Soviet delegation were confirmed. Robert Koling (Kaulin) was evidently combining the work of the head of staff of the allotment department in the delegation with that of espionage and subversive activities in Europe.[39] The police discovered in his possession a number of sealed envelopes addressed with names of well-known Communists, as well as directives from the Comintern to the Communist organizations in England. More names of high-ranking Communist representatives in the United States, Mexico, Canada, Australia, New Zealand, and South Africa were found in Anton Miller's room, premises of another Soviet agent. Among the names and addresses discovered in the raid were those of J. MacDonald, M. Spector, Tim Buck, his wife Alice, Mrs Mary Sutcliffe, and E. Pirtinnen – all associated with the Communist Party of Canada and all having Toronto addresses.[40]

Convinced that the Soviet trade delegation building (Arcos) was being used as a centre of espionage and subversive activities in the British Empire as well as in the United States and South America, the British government decided to break off all formal ties with Moscow. Consequently, Sir Austen Chamberlain, the British foreign secretary, notified M. Rosengoltz, the Soviet chargé d'affaires in London, on 26 May that England had decided to withdraw her representatives from the Soviet Union and gave Moscow ten days to recall her representatives from the United Kingdom.[41] The Norwegian government agreed to have her minister in Moscow 'take charge of British interests in Russia together with the premises and contents of the British Mission there as soon as it is withdrawn.'[42]

The members of the Opposition remained unconvinced of the alleged Soviet espionage and propaganda activities, and spoke against diplomatic rupture with Moscow. The Liberal leader, David Lloyd George, participating in a debate in the House of Commons on Anglo-Soviet relations, argued that 'to bring about a diplomatic rupture with one of the greatest

39 L.S. Amery to Lord Willingdon, 23 May 1927, no. 60951, ibid.
40 H.M. Miller to Cortlandt Starnes, 21 May 1927, DEA.
41 L.S. Amery to Willingdon, 26 May 1927, GGF.
42 Ivar Lykke to Austen Chamberlain, 30 May 1927, no. 61433, ibid.

powers in the world, is not a thing to throw caps about. It is a thing to bend knees about.' Then he went on to defend the use of the 'so-called espionage system,' claiming that England is doing this all the time: 'Are we not doing that? If the War Office and the Admiralty and the Air Force are not obtaining by every means every information about what is being done in other countries, they are neglecting the security of this country.'[43] J.R. Clynes, spokesman for the Labour party, contended that the fragmentary evidence uncovered in the Arcos raid failed to support the government's decision of severing diplomatic connections with Moscow. He suggested that a parliamentary committee be formed to investigate thoroughly all aspects of the Arcos case and thus provide the Soviets with a fair trial.[44]

In the House of Lords, Lord Parmoor regretted that the government broke off diplomatic relations with the Soviet Union on such slight evidence. Terming the severance of relations an action tantamount to a declaration of war, he envisaged Britain losing a considerable amount of trade as a result of this decision.[45] In attempting to rebut Lord Parmoor, the Earl of Balfour, lord president of the council, challenged him 'to point to a single case in which the Russian government kept its word with regard to interference in our [Britain's] affairs?'[46]

As expected, Rosengoltz registered a strong protest to Austen Chamberlain, objecting to the brutal methods used by Scotland Yard in their 'raid' on the Arcos building and the Soviet delegation premises. He claimed that England had violated article v of the Trade Agreement by sanctioning such an illegal search on the premises of Khinchuk, the official trade agent of the Soviet Union, who supposedly enjoyed diplomatic immunity from such external interferences.[47] M. Litvinov, the Soviet foreign commissar, supported Rozengoltz's protest, and expressed the fear that the British government's decision might affect world peace and general economic recovery.[48]

43 Great Britain, House of Commons, *Debates*, 26 May 1927, pp. 2195–310.
44 Ibid., p. 2231.
45 Great Britain, House of Lords, *Debates*, 31 May 1927, p. 680.
46 Ibid., p. 690.
47 Rosengoltz to Austen Chamberlain, 12 May 1927, see Jane Degras (ed.), *Soviet Documents*, vol. II, 202–4.
48 Ibid., p. 204.

The Soviet government's organ, *Izvestia* (25 May 1927), lamented that the British government's arbitrary decision would cause untold suffering to the toiling masses. On the same day the Communist paper *Pravda* expressed its utter indignation at the 'insolent violation' of the Anglo-Soviet treaty. 'Let bourgeois politicians be informed,' it stated, 'that the Union and its government, supported by millions of population, are strong enough not to brook insolence from any nation.'

The lapse of time did not modify significantly Soviet historians' views on the Anglo-Soviet rupture of 1927. In the first half of the 1940s V. Potemkin continued to maintain that Sir Henri Deterding, president of Royal Dutch-Shell, must take his share of responsibility for the unfortunate event. According to this historian, Deterding, dissatisfied with the oil transactions he had carried on in Russia, urged an economic blockade of Russia as well as a diplomatic break with her.[49] Another Soviet historian, V. Trukhanovskii, blamed the deterioration of relations on such alleged Soviet-adversaries as Winston Churchill, Lord Birkenhead, a noted British Conservative statesman and lawyer, and L.S. Amery, secretary of state for Dominion Affairs.[50]

Canada was informed of the impending Anglo-Soviet rupture on 23 May, three days before the Soviet trade delegation was requested to withdraw from England. In a dispatch labelled 'secret' the secretary of state for the Dominions asked the Canadian government what it intended to do in case Britain decided to break off relations with Moscow.[51] Although he maintained that Canada was free to make her own choice, he suggested that in making this decision she should keep in mind that Russian espionage and subversive activities had been discovered in the British Empire and that 'uniformity of action by various members of the Commonwealth concerned would present great advantages.'[52]

On 24 May the Canadian government through the governor general assured the secretary of state for Dominion Affairs that a cabinet meeting would study the findings of the 'Arcos Raid,' but pointed out that the

49 Vladimir Potemkin, *Istoria Diplomatii* (Moscow, 1941–5), p. 374.
50 Vladimir G. Trukhanovskii, *Istoria Mezhdunarodnykh Otnoshenii i Vneshnei Politiki SSSR* (Moscow, 1961–2), vol. I, 307.
51 L.S. Amery to Lord Willingdon, 23 May 1927, no. 60949 [GGF].
52 Ibid.

evidence obtained so far from the search of the premises of the Soviet delegation failed to establish any proof 'that the official agency in Canada has been a centre of espionage and subversive propaganda.'[53] Nevertheless, the dispatch asked the secretary to forward any recently discovered information on Communist activities in Canada. In addition, it inquired whether the British government had decided to terminate its relations with Moscow under paragraph one, article XIII of the Trade Agreement, which required six months' notice for such termination, or under paragraph three, which demanded immediate cessation of relations along with an opportunity for the Soviets to voice their objections.

As promised, the Canadian government gave immediate attention to the British note on 23 May regarding her decision to break diplomatic ties with Russia. The dispatch, dated 26 May, reviewed Canadian-Soviet relations, noting with satisfaction the increase of trade with Moscow in the past few years and the unblemished record of L.F. Gerus, the present Soviet agent in Canada.[54] Following this introduction, the cablegram elaborated on the method used by the cabinet to reach its decision to sever relations with Russia:

It appears possible to take two views to the effect of the termination of the Agreement made by the Government of Great Britain. In one interpretation Canada may be considered simply to have adhered to an existing Anglo-Soviet Agreement with the consequence that on the lapse of this agreement her own arrangement ceases to have a basis and lapses automatically. If this view is taken the question settles itself. In the other interpretation the Canadian agreement would be held to have an independent existence and would continue unless expressly terminated. In this case it becomes the duty of the Canadian Government to decide whether it is desirable to terminate it.

My ministers have concluded that the evidence of espionage and subversive propaganda set forth by your Prime Minister made it clear that an essential condition of the Agreement as entered into by Canada as well as by Great Britain, namely, that each party should 'refrain from hostile action or undertakings and from conducting outside of its own borders any official propa-

53 Lord Willingdon to L.S. Amery, 24 March 1927, no. 60959, ibid.
54 Ibid., 26 May 1927, no. 60968.

ganda direct or indirect against the institutions of the British Empire' has not been fulfilled. In order to remove any doubt as to whether the Agreement lapses automatically and having regard to all the circumstances, they have accordingly decided to terminate the Agreement.[55]

This lengthy cablegram also informed the secretary of state for Dominion Affairs that Canada had officially notified L.F. Gerus of the cabinet's decision. At the same time it emphasized Ottawa's wish to continue trade with the Soviet Union on an unofficial basis.

The British prime minister, Stanley Baldwin, expressed his gratitude for the Canadian government's uniform action against the Soviet Union: 'I would like to express my own thanks to you for the support you have given us, which I personally value very highly. The action of the Canadian Government in regard to relations with the Soviets will have an enormous and far-reaching effect.'[56]

The Soviet agent in Canada was obviously disappointed with the decision of the cabinet. In a personal interview with King, and by a telegram to him, L.F. Gerus attempted to persuade the Canadian government to drop its plans to sever ties with the Soviet Union. The telegram ran as follows: 'Pray once more, hesitate to abolish the Treaty with the Soviet Union. If it is inevitable, let us abolish it in accordance with the Anglo-Russian Trade Agreement which says, "before taking any action inconsistent with the Agreement the aggrieved party shall give the other party a reasonable opportunity of furnishing an explanation for remedying the default." '[57]

With the consummate skill of an experienced politician, Gerus pleaded with the prime minister not to 'break a precious thing,' meaning the Trade Agreement, for by such a termination he would commit an act of injustice against the workers and peasants of the Soviet Union. He intimated that King must be keenly aware of the pain caused by injustices perpetrated on innocent people, for his own grandfather, William Lyon Mackenzie, suffered unjustly for the sake of his fellow Canadians.

55 Ibid.
56 Stanley Baldwin to Lord Willingdon, 27 May 1927, no. 60972, ibid.
57 L.F. Gerus to King, 26 May 1927, Sessional Papers, no. 180, the Journal Section of the House of Commons, Ottawa.

Replying on behalf of King, O.D. Skelton, the under-secretary of state for External Affairs, pointed out to the Soviet agent that he was given ample opportunity to air his views on 25 May, when he had an interview with the prime minister. On that occasion King informed Gerus that after careful deliberation his cabinet was convinced that the Soviet government had failed to fulfil the terms of the treaty which specified that each partner would 'refrain from hostile action or undertakings and from undertakings outside of their own borders any official propaganda direct or indirect against the institutions of the British Empire.'[58] As a result of the obvious breach of the agreement the Canadian government considered itself free from all obligations of this treaty. Skelton emphasized the fact that there was no possibility of the cabinet's reversing its decision.

In his reply, Gerus showed his usual politeness. He mentioned that Moscow was displeased with his explanation of the Soviet position in the 'Arcos' incident, and had ordered him home immediately. 'It is with profound regret,' he concluded his letter, 'that I must notify you of my intention to close the offices of our official agency and Trade Delegation within two weeks. Thank you for your assistance and courtesy.'[59]

In an attempt to minimize the seriousness of this diplomatic rupture, King continued to maintain that Canada had never had full diplomatic relations with the Soviet Union. 'Our communications and negotiations with that country,' he held, 'have always been conducted through the Foreign Office in London, so that the net result of our action really is that certain privileges of a quasi-diplomatic character have been severed.'[60] According to King, immunity from examination of mail in sealed bags, and of telegraphic dispatches, constituted the most important privileges.

Probably the economic consequences of the termination of diplomatic ties with Moscow were more significant than the political repercussions. At the time of the 'Arcos raid' serious negotiations were being carried on between the Soviet government and Canadian citizens. Apparently Russia was anxious to buy farm machinery from Massey-Harris and 4,000 horses from western Canada. When Canada broke formal ties with Moscow, all negotiations were suspended.

58 O.D. Skelton to L.F. Gerus, 26 May 1927, ibid.
59 L.F. Gerus to King, 28 May 1927, ibid.   60 The Montreal *Gazette*, 26 May 1927.

Unquestionably, the cancellation of the farm-machinery deal with Massey-Harris by the Soviet government deprived Canada of a valuable cash transaction. But there is some doubt whether the sale of 4,000 horses to Russia would have been realized at all because of the pressure of Canadian public opinion. The influential Toronto *Globe* (25 May 1927) expressed its opposition to the sale of Canadian horses on the ground that they might be used by the Soviet government for military purposes. The *Ottawa Citizen* (26 May 1927) saw horses as having little value in a mechanized war, but maintained that machinery, manufactured goods, and raw materials would inevitably bolster the Russian economy. Since horses can be classified as a source of power for agricultural industry, the Ottawa paper, therefore, was opposed to the shipment of horses to Russia.

Despite the commercial losses that Canada would suffer as a result of the 'diplomatic rupture,' most of the Canadian newspapers lauded Mackenzie King for the prompt and decisive action he took against the Soviet government. In a convincing editorial, the *Victoria Daily Times* (27 May 1927) argued that though Canada might lose about $6,000,000 worth of trade each year as a result of the Canadian-Soviet 'diplomatic break,' this would be insignificant in comparison with the loss of national respect. The *Manitoba Free Press* (30 May 1927) termed Prime Minister Baldwin's decision to sever ties with the Kremlin 'one of the most momentous decisions of his career.' The Toronto *Globe* (26 May 1927) viewed King's diplomatic act as a gesture 'to show Moscow the ineffectiveness of its campaign to dismember the British Empire.' Then the editor added that the Canadian prime minister 'has earned the gratitude of the country in thus declaring promptly and definitely the position of Canada.' The Conservative party organ, the *Mail and Empire* (26 May 1927), commended King for his courageous action, but at the same time denounced his independent attitude of making decisions without express authorization from England. The *Montreal Daily Star* (26 May 1927) argued that Canada's inevitable termination of relations with Moscow would not seriously jeopardize the chances for further trade with Russia, since the Soviet government fully realized that it could buy goods cheaper in Canada than anywhere else in the world. The Montreal *Gazette* (26 May 1927), following the line of other Liberal newspapers, maintained that 'public opinion in Canada will very heartily endorse the action taken by the Ottawa Government in terminating the trade agreement with Russia.' Rather sarcastically, Montreal's *La Presse* (27 May 1927) referred to the Russians as 'wolves' whose subversive activities were checked by Great Britain. In a seemingly impartial manner, the *Halifax Chronicle* (3 June 1927) related the circumstances of the Anglo-Soviet diplomatic rupture as well as Canada's reaction to the findings of the 'Arcos raid.' In a rather philosophical tone it concluded that the Soviets would undoubtedly suffer more from the 'diplomatic break' than would the English or the Canadians.

Various news organs of Canadian labour also expressed their views on the current Canadian-Soviet rupture. The *Payroll* (2 September 1927), quoting Lewis E. Pierson, president of the United States Chamber of Commerce, declared that trade relations with the Russians were virtually impossible because of their conflicting and confiscatory edicts and persistent bad faith. Another non-Communist paper, the *Labor Leader* (7 June 1927) dismissed the loss of trade with Russia as an insignificant 'ripple': 'Our trade with Russia is negligible, and even if Russia retaliates by refusing to buy our goods it would scarcely cause a ripple in commercial circles.' The Communist party of Canada organ, the *Worker* (1 June 1927), following the established pattern of its master models, *Pravda* and *Izvestia*, viewed the official severance as an inevitable step towards an imperialistic attack on the Soviet Union. Characteristically, it called on all Canadian workers to respond to the threatening capitalistic challenge 'with all their power, for now more than ever have we the evidence that Canada is but a vassal of Britain, the beautiful phrases of the last Imperial Conference notwithstanding.'

In addition to the left-wing newspapers, a number of organizations argued against the termination of the Trade Agreement on economic and political grounds. The Workers and Farmers of Central Ontario, a leftist organization, deplored the loss of trade that would result from Ottawa's course of action in which she uncritically imitated Great Britain.[61] Supporting this same view, the Independent Labour Party of Manitoba[62] and the Sinn Fein Club of Toronto[63] denounced King's questionable action of slavishly following the mother country despite the fact that the 'Arcos raid'

61 John Wirth to King, 2 June 1927, Sessional Paper, no. 180.
62 William Ivens to King, 5 June 1927, ibid.
63 Sinn Fein Club of Toronto to King, 6 June 1927, ibid.

found no evidence of Soviet espionage in Canada and in spite of Canada's status of equality gained at the Imperial Conference of 1926.

With the opening of Parliament following the Christmas recess, discussions on the recent Canadian-Soviet 'rupture' shifted from the newspaper rooms and offices of private organizations to the floor of the House of Commons. In the debate on the speech from the throne H.B. Adshead (Labour – East Calgary) queried whether Canada 'severed relations with Russia simply because Mr Baldwin did it, or, as the honourable member for Labelle [Henri Bourassa] said last year, if we simply put up our umbrellas because it is raining in London, then ... we are certainly exhibiting an inferiority complex.'[64] Repeating in substance the arguments advanced by Adshead, A.A. Heaps (Labour – Winnipeg North) questioned the degree of independence given to Canada by the Imperial Conference of 1926. '... And yet almost immediately that (*sic*) the new status had been achieved,' he declared, 'at one of the first opportunities the government had of showing the new status, it meekly followed the example of the British government. There was no reason why Canada should have broken relations with Russia.'[65]

In order to discover the background for Canada's policy towards Russia, Heaps asked the government on 16 February 1928 to table all the correspondence, telegrams, orders-in-council and other relevant documents pertaining to the diplomatic rupture. Prime Minister King tabled the requested documents after securing permission from the British government.

Henri Bourassa (Independent – Labelle) began the debate on Canadian-Soviet relations on 28 May 1928 when he disagreed with the Canadian government's practice of asking the permission of the British government to use documents on Canadian-Soviet relations. But his main attack on the Canadian government centred around the lack of substantial evidence of Soviet subversive activities in Canada which warranted a break with Moscow. Bourassa pointed out that Canada severed ties with Russia 'without having in its possession any of the evidence gathered by the police of London ...' He observed acutely, to the embarrassment of

64 Canada, House of Commons, *Debates*, 1928, p. 143.
65 Ibid., p. 223.

King, that the secretary of state for Dominion Affairs had encouraged the Canadian government to break relations with Moscow in order to present a 'uniformity of action' of the members of the Commonwealth against the Soviet Union. Finally, he reminded the House of Commons that Prime Minister King, in his dispatch to the Dominion Office and in his communication with the Sovet agent L.F. Gerus, acknowledged his satisfaction with the conduct of the members of the Soviet trade delegation in Canada.[66]

J.S. Woodsworth (Labour – Winnipeg Centre) entered the debate by outlining the progress made by the Soviet regime in education and in economy. He referred to the flourishing trade between Great Britain and Russia since the conclusion of the Anglo-Soviet Treaty of 1924. He regretted that Canada followed the 'lead of Great Britain and indirectly the behest of the oil kings ... [the Royal Dutch-Shell Company of Great Britain] when she severed relations with Russia[67]

King's rebuttal illustrated the characteristics of a master parliamentarian. In his review of Canadian-Soviet relations he elaborated on the two irregularities associated with the arrival of the Soviet delegation in Montreal, namely: that of the importation of Communist literature and that of the forgeries of Canadian bank notes. Finally, he emphasized the fact that Moscow was spreading anti-British propaganda throughout the British Empire and in direct violation of the Anglo-Soviet Trade Agreement, to which Canada adhered.

In reply to those members of Parliament who accused him of slavishly following Great Britain in severing relations with Russia, Prime Minister King pointed out that, in the matter of time, Canada broke with Moscow before England did. It was precisely to exercise her new status of an autonomous Dominion, said King, that Canada on her own initiative terminated the quasi-diplomatic ties without waiting for the complete evidence gathered by police at Arcos. Appealing to their common sense, he asked the members of Parliament to picture Canada in the embarrassing position of being the only English-speaking country to have formal ties with Moscow after England had broken with Russia, and her neighbour, the United States, had never established formal relations with her. Finally,

66 Ibid., p. 3449.   67 Ibid., pp. 3458–63.

to calm the fears of those who lamented that Canada would suffer large economic losses because of the rupture, he referred to the United States as an example of an industrial nation which did not establish diplomatic relations with the Soviets and yet enjoyed flourishing trade with them.

R.B. Bennett, the leader of the Opposition, congratulated King on a decision with which 'all right-thinking Canadians' would agree. 'After all,' he concluded, 'there can be no comity between nations when the representatives of one nation are concerned with destruction of the government to which they are accredited.'[68]

With the termination of the full-scale debate in the House of Commons, one of the most controversial events in the history of Canadian-Soviet relations came to an end. Canada's fear of Communism and of everything it stood for appeared again on the Canadian scene. Equally influential in determining Canada's relations with other countries was the feeling of independence she had begun to enjoy as a result of the Imperial Conference of 1926. Was it not the tension created by these two national emotions that formed the very essence of the controversy on the diplomatic rupture?

68 Ibid., p. 3477.

CHAPTER SIX

Limited Diplomatic Relations Restored

Two months before the official restoration of relations between Moscow and London in May 1929 Canada contemplated the resumption of trade and, if need be, diplomatic relations with the Soviet Union. Prime Minister King, urged by Colonel C.H. Mackie, Labour members of Parliament, and manufacturing firms, asked the British government whether an exchange of consular officials with Russia meant the full resumption of relations with that country.[1] At the same time the Canadian prime minister notified London that he did not intend to take any action until after the general elections in the United Kingdom.

One of the most insistent promoters of trade with Moscow was Colonel Mackie. He argued that Canada ought to take the advantage of the opportunity for trade by regularizing her ties with Russia. Fresh from his visit to Russia where he perceived renewed interest in Soviet commerce by the touring British businessmen, Mackie attempted to stimulate similar enthusiasm among Canadian firms.[2] Most of the firms responded positively, but like Massey-Harris, they felt that private transactions with the Soviet Union would be a risky venture unless the Canadian government backed them up through official channels.[3]

To acquire parliamentary approval for his project he solicited the help of Labour members of Parliament and of S.W. Jacobs (Liberal – Mercier).

1 From the Dominion Office to the Foreign Office, 8 May 1929, N2613/1387/38, Public Record Office, London, England.
2 From W.H.J. Clark, British high commissioner to Canada, to L.S. Amery, secretary of state for Dominion Affairs, 20 March 1929, ibid.
3 From Clark to Amery, 15 April 1929, ibid.

In addition he persuaded the Mennonite leaders to write Ottawa petition-
ing the government to establish diplomatic channels which would help the
release of thousands of Mennonites sentenced to death or extermination.[4]
Possibly, too, Canada would, if for no other reason than humanitarianism,
permit these hapless people to migrate to Canada.

The British Foreign Office was annoyed by the news of Canada's intention to restore relations with Moscow. It informed the Canadian prime
minister that, though the appointment of Soviet consuls in Canada would
not necessarily be equivalent to the renewal of relations with Russia, nevertheless, it would be a provisional and an informal manner of sanctioning
such relations. Because of the implied recognition of the Soviet government, the British government strongly deprecated such a move.[5] This
firm stand was made in light of the fact that the United Kingdom did not
herself regularize her ties with Moscow and that such restoration would
only encourage the revolutionary activities of the Third International in
India. Moreover, London financial circles were of the opinion that Russia
was heading towards bankruptcy and therefore would not be able to repay
the loans Canada would be forced to accord her in order to carry on trade.
From the practical angle it was not necessary to renew diplomatic relations
with Moscow for expediting trade since the experience of the United States
attested to the fact that no official relations were essential for a successful
conduct of commerce with Russia.[6]

Members of the Department of External Affairs were criticized by the
British high commissioner to Canada. In his opinion some of the members
of the department were responsible for the conciliatory position taken by
the Canadian government towards Soviet Russia. He maintained that
the Department of External Affairs was staffed by university-trained intel-
lectuals who expressed 'lurking sympathy' for the Communist experiment
as displayed in Russia, even though they disapproved of the methods used
to implement the Communist principles.[7] However, he felt that these sym-

4 From R.H. Hardlow of the Foreign Office to C.W. Dixon of the Dominion Office,
   19 April 1929, ibid.
5 From the secretary of state for Dominion Affairs to the British high commissioner in
   Canada, 11 April 1929, ibid.
6 A copy of a letter sent to Prime Minister M. King by W.H.J. Clark, 15 April 1929,
   ibid.
7 From W.H.J. Clark to L.S. Amery, 20 March 1929, ibid.

pathies were counteracted by a strong anti-Communist feeling shown in Ontario and in Quebec.[8] Consequently, the strong opposition to Communism and to Soviet Russia persuaded the government to defer the resumption of ties with Moscow until this subject was introduced in the British-Soviet discussion following the elections in the United Kingdom. This postponement brought a comment from one of the members of the British Foreign Office who rejoiced that 'Mackie's effort will continue to be in vain ...'[9] – a fitting result for one whom he described as 'not too trustworthy nor scrupulous.'[10]

Diplomatic ties between Moscow and London remained severed until 1929, when Ramsay MacDonald became prime minister and restored full diplomatic relations with the Soviet Union, including exchange of ambassadors. Although Canada did not have representatives at the negotiation conferences at which all aspects of diplomatic restoration were discussed, she was, however, duly informed of the progress of the talks and even consulted on certain terms of the proposed treaty between Russia and Great Britain. But despite the collaboration between London and Ottawa and the warm invitation of the Soviet Union, Canada refused to re-establish the quasi-diplomatic relations she enjoyed with Moscow from 1924 to 1927.

The British general election of May 1929 brought Ramsay MacDonald and his Labour party into power by a narrow margin of three seats over the Conservatives. With the promised support of the majority of the Liberals, Macdonald agreed to head the minority government. Although the Liberals and the Labourites differed with one another on several minor issues, they did, however, agree on many important ones. Both favoured an increase in foreign trade, and an immediate resumption of diplomatic relations with the Soviet Union.[11] On 5 November, following a general debate in the House of Commons, the Labourites supported by the Liberals and three Conservatives voted by a substantial margin of 324 to 199 to restore formal ties with Moscow.

The Soviet Union, too, was anxious to re-establish relations with Eng-

8 Ibid.
9 Comment by S. Harcourt-Smith of the Foreign Office, 8 May 1929, ibid.
10 Comment of S. Harcourt-Smith, 23 May 1929, ibid.
11 Alfred F. Havighurst, *Twentieth Century Britain* (Evanston, 1962), p. 211.

land. In 1928 Stalin was beginning to effect his policy of 'socialism in one country' by inaugurating his First Five-Year Plan. The aims of the plan were twofold: to industrialize Russia rapidly and effectively and to collectivize agriculture. The plan was but a means used by Stalin to convert backward Russia into a powerful industrialized and military 'socialist state,' a base from which Marxist-Leninist ideology could influence adjacent countries.[12] This strategy was in direct opposition to Trotsky's idea of fomenting socialist revolutions in other countries without being overly concerned about Russia's economic development or her military strength.

Following the forced exile of Trotsky in 1927, Stalin pursued his policies of planned economy with ruthless determination. He organized the Gosplan, a supreme agency entrusted with the co-ordination of the various organs which worked towards the successful execution of the Five-Year Plan. This agency set the wages of the workers, determined the number, kinds, and sites of new factories, secured raw material for factories, regulated trade, and distributed manufactured goods.

From its very early stages the directors of the Gosplan realized that they could not successfully execute their plan without the help of Western countries. To erect factories and to cultivate the huge collective farms, each averaging about a thousand acres, Russia needed factory equipment, electrical appliances, chemicals, and heavy farm machinery. She also had an urgent need for skilled technicians and engineers to teach the native workers how to erect factories and operate the complicated factory and farm machines.

The Communist party of the Soviet Union and the Comintern through its Communist parties in Western countries were directed by Stalin to initiate friendly relations with the non-Communist nations in order to aid in the fulfilment of the five-year plans. At the Fifteenth Congress of the Communist party held in Moscow in December 1927, the following resolution was drawn up: 'We must base our policy on the idea of maximum development of our economic relations with foreign countries so far as such relations (expansion of foreign trade, foreign credits, concessions, employment of foreign technical advisers) contribute to the economic strength of

12 Jan F. Triska, 'A Model for Study of Soviet Foreign Policy,' *American Political Science Review*, vol. 52, March 1958, 72.

the Union.'[13] The Sixth Congress of the Comintern, meeting in September 1928, also urged Communist parties throughout the world to work incessantly towards encouraging trade between their own countries and Russia and towards maintaining peace between the Soviet and capitalist states.[14]

Sensing Russia's conciliatory attitude towards Western countries and her eagerness for foreign trade, Great Britain made overtures to Moscow on the re-establishment of normal diplomatic relations. In a dispatch from London dated 13 July 1929, sent through the Norwegian chargé d'affaires in Moscow, the British Labour foreign minister, Arthur Henderson, expressed his government's willingness to restore normal ties with Russia, provided that 'the reciprocal rights and duties which International Law recognizes' would govern preliminary negotiations.[15] The note further invited Russia to send a responsible representative to London to discuss with the foreign minister 'the most expeditious procedure for reaching as rapidly as possible a friendly and mutually satisfactory settlement of the outstanding questions between the two countries, including those relating to propaganda and debts.'[16]

Eight days after the receipt of the invitation, the Soviet government notified London that it was most anxious to restore diplomatic relations. The cablegram, however, reminded the British government that the severance of ties in 1927 was 'not the consequence of the fault or desire' of the Soviet government in the first place. But 'in the interest of both countries and of the cause of peace' it was willing to forget the regrettable incident and work towards a better understanding between the two states. Finally the cable informed England that Valerian Dovgalevski, Soviet chargé d'affaires in Paris, would travel to London to initiate the discussions.[17]

The preliminary talks between V. Dovgalevski and Arthur Henderson

---

13 Michael Florinsky, 'Soviet Foreign Policy,' *Slavonic Review*, vol. XIII, 1934, 545.
14 Alvin Z. Rubenstein, *The Foreign Policy of the Soviet Union* (New York, 1960), pp. 84–5.
15 Dispatch from the government of Great Britain to the government of the Soviet Union, 15 July 1929. Great Britain, HMSO, *Accounts and Parliamentary Papers*, cmd. 3418, Russia no. 2, p. 3.
16 Ibid.
17 Dispatch from the government of the Soviet Union to the government of Great Britain, 23 July 1929, ibid., p. 4.

were stalled by the thorny problem of procedure. The Soviet representative insisted that no negotiations could be carried on without the immediate exchange of ambassadors, whereas the British representative considered the organization of committees dealing with debts, war claims, propaganda, and trade as prerequisite requirements for full-scale negotiations. A compromise was finally agreed upon whereby both parties agreed to an immediate exchange of ambassadors, with Gregori Sokolnikov coming to London and Esmond Ovey going to Moscow, and to a reciprocal confirmation of the pledge with regard to propaganda contained in article XVI of the Treaty signed on 8 August 1924, between Great Britain and the Soviet Union. Article XVI read as follows:

> The contracting parties solemnly affirm their desire and intention to live in peace and amity with each other, scrupulously to respect the undoubted right of a State to order its own life within its own jurisdiction in its own way, to refrain and to restrain all persons and organizations under their direct control, including organizations in receipt of financial assistance from them, from an act overt or covert liable in any way whatsoever to endanger the tranquillity or the prosperity of any part of the territory of the British Empire or the Union of Soviet Socialist Republics, or intended to embitter the relations of the British Empire or the Union with their neighbours or any other country.[18]

In keeping with its promise, made in a cablegram dated 24 June 1929, the British government informed Ottawa fully of the progress of the ensuing negotiations that were carried on in London between the Soviet and British representatives. The same note expressed its intention to consult with the Dominions before resuming diplomatic relations with Moscow. Consequently Canada was asked by the British government whether she agreed with the inclusion of the Fur Sealing Protection Convention of 1911 in the protocol of the proposed treaty and whether she approved article V on fisheries as found in the General Treaty of 1924. This article stated that 'citizens of the Soviet Union shall enjoy exclusive rights of fishery not only within three miles of the coast (measured in the case of

18 Gregori Sokolnikov to Arthur Henderson, 20 Dec. 1929, cmd. 3467, ibid., p. 3.

bays from a straight line drawn across bays at the first point nearest entrance where width does not exceed ten miles) but also in waters of the White Sea and its entrance, lying to the southward parallel 67 degrees 40 minutes north latitude.'[19] Ottawa found nothing objectionable in either of these articles.

Early in November the British Foreign Office sounded out the governments of the Dominions on their desire to adhere to article xvi of the treaty. After obtaining a positive response from the Dominions, Henderson notified the Soviet government on 28 November that the Dominions expressed their wish to adhere to the 'undertaking contained in Article xvi of the Treaty signed on August 8, 1924.' The Soviet government was puzzled by this request of the British foreign minister. It was unable to understand how Canada, which had not resumed relations with Moscow since the rupture of 1927, and the other Dominions which never had established formal ties with the Soviet Union, could possibly adhere to article xvi of the treaty. However, the note optimistically added: 'When normal relations have been established between the Soviet Government and the Dominions, the Soviet Government is willing to effect a similar exchange of notes [similar to the notes exchanged between the British and the Soviet representatives during the negotiations] with each of them and asks the British Government to be so good as to investigate the attitude of Dominions to this.'[20]

The British Foreign Office investigated the attitude of the Dominions towards the establishment of, and in the case of Canada the resumption of diplomatic relations with Moscow. It then notified Litvinov, Soviet deputy foreign commissar, that Canada, Australia, New Zealand, South Africa, the Irish Free State, and Newfoundland were ready to exchange notes similar to those effected between Great Britain and Russia. Because none of the Dominions had the appropriate diplomatic offices for negotiations, all diplomatic transactions were to be carried out by the British ambassador in Moscow. The Soviet government readily accepted this arrangement for future negotiations with the Dominions, but wanted assur-

19 Secretary of state for Dominion Affairs to the secretary of state for External Affairs, 28 Nov. 1929, no. 63920, GGF, no. 34691, vol. (2b) 1925–9.
20 Ibid., 6 Dec. 1929, no. 63979.

ances that the problems of war claims, debts, fishing rights, and treaties as outlined in articles I and II of the Protocol would be fully discussed prior to any official agreement.[21]

Canadian press reaction to the British resumption of relations with Russia and a possible similar restoration with Canada ranged from mild optimism to gloomy scepticism. The Toronto *Globe* (7 November 1929), commenting on the re-establishment of ties between London and Moscow, expressed its surprise at the change of heart of Great Britain, which considered Soviet Russia her 'arch enemy.' 'All this, however, is forgotten,' concluded the editorial, 'in a gesture of friendliness to Britain's most implacable enemy, and in an attempt to get a few more million pounds of trade for which payment cannot be certain.' Nine days later another editorial in the same paper quoted *Pravda*'s repudiation of all obligations to control propaganda spread by the Communist International and positive denial of a possible settlement of the debts problem as suggested by the Anglo-Soviet Treaty of 1929. The Toronto newspaper saw nothing surprising in the statements made by the Soviet organ, but it did express astonishment 'that British statesmen should be so simple-minded as to believe they could get a square deal from the Soviets.'

The *Ottawa Journal* (13 October 1929) opposed the newly concluded Anglo-Soviet agreement on the grounds that such a restoration of relations would only deprive Canada of British markets for her wheat and manufactured goods. The editorial agreed with H.A. Gwynne, editor of the London *Morning Post*, who, in an address to the Canadian Club of Montreal, warned Canadians that the unbelievable changes in Russian agriculture would eventually interfere with Canadian wheat markets. 'When that happens' (a thorough cultivation of Russia's vast farmlands and her return to ordinary commerce), he emphasized, 'there will be open next door, as it were, to the Old Country a vast wheat field, producing almost as much as the Prairie Provinces of Canada, and at a much lower cost of production and transportation.'

A rather neutral attitude towards the restoration of diplomatic relations was taken by the *Montreal Daily Star* (4 July 1929). The editor did not know whether such a resumption would affect Canadian business, since

21 Ibid., 13 Dec. 1929, no. 63999.

trading between Canada and the Soviet Union did continue despite the rupture of 1927. He summarized his attitude in the following manner: 'However, if Mr. King feels like co-operating with Ramsay MacDonald and having Canada become less distant to Russia, it will probably cause no harm. The Soviets may send a few bewhiskered individuals here who will try to convert us to Bolshevism, but that will be about as easy as converting us to Buddhism. Although we are pretty crazy at times, we're not quite as crazy as that.'

The *Victoria Daily Times* (24 July 1929) outlined the usual arguments used by the enemies of Soviet Russia against countries who restored diplomatic ties with Moscow. Among the most frequently mentioned was the dissemination of Communist propaganda among the countries of the British Empire with the sole purpose of undermining its strength and prestige. The editor, however, disagreed with this type of argument. He defended Ramsay MacDonald's policy towards the Soviet Union and held that Great Britain would not 'allow the internal affairs of another country to interfere with the normal business relationships.' He went on to say that Russia's contact with the Western world would help considerably towards her rehabilitation.

In a similar manner the *Halifax Chronicle* (6 November 1929) looked upon the resumption of commercial relations with Soviet Russia as a means of exerting a moderating influence on her: 'Trade will be resumed in greater measure and Russia once more will take her place and be subjected to the moderating influence of other nations. This all makes for betterment and it is well that now when the world is settling down, that Russia is coming again to take a place with the others. There can be no question but that it will make for better feeling and eventually react for the good of all concerned.' The editorial argued that there was definite evidence of increased freedom and of general toleration in the Soviet Union. It bitterly denounced those who considered the Soviet Union an enemy, particularly after her outstanding contribution to the Allied victory during World War I.

The restoration of relations was first broached in the House of Commons when J.S. Woodsworth asked whether Prime Minister King, in view of the favourable reports of Col. H.J. Mackie of Renfrew, was contemplating the renewal of relations with Russia. It was rumoured that Mackie informed King that Russia had a market for Canadian wheat, flour, horses, and for such manufactured articles as binder twine, agricultural implements, electrical and railway equipment.[22] King replied that his government was 'giving consideration to the matter.'[23]

On 14 March H.E. Spencer (United Farmers of Alberta – Battle River) urged the government to follow England and investigate the immense potential markets of Russia.[24] The same kind of advice was voiced by A.A. Heaps, who informed the House that, whereas Great Britain had about twenty-three trade agencies in Russia, Canada did not have a single one. 'I cannot understand,' added Heaps, 'why our Minister of Trade and Commerce, who seems so anxious to develop trade in all parts of the world, has allowed the occasion to slip by of adding a Canadian representative to the British trade delegation which is now visiting Russia.'[25]

As promised, King did give serious consideration to the question of restoring the 1924–7 quasi-diplomatic relations. He decided not to send a trade representative to Moscow or to allow a Soviet trade delegation to come to Canada. Instead, the British ambassador in Moscow looked after Canada's economic and political interests.

Canada's decision not to restore the pre-1929 arrangement with the Soviet Union appeared to be influenced by the American policy towards Moscow and by Canada's growing concern with widespread Communist activities in various parts of the country as well as by the Soviet government's attitude towards religion. In the spring of 1929, Vincent Massey, Canadian minister in Washington, sounded out the American government on its attitude towards the restoration of formal diplomatic relations with Russia.[26] The American government felt that such formal relations were neither advisable nor necessary, for the existing commercial organizations in the United States could adequately transact business with Moscow. On 14 March 1929, the London *Morning Post* scoffed at this American policy and intimated rather sarcastically that Canada should follow her 'beloved

22 Memorandum of O.D. Skelton, 12 March 1929, no. 101048, King Papers, MG 26, vol. 139.
23 Canada, House of Commons, *Debates*, 22 Feb. 1929, p. 355.
24 Ibid., p. 969.   25 Ibid., p. 1295.
26 Vincent Massey to King, 2 March 1929, no. 101052, King Papers.

United States' in studiously refraining from any official relations with the Soviet Union. On the other hand, the Montreal *Gazette* (6 November 1929) assumed that Ottawa's decision was influenced by her concern with widespread Communist activities in Canada and the Communists' attitude towards religion.

Admittedly, Ottawa was made fully aware of the Communists' activities by the reaction of the provincial and local police. In January 1929 a Communist meeting, which was to be held in the Toronto Standard Theatre, was banned by the Toronto police commissioner on the ground that the aim of the gathering was to spread seditious propaganda. A month later six Communist supporters were arrested in Toronto for obstructing traffic. In February, Aaroo Vaaro, editor of *Vapaus*, a Finnish Communist paper published in Sudbury, was committed to jail for spreading Communist propaganda of 'seditious, immoral, anti-Christian, anti-Canadian, anti-British' nature among the Finnish immigrants. In April, the Canadian Communists suffered another setback when, on the recommendation of its Executive Committee, the Trades and Labour Council of Toronto expelled Communist representatives of unions affiliated with the council on the charge 'that the latter stood for dual organization and had attempted to disrupt the existing unions.'[27] Communist delegates were also expelled from the Windsor Trades and Labour Council and from the Brotherhood of Railway Carmen.

One of the main reasons for the ejection of Communist members from labour unions was their close affiliation with the Comintern and the Communist party of the Soviet Union. Both the union executives and the Canadian government knew that the Communist party of Canada took orders from the Comintern located in Moscow. Many of the Canadian Communist leaders attended annual meetings held in the Soviet capital. In 1928 two outstanding Communist party members, Maurice Spector and John MacDonald, represented the Communist party of Canada at the Sixth Congress of the International held in Moscow.

The Canadian government was, no doubt, cognizant of the anti-religious legislation passed by the Soviet government in 1929. A decree of the All-Russian Central Executive Committee and Soviet of the Peoples' Com-

27 CAR, 1928–9, p. 543.

missaries of the RSFSR excluded the teaching of religion from all public and private institutions: 'The teaching of any kind of religious faith in government, public and private establishments for instruction and education is forbidden.' Only selected teachers, and inspectors of anti-religious propaganda were to be hired. In addition, the decree sanctioned 'the liquidation of prayer buildings, when occasion arises ...'[28] Needless to say, King, ever sensitive to the voters' feelings on religious matters, did not wish to give the impression that he condoned the Soviet Union's anti-religious decrees by regularizing diplomatic relations with Moscow.

The Soviet government organ, *Izvestia* (26 November 1929), expressed its indignation at Canada's decision not to restore diplomatic relations with Moscow. It regarded Prime Minister King's attitude as inconsistent and incomprehensible, for on the one hand he encouraged trade with the Soviet Union, while on the other he deliberately prevented such trade by refusing to exchange trade delegations with Russia. At the same time *Izvestia* considered such a dubious policy to be consistent with the character of the prime minister who in 1927 severed ties with Moscow for no other reason than his inability to refuse the demands of the British Foreign Office, which clamoured for this diplomatic rupture.

Not only did the Canadian government refrain from exchanging diplomatic representatives with Russia but the members of the Canadian legations in Paris and Tokyo refused to visit the delegates of the Soviet embassies in these two cities.[29] Strictly speaking the Dominion representatives abroad were not required to associate with the Soviets, for the renewal of relations between the United Kingdom and the Soviet Union was applicable to the British Dominions on their own requests. However, the British government argued that for the sake of Commonwealth uniformity and for the enhancement of social life among the members of the diplomatic corps it would be advisable for the representatives of Canada, the Union of South Africa, and the Irish Free State to develop cordial social relations with the Russians.[30] The Dominion Affairs Office did not fully

28 Decree of the All-Russian Central Executive Committee and Soviet Peoples' Commissaries of the RSFSR respecting Religious Associations, quoted in *Izvestia*, 26 April 1929.
29 From H.J. Seymour of the Foreign Office to Sir W. Clark, 20 March 1930, N3760/114/38, Public Record Office, England, FO 371, vol. 14869.
30 Ibid.

share this view, maintaining that Canada and other Dominions were not obliged 'to speak and act in consonance with the British Legations and Embassies.'[31] To avoid unnecessary conflict the Foreign Office discreetly inquired whether the Dominions had any objection to social relations between their representatives and those of the Soviet legations in the countries where the Russian embassies were located.[32]

The Canadian government acted positively, agreeing with the suggestions of the British government. It denied any alleged animosity towards the Soviet Union and emphasized that Ottawa was most anxious to maintain friendly relations with the Union of Soviet Socialist Republics as evidenced by the exchange of notes with the Soviet government regarding article XVI of the treaty signed on 8 August 1924. To fulfil the spirit of this treaty the Canadian representatives in Tokyo were asked by the Department of External Affairs to initiate social visits with the Soviet representatives in that city beginning with the junior members.[33] A similar request was dispatched to the Canadian legation in Paris.

31 Minutes of the Dominion Office, 3 April 1930, ibid.
32 From E.J. Harding to Sir William Clark, 3 April 1930, ibid.
33 From O.D. Skelton to H.M. Marler, Canadian minister to Japan, 25 April 1930, ibid.

CHAPTER SEVEN

Preliminary Skirmishes

The British initiative in resuming diplomatic ties with the Soviet Union provided Canada with the opportunity of regularizing her relations with Russia. But, instead of improving, relations degenerated into a minor economic war in the early 1930s. This new situation can be understood only in the context of Canada's attempt to cope with the profound economic problems of the Great Depression and Stalin's determination to industrialize Soviet Russia by means of the five-year plans.

During the decade following the Wall Street crash of 1929, Canada experienced large-scale unemployment, disrupted production, falling prices, and shrinking of her overseas markets. The number of unemployed in the Canadian working force increased from 5.7 per cent in 1929 to 11.1 per cent in 1930 and reached 16.3 per cent in June of 1931.[1] Canadian foreign trade during the fiscal year ending 31 March 1930 amounted to $2,393,212,000 as compared with $2,654,575,000 in 1929.[2] Agricultural exports seemed to be most adversely affected by the depression. Canada's total external trade in farm products for the fiscal year ending 31 March 1930 was valued at $639,528,184 as compared with $924,557,208 in 1929 – a significant decrease of $285,029,024, or 30.8 per cent.[3]

During the election campaign of June and July 1930 both major political parties in Canada expressed confidence in their ability to solve the crises precipitated by the depression, and made promises to do so. Richard B. Bennett, leader of the Conservative party, assured the voters that, if his party were elected, it would immediately come to grips with the economic problems by raising tariffs to protect Canadian industries, by convening a special session on unemployment, and by 'blasting' its way into the

[1] CAR, 1930–1, p. 440.   [2] Ibid., p. 190.
[3] Ibid., p. 250.

markets of the world.[4] He pledged to foster trade with the British Empire, but not at the expense of Canada's welfare.[5]

Mackenzie King, leader of the Liberal party, attempted, in turn, to woo the voters by reminding them of the wonderful record of the Liberals, who had been in power from 1921 to 1930 (except for three months in 1926 when Meighen's Conservatives formed the government), and by suggesting the convening of an imperial conference as a means of increasing trade among the Commonwealth countries. However, the Liberals were defeated in the general election of 28 July – a set-back which King later considered a stroke of good fortune. Even as leader of the Opposition in the House of Commons he came to realize the difficulties facing the government.[6]

As he had promised during the election campaign, Bennett convened a special session of Parliament to deal with the current economic crisis. The government proposed legislation which attempted to aid the unemployed and protect domestic industries. After a short debate, Parliament voted $20,000,000 'for the relief of unemployment in constructing, extending or improving public works and undertakings, railways, highways ... that will assist in providing useful and suitable work for the unemployed.'[7] To protect Canadian industries, the Customs Act was amended, authorizing the government to place a dumping duty of 15–50 per cent on any imported goods that would compete unfairly with Canadian products.

While Canada was struggling to remedy her economic ills, the Soviet Union was in the throes of one of the most stupendous economic experiments in the history of mankind. The Soviet government was attempting to convert a backward, agricultural Russia into a highly industrialized modern state by means of the five-year plans. The First Five-Year Plan, which came into force on 1 October 1928 undertook the development of heavy industries, the collectivization of all forms of agriculture, and the gradual abolition of capitalism within the state. Nothing seemed too precious to sacrifice for the success of the plan. Labour was mobilized as

4 The Montreal *Gazette*, 19 June 1930.
5 The *Calgary Daily Herald*, 13 June 1930.
6 H.B. Neatby, *William Lyon Mackenzie King, the Lonely Heights, 1924–32* (Toronto, 1963), p. 341.
7 CAR, pp. 33–41.

thousands of workers were encouraged and, in some cases, indirectly forced to work on government projects. Such faults as failure to ensure a timely supply of manpower, the refusal to carry out the decisions of the production committee, or the wrong utilization of raw materials were considered serious criminal offences.[8] The emphasis placed by the plan on heavy industry led to a chronic shortage of consumer goods which was keenly felt by the population as a whole. Shortage of housing for workers in the new industrial areas became acute. Furthermore, domestic fuels and foodstuffs that were in short supply were exported by the Soviet government in order to obtain credits to buy heavy factory and agricultural equipment abroad.

One of the aims of the First Five-Year Plan was to increase the production of agricultural products. Consequently, farms were collectivized and mechanized farm machinery introduced. The initial objectives of the Soviet government were not entirely realized, as the rich peasants or kulaks resisted collectivization, and thousands of horses and livestock were slaughtered by them. In 1934 Stalin disclosed at the Seventeenth Party Congress that the horse population had decreased from 34 to 16.1 million in 1933. In addition, some 30 million head of cattle and almost 100 million sheep and goats had been slaughtered by the rebellious kulaks.[9]

Admittedly during the period of the Five-Year Plan the sown acreage had increased by some 100 million acres, but the yield per acre had significantly decreased. One author claims that crop production dropped by 10 per cent and gross farm output by 15 per cent during the years 1928–32.[10] Other factors that contributed to this decrease in farm production were the inefficiency in the organization of collective farms, faulty distribution of labour, and the lack of trained technicians.[11]

The First Five-Year Plan was more successful in industrial expansion than in agricultural output. One Soviet source claims that the production of farm machinery increased fivefold from 1928 to 1932; hydroelectric power increased four times, and the production of iron increased by three

8 Alexander Baykov, *The Development of the Soviet Economic System* (Cambridge, 1950), pp. 150–1.
9 Joseph Stalin, *Problems of Leninism* (Moscow, 1945), p. 480.
10 Naum Jasny, *Soviet Industrialization, 1928–52* (Chicago, 1961), p. 97.
11 Baykov, *Soviet Economic System*, pp. 202–3.

and a half times.[12] Another Soviet author maintains that, if the production of industrial goods in 1928 is taken as 100 per cent, then industrial production in 1929 was 120 per cent; in 1930, 146 per cent; in 1931, 176 per cent; and in 1932, 202 per cent. The same author stresses the amazing increase in industrial production in spite of continuous attempts on the part of the United States, England, France, Japan, and other countries to interfere with the plan.[13] An English economist agreed that quantitatively industrial production did increase substantially during the First Five-Year Plan. However, he is quick to point out that the fulfilment of the plan was rather uneven. For instance, the output of industries manufacturing machinery and electrical equipment totalled 157 per cent of the amount demanded by the First Five-Year Plan for 1932–3, but the output of heavy metallurgy (pig iron, steel, rolled metal) was only 67.7 per cent, that of the coal industry 89.2 per cent, of the chemical industry 73.6 per cent, and of consumer goods only 73.5 per cent of the respective planned quantities.[14]

Because the non-Communist world was unable to secure objective information on the progress of the First Five-Year Plan, some Western observers, influenced by the official Soviet reports which lauded the unprecedented successes of the plan, became alarmed at the prospects of the re-entry of Soviet goods into the world's markets. The *New York Times* considered the Five-Year Plan to be the 'biggest social and economic piece of business in the world today,' and added, 'if it succeeds, all the capitalistic countries of the world will pay the price of its success.'[15] W.S. Wasserman, a prominent French economist, also warned the world of the impact of Russian goods on the world market: 'The return of Russian products to the world market has created a situation which will probably require important readjustment of world trade and will undoubtedly prolong the present depression.'[16] The *Round Table*, a quarterly review of the politics of the British Commonwealth, deplored Great Britain's increased trade

12 Efraim Ludovich Lokshin, *Ocherki Istorii Promyshlennosti, SSSR (1917–40)* (Moscow, 1956), p. 207.
13 Ivan Fedorovich Ivashin, *Ocherki Istorii Vneshnei Politiki, SSSR* (Moscow, 1958), p. 194.
14 Baykov, *Soviet Economic System*, p. 166.
15 *New York Times*, 6 Dec. 1930.
16 W.S. Wasserman, 'Russia as a World Factor,' *L'Europe Nouvelle*, reprinted in *International Digest*, May 1931, p. 55.

with the Soviet Union. 'This is the more regrettable,' it argued, 'because should the Soviet Five-Year Plan follow its present lines, Russian exports will undoubtedly constitute an economic problem which will have to be treated without prejudice of any kind.'[17] One writer considered the Five-Year Plan 'a gigantic weapon for an economic war on capitalism throughout the world.'[18] The official organ of the Canadian Bankers' Association cautioned Canadians to prepare themselves for an unlimited export of cheap Russian goods.[19] Understandably, the Canadian government was concerned about the possibility of the Soviet Union flooding the markets. One of the most alarming pieces of news regarding the Soviet projected agricultural and industrial production came from 'Luboff's Russian News Service' established in London, England, by Dr Edouard Luboff, alleged to be a well-known authority on Russia, to inform English-speaking businessmen about the latest economic and political developments in Russia. Luboff's News Service Bulletin notified the Canadian Department of Trade and Commerce of the Soviet projected outputs in wheat, coal, oil, asbestos, and lumber for the year 1931. To ascertain the extent to which Soviet products were competing with Canadian goods, the director of the Commercial Intelligence Service of the Department of Trade and Commerce mailed photostatic copies of Luboff's Bulletin to Canadian trade commissioners scattered throughout the world, asking them to investigate the effect of the appearance of Soviet-made products on the sale of Canadian produce.[20]

Most of the trade commissioners found the contents of the photostats interesting but by no means alarming. The Canadian trade commissioner in the West Indies observed that British flour milled from Russian wheat was competing with Canadian wheat in the Caribbean area.[21] Simi-

17 'Great Britain: Economy and Unemployment,' the *Round Table* (London, 1931), vol. XXI, 389.
18 White J. Baker, 'The Soviet Five Year Plan,' *National Review*, 1931, vol. 96, 756.
19 W.B. Allan, 'The Shadow of Russia,' *Journal of the Canadian Bankers' Association*, vol. XXXVIII, 1930–1, 307–13.
20 C.H. Payne, director of the Commercial Intelligence Service, Department of Trade and Commerce, to all trade commissioners, 30 Sept. 1931, file no. 22320, PAC Record Centre, Ottawa.
21 W.F. Bull, Canadian government trade commissioner for Trinidad, Barbados, British and Dutch Guiana, Windward and Leeward Islands, Martinique, and Guadeloupe, to C.H. Payne, 30 Oct. 1931, ibid.

larly, Russian asbestos did compete with Canadian asbestos in Japan.[22] The trade commissioner stationed in Glasgow, Scotland, disclosed that, although Russia was accumulating large sterling credits in London from the sale of produce to Great Britain and other countries in order to buy machines necessary for the success of the First Five-Year Plan, there appeared to be little reason for undue concern about Soviet flooding; in fact the consensus in some business circles predicted the failure of the plan.[23] A similar impression was given by the Canadian representative in Dublin.[24]

Two trade commissioners questioned the reliability of Luboff's report. The one at Shanghai pointed out that the projected production could not be reliable, for it would mean that Russia was in a position to produce more wheat than all the other wheat-producing countries of the world.[25] The trade commissioner at Melbourne, Australia, also challenged Luboff's report, arguing that the Soviet government could not possibly have obtained 120,000 tractors for agricultural purposes in such a short space of time.[26] The trade commissioner at Calcutta, India, although not discounting the danger of Soviet dumping, pointed out that such words as 'huge' and 'immense' so liberally used throughout the report seemed to suggest gross exaggeration of the estimates.[27]

However, the Canadian trade commissioner at Cape Town, Africa, considered Luboff's information reliable. He recommended that Canada, instead of decrying Russian competition in world markets, should meet it positively by agreeing to an arrangement of preferential imperial tariffs. He felt that Canada had gutted her natural resources for 'a hireling's profit,' and sold the produce in markets which she thought would last forever. Now she was forced to compete with 'a ruthless collectivistic state

22 P.V. McLane, Canadian government trade commissioner to Japan, to C.H. Payne, 27 Oct. 1931, ibid.
23 G.B. Johnson, Canadian government trade commissioner in Glasgow, to C.H. Payne, 13 Oct. 1931, ibid.
24 John H. English, Canadian government trade commissioner at Dublin, to C.H. Payne, 22 Oct. 1931, ibid.
25 Bruce A. Macdonald, acting Canadian government trade commissioner at Shanghai, to C.H. Payne, 29 Oct. 1931, ibid.
26 D.H. Ross, Canadian government trade commissioner at Melbourne, Australia, to C.H. Payne, 10 Nov. 1931, ibid.
27 R.T. Young, Canadian government trade commissioner at Calcutta, India, to C.H. Payne, 3 Nov. 1931, ibid.

which refuses to sacrifice economic efficiency to sociological or cultural considerations.' 'Our primary industries,' he stated, 'lacking industrial or commercial cohesion, weakened through speculation, and in many cases bled white through adherence to the silly American ideal of cramming goods down people's throats by advertising, are in no condition to meet as ruthless and efficient a competitor as Russia in the open markets of the world. It is like sending a man against a machine.'[28]

On the other hand, many observers of the Russian economic policy forecast universal benefits from the First Five-Year Plan. George Pendle, a prominent British businessman, regarded the economic program initiated in the Soviet Union as an experiment 'of incalculable significance for the whole world, and we can only profit by that experiment if we possess the courage to examine it clearly and honestly.'[29] He regretted that the vision of many Western observers was obscured by the irrational fear of Soviet competition. The *Canadian Congress Journal*, the official magazine of the Trades and Labour Congress of Canada, enthusiastically maintained that the First Five-Year Plan would inevitably raise the standard of living in Russia, increase the Russian demand for capital and consumer goods, and thus provide a huge market for Canadian farmers and manufacturers.[30]

European countries felt the impact of the First Five-Year Plan for the first time in September 1930, when Russian wheat began pouring into Italy and France at a price 5 per cent lower than that prevalent in Central European countries. The influx of huge quantities of cheap wheat into the European market alarmed Canadians, whose grain elevators already bulged with 264,000,000 bushels of surplus wheat.[31]

The fear of Soviet wheat dumping was intensified by the announcement of the American secretary of agriculture on 24 September that Soviet agents were engaged in a campaign of 'short selling' on the Chicago Grain Exchange.[32] The Soviet government had already chartered some 170 British ships to handle the grain it planned to export to the United States.

28 G.R. Stevens, Canadian government trade commissioner at Cape Town, Africa, to C.H. Payne, 10 Nov. 1931, ibid.
29 George Pendle, 'Commonsense about Russia,' *The Review of the River Plate*. Reprinted in *International Digest*, Nov. 1931, p. 22.
30 'Report of Albert Thomas on the Economic Depression: Its Extent, Causes and Possible Remedies,' *Canadian Congress Journal* (Ottawa, 1931), vol. x, 17.
31 CAR, 1930–1, p. 351.
32 Ibid.

To counteract this Soviet plan, the American government announced that it would purchase Russian wheat in order to stabilize prices. On 27 September, further Russian grain transactions were barred from the Chicago Exchange.

The Soviet government was not easily discouraged in its effort to obtain credits to buy necessary machinery by selling its wheat. In February 1931, the Soviet agency purchased a seat on the Vienna Stock Exchange and offered to sell its wheat at 5 per cent less than the current price in Eastern Europe. As a result of this Soviet action, the Balkan countries immediately held two conferences in Paris at which the question of grain surpluses was thoroughly discussed, but no definite measures were adopted.[33]

Canada, too, showed marked concern over Soviet dumping and the possible decrease of markets for her wheat. Robert Weir, minister of agriculture, held that the menace of Russian wheat lay not so much in the volume of grain dumped, but in the methods the Soviets used: 'They [the Russians] take a quantity of wheat and dump it on the market all at once and give the impression of having an unlimited volume. This breaks the market and creates panic among growers. They think that there is no outlet for their wheat, whereas, there is, of course, always an outlet.'[34]

Bennett was advised by Col. H.J. Mackie, former Conservative member of Parliament for Renfrew North, that the Russians fully realized the harmful effects of their price cutting and that they had expressed their desire to co-operate with Canada in solving the current wheat problem. 'Following up this trend of feeling,' Mackie wrote, 'I have uncovered a decided willingness on the part of the Soviets to participate in a Conference with Canada to discuss, say, ways and means to stabilize the wheat market, to prevent future flooding of the market and to maintain a price of grain that would be remunerative to the producers and honest to the consumers.'[35] He further suggested that Canada should take the initiative in convening the conference which would bring glory to the Conservative party and prosperity to Canada.

33 Ibid., p. 352.
34 Quoted in the *Montreal Daily Star*, 17 Sept. 1930.
35 Col. H.J. Mackie to R.B. Bennett, 8 Dec. 1930, Collected Papers of R.B. Bennett (hereafter cited as Bennett Papers), Box 252, vol. 285, file u-150, 1930–1, Harriet Irving Library, University of New Brunswick, Fredericton. Presently the Bennett Papers are being microfilmed by the Public Archives of Canada, but will be returned to the Harriet Irving Library as soon as the work is completed.

Seventeen months later Canada did send representatives to the Second World Wheat Conference held in Rome on 26 March 1932, and to the London Conference in May of the same year. The Canadian delegates to the conference, held in Rome, were G. Howard Ferguson, the Canadian high commissioner for Canada to the United Kingdom, W.A. Riddell, Canadian advisory officer to the League of Nations, and D.L. Smith, the London representative of the Canadian Co-operative Wheat Producers.[36] This conference failed to reach its objectives, for the Canadians refused to accept the Austrian suggestion that Canada limit her sale of wheat to China and Africa and leave the European market to the Europeans.

At Ferguson's invitation, another conference of exporting countries met in London on 18 May 1932. The delegates, representing eleven countries, hoped to work out some means of disposing of their stored stocks of wheat and of improving methods for handling the distribution of wheat surpluses in the future. The Russian delegate rejected the Canadian proposal to reduce acreage and to arrive at a minimum price per bushel. He agreed, however, to fixed export quotas, provided some means were arranged to guarantee adequate credits for financing subsidies to owners who could not dispose of their surplus wheat.[37] The Soviet proposals were rejected by a majority of the delegates. The only worthwhile result of the conference was the creation of a committee, under Ferguson's chairmanship, which would provide the participating governments with definite information on wheat supplies, the quantities of wheat unloaded at importing points, the acreage sown, and the crop prospects. In addition the committee was to explore all possible markets for wheat.

Wheat-producing countries, particularly Canada, breathed a sigh of relief when they learned that Stalin and Molotov had ordered the *kolkhozes* (collective farms) to reduce their wheat acreage and to refrain from increasing the land under cultivation. Apparently, the available tractor power and the number of farm labourers could not cope with the larger acreage without risking the possibility of poorer yields.[38]

The possibility of Russian dumping of anthracite coal on the world market was a second area of concern for Canadians, particularly for those from the Maritimes. In the fall of 1928 a shipload of Soviet coal was

36 CAR, 1930–1, p. 353.   37 Ibid., p. 354.
38 Stalin, *Problems of Leninism*, p. 326.

refused admission to the United States, but was accepted at Montreal where it was discharged free of duty. In 1929 some 115,000 tons of Russian anthracite were imported into Canada.[39] The importation of Russian anthracite was debated in the House of Commons during both the Liberal and Conservative administrations. One of the most vociferous opponents of the policy of importing Russian coal was Thomas Cantley (Conservative – Pictou). In a debate on 7 March 1929, he deplored the fact that Russian anthracite, mined under conditions of virtual serfdom, was being admitted duty free into Canada in competition with Nova Scotian and Albertan coal. He appealed for immediate action on the part of the Canadian government:

Is this government to sit still; are all the resources of this government of no avail to deal with this matter? Canada is said to possess one-tenth of the total coal resources of the world, yet with many of our coal miners idle to-day our beneficent government allows coal to come into Canada from a Soviet controlled country, transported over a distance of about 6,000 miles to enter into competition with Canadian coal, in direct disregard of all business economic principles.[40]

Cantley's plea for government action brought a reply from Col. J.L. Ralston, the minister of national defence, who emphasized that Russian anthracite was displacing American, not Canadian, anthracite. He pointed out that Canada possessed only small deposits of anthracite, most of which were located in British Columbia, the Yukon, and Alberta, but none in the Maritime provinces. Evidently Ralston's explanation did not satisfy Cantley, for he returned to the question of Russian coal on 2 April 1930 during a debate on unemployment. He informed the House that there were confirmed reports that one-quarter million tons of Russian coal were to arrive in Canada by the end of the year, and he posed the question: 'Should our miners in Nova Scotia be asked, and they are being asked, to compete with Soviet labour under all the degrading conditions that prevail in regard to that particular class of labour in Russia?'[41]

39 Canada, House of Commons, *Debates*, Special Session 1930, p. 332.
40 Canada, House of Commons, *Debates*, 1929, p. 880.
41 Ibid., 1930, p. 1211.

During this debate several members of Parliament from the Maritimes came to Cantley's assistance. Finlay MacDonald (Conservative – Cape Breton South) remarked that Canada had ample coal resources to meet all domestic needs without importing any from Russia. But his main argument was designed to rally the support of the Prairie members: 'The newspapers tell us that within the last year or so hundreds of millions of dollars have been spent in the United States for agricultural implements for Russia. Who dare to say that within four or five years from now the great agricultural lands of Russia will not be developed to such a degree that, if they can replace our coal now, they will not then be in position to replace our Canadian wheat?'[42] F. Patrick Quinn (Conservative – Halifax) accused the government of being remiss in its duty to help the miners of Canada by forcing them to compete with the miners of the Soviet Union. He suggested a protective tariff in order to stop the importation of Russian anthracite.

The members of the cabinet dismissed the problem with brief and inadequate comments. C. Stewart, minister of the interior, disagreed with Cantley's statement that Russian coal was sold at $6.00 per ton whereas the Americans and the English were selling theirs at $11.50. Stewart claimed that the price of the Russian coal was almost identical with the price of American and English coal. In answer to Robert K. Smith (Conservative – Cumberland), who asked whether the government was taking steps to prevent the entry of Soviet anthracite under conditions of 'sweated labour,' Mackenzie King promised to investigate the reports.

King did not have an opportunity to disclose the results of his investigation, for the Liberal party was defeated in the general election of 1930. But at the special session of Parliament convened by Bennett in September the question of Soviet coal appeared as an important item of discussion. According to Alfred Edgar MacLean (Liberal – Prince), Bennett had promised during the election campaign to stop the importation of Russian coal. MacLean disagreed with this proposal on the grounds that Soviet anthracite was needed in Canada and that it did not compete with Canadian bituminous coal.

The most elaborate defence for the continued importation of Russian coal came from J.S. Woodsworth (Labour – Winnipeg North Centre).

42 Ibid., pp. 1269, 1356, 2726; Special Session, p. 471.

He argued that Russian anthracite was decidedly superior to American and was of much the same quality as British. He disclosed that the Americans lifted their ban on Soviet coal following an investigation into the charges that Russian coal was mined by convict labour. No positive proof could be found to substantiate these charges. Woodsworth further maintained that the Canadian government should encourage trade with Russia rather than stifle it by an embargo. 'It would seem,' he concluded, 'that we are adopting a very short sighted policy if because of prejudice we do not permit the opening up of a market which might absorb a great many of the products we are producing in larger quantities than we can dispose of in the home market.'[43]

Although the special session of Parliament gave the government the authority to prohibit importation of goods which competed with Canadian products, no action was taken until the second week of October. The government decided against an immediate embargo on Soviet coal; instead it asked the coal importers to refrain from buying any more anthracite during the autumn and winter months, although the cargoes of Russian coal already on their way to Canada were permitted entrance. Sir George Perley, the acting prime minister, described the government's decision in the following manner:

The government having fully considered the desirability and necessity of stopping the importation of Russian coal, so notified the importers who have now given an undertaking that only cargoes now afloat will be brought in. There are only seven boats now on the way and as they are chartered to load cargoes of grain at Montreal for Europe, it would seem undesirable to enforce diversion of them elsewhere. Steps have been taken to ensure that no more coal from Russia will be shipped this fall or winter and should the undertaking given be for any reason not fulfilled action will be taken by the government under the dumping clause of the Customs Act to prevent any further unloadings.[44]

Mixed public reaction greeted the government's announcement. The *Montreal Daily Star* (24 October 1930) praised the Conservative ad-

43 Canada, House of Commons, *Debates*, 1930, p. 480.
44 Quoted in the *Ottawa Morning Citizen*, 14 Oct. 1930.

ministration for taking positive steps to cope with a nation 'that sells its surplus without reference to profits.' After giving a statistical survey of the amount of Russian coal imported into Canada during the past two years, the editorial ended with an observation that 'there was no reason why Canada should deliberately aid Bolshevist Russia to sell her coal in view of the unfair tactics which Bolshevist Russia was adopting in its effort to hammer down the price of Canadian grain.' The Montreal *Gazette* (14 October 1930) supported this view by maintaining that Canada could obtain the necessary amounts of anthracite from either the United States or Wales and that Canadian farm implements sold to Russia could still be paid for, provided Moscow spent some of its money on machinery instead of using it 'to finance political disturbances in foreign countries.'

On the other hand, L.G. Mickles, president of the F.P. Weaver Coal Company Ltd., of Montreal, speaking on behalf of importers of Russian coal, disagreed with the government's policy, and argued that a ban on Russian coal could not possibly affect the current unemployment situation in the Maritimes since the imported anthracite did not compete with Maritime coal. He reminded the prime minister that many Canadians were, like himself, convinced that the unnecessary boycott would eventually harm the Canadian economy.[45]

Far from relenting in his attitude towards the existing ban on Soviet anthracite, Bennett was prepared to invoke the dumping clause of the Customs Act if the coal importers failed to keep their promises of refraining from buying any more Russian anthracite. The amended Customs Act provided discretionary powers to prohibit the importation of goods into Canada from any country which was not a party to the Treaty of Versailles. Soviet Russia belonged in this category.

45 L.G. Mickles to R.B. Bennett, 7 Feb. 1933, Bennett Papers, box 255, vol. 2, file U-151-T.

CHAPTER EIGHT

The Undeclared Economic War

Despite the promise of the Canadian importers to refrain from buying Russian coal, the Soviet product continued to flood eastern Canada. A number of Canadians considered the existing embargo a farce since it was enforced during the season when no ships could travel down the St Lawrence. As one Lachine resident put it in his letter to Bennett: 'Some sort of arrangement was made this fall, but it did not prevent cargoes of Russian coal from being unloaded at St Lawrence ports, right up until the close of navigation.'[1] Then he went on to challenge the Conservative prime minister by asking him whether he was 'strong enough' to deal with the situation. A letter from Quebec City accused Bennett of permitting some fifty 6,000-ton Russian vessels to unload their cargoes of coal, using the lame excuse that the government had no other choice. 'That way you, Bennett, will try to fool the public,' the writer added, 'the same way you tried this fall by stopping the coal after the river froze up and they couldn't bring any more anyway.'[2]

Bennett began to realize the ineffectiveness of the existing ban on Russian products, but before embarking on the more drastic expedient of a complete embargo, not only on coal but on other Soviet goods as well, he asked officials of the Department of External Affairs to make a thorough study of Soviet dumping in other countries, of the alleged use of slave labour by the Soviets, and of the current American and English attitudes towards Russian trade practices. The major portion of the task was entrusted to Lester B. Pearson, who was first secretary to O.D. Skelton.

1 W. Wilson to R.B. Bennett, 13 Jan. 1931, Sessional Paper, no. 442 (a), Journal Section of the House of Commons, Ottawa.
2 A. Bourbonnais to Bennett, 6 Jan. 1931, ibid.

Pearson's memorandum to Bennett began with a general survey of attitudes in the United States. American opinion seemed to be fairly equally divided between two groups. Importers, shippers, paper and steel manufacturers favoured increased trade with Russia, while local producers and anti-Communist groups opposed all dealings with Moscow. Advocates of continued trade, such as the International Paper Company, pointed to the high quality of Russian pulpwood. The director of the Lumber Division of the Department of Commerce frankly admitted that Russian pine and spruce lumber surpassed in quality not only European lumber but Canadian as well. Furthermore, the supporters contended that such commerce would supply healthy competition for Canadian producers. The opponents of further trade with Moscow alluded to the widely held opinion that Russian lumber was produced and transported by convict labour.[3]

With definite evidence of slave labour being used in the lumbering industry of certain sections of the Soviet Union, the United States Treasury Department on 10 February 1930 issued a regulation prohibiting the importation into the United States of lumber and pulpwood from the Kola Peninsula, including the Murman Coast, the Karelian Autonomous Republic (the northern area), and the Zyryan (Komi) Autonomous Republic, unless the importer could prove that only free labour was engaged in the production, unloading, and transportation of these lumber products.[4] On the same day, the Committee of Ways and Means of the United States House of Representatives, in an executive session, agreed to amend section 307 of the Tariff Act of 1930, extending the embargo to all convict-made goods.

England also was reportedly divided on the question of the Soviet embargo. For some time, moderate agitation was carried on in the United Kingdom for a ban on Russian-made goods on humanitarian grounds. As in the United States, English importers and shippers strenuously opposed the proposed boycott for economic reasons. Unlike the American supporters, the British expressed sympathy for the British Columbian

3 Lester B. Pearson, 'Memorandum on the Question of Soviet Imports and Forced Labour,' Collected Papers of R.B. Bennett (hereafter cited as Bennett Papers), box 252, vol. 286, file U-150, 1930–1, Harriet Irving Library, University of New Brunswick, Fredericton.
4 Ibid.

lumbermen who would be adversely affected by increased trade between Russia and England. Like the Americans, the British experts maintained that convict labour was being employed in the region of Archangel, where some ten thousand prisoners were forced to work in the lumbering industry under the harshest conditions.

The Pearson memorandum showed that Soviet dumping practices were not confined to Canada and the United States, but were also being carried on in Europe. In 1929 petroleum, glue, and galoshes were dumped on the Polish market. This practice was extended the following year to superphosphates, tiles, and china. Moscow's attempt to undersell cotton thread, however, met with stiff opposition from the Polish Textile Federation. The Baltic countries also reported dumping of Russian sugar, galoshes, salt, and cement, but in view of their proximity to Russia and the growing political prestige of the Kremlin, the Baltic states refrained from passing any restrictive laws. On the other hand, Belgium introduced new tariff laws on 30 April 1930 regulating the importation of Soviet flax and matches, and in October of the same year subjected Russian grain and flour to the new restrictions. France, too, regulated the importation of Russian cereals, meat, poultry, eggs, sugar, lumber, and flax by requiring importers to possess licences for such goods. Because of the existing high tariffs, Bulgaria remained unaffected by Soviet commercial practices, and in the Netherlands, Italy, and Germany no embargo was contemplated. This attitude was, in part, understandable since Germany was thriving on the sale of farm implements and metal goods to Russia, and Italy was purchasing from the USSR at low prices the grain and petroleum it badly needed.

Pearson's memorandum contained, in addition, British and Soviet views on the definition and consequences of the dumping practices. William Strang, head of the Middle-European division of the British Foreign Office, was sent to Moscow to investigate the practice of dumping. In a letter to Arthur Henderson, the British foreign secretary, he intimated that every European country influenced by economic nationalism was guided by the principle of *chacun pour soi*. The Soviet Union, of course, was no exception. Strang stressed the fact that the Soviet government, eager to finance the purchases of foreign machinery upon which the success of the Five-Year Plan depended, was forced to sell her products, particularly grain, as quickly as possible and at as high a price as possible.

The Soviet's reply to the accusation of indiscriminate dumping was contained in an article in *Izvestia*, 21 October 1930. The article denied the allegation that the Soviet government purposely lowered prices on her exports to aggravate and hasten world economic crisis. It maintained that all capitalist trusts, cartels, and concerns carry on a policy of dumping. To illustrate capitalist underselling it singled out the German metallurgical trusts which allegedly sold their goods abroad 50 per cent cheaper than in Germany, and the Canadian Wheat Pool, which presumably sold its wheat 40 per cent cheaper to other countries than in Canada. The article attributed the low selling prices of Soviet products to the elimination of such middlemen as brokers, traders, and jobbers, and contended that the campaign against the so-called Soviet dumping was simply a means used by the capitalist countries to divert attention from the relentless plundering of their own peasants, and to rally world support against the Soviet Union.

Pearson also included in the memorandum a lengthy discussion of forced labour in Russia. He enumerated the different types of Russian labour, among them voluntary labour for hire, forced labour imposed by judicial or administrative organization for punishment of crime or misdemeanour, mobilized labour used at a time of emergency, and prison labour imposed in the places of incarceration. He also quoted article 61 of the Soviet Criminal Code, as amended on 28 June 1930, which made those who refused to do forced service, national tasks, or work of national importance subject to fines and imprisonment. In addition, the Decrees of 22 March 1930 and 9 October 1930 provided for cancellation of unemployment benefits to those individuals who refused to load or unload goods.

The memorandum mentioned the difficulties experienced by Western experts in classifying forced labour since Soviet legislation could be interpreted in a number of ways. It did, however, list the Finnish memorandum to the League of Nations, December 1930, the British Embassy dispatch containing highly confidential information on convict labour, and the *New York Times* article written by Walter Duranty as evidences that convict labour was being used in such northern Russian regions as Murmansk, Archangel, and the Kola Peninsula.

The memorandum mentioned the difficulties experienced by Western information on the Soviet dumping practices exercised in North America and Europe. He realized that the United States and the United Kingdom, countries which in the past had influenced Canadian foreign policy, did not intend to impose an unlimited embargo on Russian merchandise; on the contrary, organized groups in both of these countries supported increased trade with Moscow. But Bennett clearly understood that the decision to place an embargo on Soviet products, in the final analysis, must be made in the context of the current economic, social, and political situation in Canada. He was fully aware of the fact that the two areas, the Maritimes and Quebec, which were clamouring for a ban on Soviet goods, provided him with about one-third of his Conservative members of Parliament. In the general election of July 1930 the Maritime provinces returned 23 Conservative members out of a possible 27, and Quebec sent 24 Conservatives to Ottawa out of a possible 65. In addition, in Halifax on 3 July he promised the people of the Maritime provinces that he would enact effective measures to curb all unfair competition if he were elected: 'I will not sacrifice the coal industry of this province or the steel of this province to any country in the world. We will not tolerate the importation of Soviet coal when we take office.'[5]

Quebec considered his promise an important one. One citizen termed it 'a mandate of the people,' whereas another cynically remarked that the Canadian people were waiting to see whether the prime minister would 'really stand by' his election promise or 'just try some other trick to fool the public.'[6] One of the most thought-provoking statements on the subject was made by the proprietor of the George E. Brunelle Coal Company, Montreal, who alleged that 'one of the reasons strongly influencing the Conservative votes cast in Quebec during the General Election of July 1930 was the promise that the Conservative Party would impose and maintain an embargo on Russian coal.'[7] This view was upheld by the *Manitoba Free Press* (30 March 1930) which claimed that the Conservative prime minister felt that he was morally bound by his election

5 The *Herald*, Halifax, 3 July 1930.
6 A. Bourbonnais to R.B. Bennett, 6 Jan. 1931, Sessional Paper no. 442 (a).
7 G.E. Brunelle to Bennett, 30 Dec. 1930. ibid.

promise to impose an embargo on Soviet goods, even though the facts on hand did not warrant such legislation.

The prime minister's desk was flooded with requests from private citizens, as well as from associations and firms, demanding an embargo on Soviet-made goods. The letters, most of which came from Quebec province, asked for this ban on religious, political, and economic grounds. Trade with Russia is 'bad for the Catholic religion,' ran one letter. Such commerce with the Communists, wrote a Montrealer, would help them in their 'campaign against religion, which has already almost destroyed Christianity in Russia.'[8] Another Montrealer, D.C. Cool, manager of Cool Brothers, calculated that under ordinary conditions Russia could earn four million dollars annually by her trade with Canada. He maintained that the profit from such trade would most likely be spent on producing asbestos, wheat, salmon, and furs in order to dump them on the Canadian market. But most unfortunately, continued his letter, a good portion of this profit would be used 'to pay the OGPU to stir up uprising in China and massacre our priests, or to pay agents to poison the minds of good Canadians with their fiendish communistic doctrines, or to help cover the cost of tearing down churches and destroying religion in Russia itself.'[9]

Some letters urged Bennett to impose an embargo because the Communist regime, economically strengthened by Canadian trade, might eventually destroy all Canadian democratic institutions. A Montreal coal merchant fervently hoped that 'Canadian money will not go to Russia to help our Red enemies undermine our political institutions and our faith.'[10] A representative of Davis and Lynch of Montreal, a coal-dealing corporation, expressed the fear that the Third International might cause a 'political disintegration in Canada if it is supported by profits from Canadian-Soviet trade.'[11] Supporting a similar view, a resident of Nicolet, Quebec, held that the Communists wanted to develop trade with Canada in order to obtain money 'to foment discord and revolt against civil authorities.'[12]

Judging by the volume of correspondence reaching Bennett, the sources

8 Perrault to Bennett, 4 Jan. 1931, ibid.
9 D.C. Cool to Bennett, 4 Jan. 1931, ibid.
10 Jas. Quesnel to Bennett, 8 Jan. 1931, ibid.
11 Davis and Lynch Company to Bennett, 6 Jan. 1931, ibid.
12 J.B. Lemay to Bennett, 6 Jan. 1931, ibid.

of these requests, and the editorial comments of the newspapers, the most important reason for a ban on Soviet merchandise was economic. On 28 December 1930 the Canadian Furriers' Guild informed the government that the Soviets had a deliberate plan to destroy the fur industry throughout the world,' and particularly the Canadian fur market, by means of flooding. At the annual meeting of the Canadian Forestry Association held in Montreal on 23 January 1931 a resolution was adopted unanimously, requesting the government to take steps to protect Canadian forest products against the importation of lumber cut and shipped by forced or conscript labour in Russia. Furthermore, in his presidential address to the annual meeting of the Montreal Board of Trade on 26 January, Walter Molson denounced the Soviet practice of dumping, particularly in connection with Russian pulpwood, which was competing with Canadian pulpwood on the American market.[13]

Private letters supported the views on the embargo expressed by such important organizations as the Canadian Furriers' Guild, the Canadian Forestry Association, and the Montreal Board of Trade. A letter from a Sherbrooke resident blamed the existing economic crisis on unfair Russian practices: 'Canada is suffering and will suffer to a greater degree than other nations, because ... [it is] faced with the ruinous Russian competition.'[14] A Montrealer observed that 'the Soviet Republic is out to compete in the markets of the world on a cut-price, cut-throat basis and Canada will suffer more than any other nation because of this relentless competition.' This letter concluded with a plea for action 'in enforcing the will of the Canadian people and keeping out Russian coal ...'[15]

Some but not all Canadian newspapers supported the request for a ban on Soviet-made goods. Commenting on the demand of eleven Maine timberland owners for an immediate embargo on Russian pulpwood and pulp which they claimed was produced by slave labour, the *Ottawa Journal* (29 January 1931) intimated that Canada was sincerely interested in the cause of the Maine timberland owners since she too was suffering from Moscow's flooding of Canadian markets. The Toronto *Globe*

13 CAR, 1930–1, p. 518.
14 R.R. Langis to H.H. Stevens, 3 Jan. 1931, Sessional Paper, 442 (a).
15 E.W. Caron to H.H. Stevens, 3 Jan. 1931, ibid.

(27 January 1931) dismissed the supposedly great financial loss that Canada might suffer from such a boycott, claiming that the benefits would outweight any economic disadvantages: 'As long as Canada buys from Russia, she is supplying the Communists of that country with funds to further the economic disruption of the Dominion. If the other nations are so eager for a few dollars, or kopecks, or whatever it is they get, that they are willing to sell their soul to get them, let Canada at least set an example in self-respect by shutting out Soviet products.'

On the other hand, such newspapers as the *Halifax Chronicle* (22 January 1931) and the *Manitoba Free Press* (30 March 1931) refused to believe that Russia was deliberately attempting to disrupt the world market by its dumping methods. These news organs held that the Moscow government was forced to sell goods at ridiculously low prices in order to obtain the necessary credits for carrying out her vast industrial program.

Two leftist-inclined authors maintained that it would be, indeed, unbusinesslike for the Soviet Union to lower prices on goods with the sole purpose of fomenting discontent at a time when she urgently needed credits to buy machinery. The authors argued that Russian trade, which constituted about 2 per cent of world trade, would have but insignificant effect on world market prices.[16] This view was officially supported by Molotov. In his address to the Sixth Congress of the Soviets, Molotov categorically denied the allegation that Russia was flooding world markets with her products for the purpose of creating economic chaos.[17] However, his statement seems to contradict the resolution passed by the Sixteenth Congress of the Communist Party held in Moscow in June 1930, which suggested that the Communists take full advantage of the economic crises in the capitalist countries by cultivating socialist revolutions in them.[18]

By the middle of February 1931, Bennett and his cabinet were aware of the requests of important organizations and business firms, the demands of the Maritime and Quebec residents, and the desire of some of the Cana-

16 J.M. Budish and Samuel S. Shipman, *Soviet Foreign Trade, Menace or Promise* (New York, 1931), p. 165.
17 Molotov's Address to the Sixth Congress of Soviets, *Soviet Union Review*, vol. IX, 1931.
18 Resolutions to the Sixteenth Congress of the Communist Party of Russia, June 1930, *Kommunisticheskaia Partiia Sovetskogo Soiuza* (Moscow, 1954), vol. III (7th ed.), 33-4.

dian newspapers for an effective embargo on Soviet merchandise. The events that took place during the latter part of February reached a climax on February 27 when the Canadian government placed an embargo on Soviet products.

On 25 February Frank Carrel in the Upper Quebec House and Athanase David in the Lower House proposed motions aimed at drawing the attention of the federal government to 'the increasing inroads of Russian imports produced under abnormal and unethical conditions with convict labour, in competition with Canadian products, thereby increasing ... Canada's unemployment problem.'[19] Ottawa was asked to take immediate steps to remedy the deplorable situation by prohibiting the importation into Canada of Soviet goods which competed with Canadian products.

It was on 25 February that Col. H.J. Mackie disclosed the generous trade offer of the Soviet government. Moscow was ready to purchase $10,000,000 worth of agricultural machinery from Canada, on condition that Canada would take one-third of the payment in Russian coal and other goods, and the balance in gold exchange. On the same day Sir Herbert Holt, president of the Royal Bank of Canada, cautioned against such a transaction. 'If Canada were to accept the Russian overtures now before the Dominion Government and exchange her machinery for Soviet coal and gold,' he declared, 'she would simply be expediting her own economic ruin; since she would be supplying Russia with the means of becoming a more formidable competitor than ever.'[20]

Two days after Russia's machinery-coal-gold deal offer the Canadian government formally rejected it, and instead placed an embargo on seven Soviet products. The order-in-council sponsored by E.B. Ryckman, minister of national revenue, and dated 27 February 1931 spelled out the nature and the reasons for the embargo. The introduction specified that section 2, chapter 3 of the 21, George v (Second Session) of the act that amended the customs tariff authorized the governor general-in-council from time to time to prohibit 'the importation into Canada of any goods exported directly or indirectly from any country not a contracting party to the Treaty of Versailles ...' Then the order-in-council stated that since

19 The Montreal *Gazette*, 18 Feb. 1931.   20 The *Manitoba Free Press*, 9 March 1931.

Soviet Russia was not a signatory of the Treaty of Versailles, it was 'in the public interest that the importation into Canada' ... from Russia 'of coal, woodpulp, pulpwood, lumber and timber of all kinds, asbestos, and furs, should be prohibited.'[21]

Other reasons for the government embargo not stated in the official order-in-council were explained by the minister of national revenue. He pointed out the evidence of forced labour in Russia and the general fear of Communist doctrine:

The government is convinced that there is forced labour in the cutting and transport of timber and in the mining of coal, that political prisoners are exploited, that the standard of living is below any level conceived of in Canada and that broadly speaking all employment is in control of the Communist government, which regulates all conditions of work and seeks to impose its will on the whole world.

This is Communism, its creed and its fruits which we as a country oppose and must refuse to support by interchange of trade.[22]

The newly imposed embargo was condemned and praised with equal vehemence. John Toyne, president of the Canadian Trading Corporation, was fully convinced that the government's action would only strengthen the Communist party of Russia. A prosperous Russia rejuvenated by foreign trade and by the Five-Year Plan, he maintained, would eventually become discontented with the Communist regime and revolt against it: 'It is very evident that should the "Five Year Plan" in Russia be successful and lead the way to gradual increase of prosperity in Russia, then the days of the Communist Regime are numbered, as Communism certainly cannot exist in any prosperous country. I am just as convinced that Russia, prosperous, will elect a government committed to a policy of co-operativism.'[23]

Some business firms, coal dealers, and labour organizations argued that the embargo would only increase the existing unemployment situation.

21 Order-in-council, 27 Feb. 1931, Sessional Paper 442 (a).
22 The Montreal *Gazette*, 28 Feb. 1931.
23 John Toyne to R.P. Sparks, 18 Feb. 1931, Bennett Papers.

On behalf of the International Association of Machinists, J. Cupello, the business agent, notified Bennett that it was the opinion of the association that the government's action would be detrimental to the welfare of the machinists and to the workers of Canada who were already suffering from unemployment.[24] Reiterating the old arguments of some of the Maritime members of Parliament, J.E. Masters, manager of the Masters Company of Moncton, New Brunswick, a large firm dealing in soft and hard coal, maintained that the government's legislation would not help the Nova Scotian producers, for they did not mine anthracite. He further held that the embargo not only deprived 'the people of Canada of the use of the best domestic fuel ever produced,' but also aided the United States coal producers and manufacturers: 'You [Bennett] are assisting, and very materially, the American anthracite producer who exports into Canada yearly about three and a half million tons of this product, and playing right into the hand of the American manufacturer who will very quietly grasp the many million dollar orders that Canada might have, to say nothing of the employment required to fill such orders.'[25]

J.E. Masters's views were shared by the *Vancouver Sunday Province* (11 March 1931). After astutely reviewing the possible reasons for the boycott, the editor demonstrated the evident inconsistency of Bennett's administration, which barred Russian anthracite of superior quality and encouraged the importation of inferior American coal. 'What interest have we in protecting the Pennsylvania mine owner?' he asked. 'Has the Smoot-Hawley tariff been so kind to us that we must rebuff a possible customer in the interests of Uncle Sam?' The editorial asserted that the Russian coal Canada refused would eventually find an outlet in Great Britain, the United States, and Germany.

Such Communist organizations as the Canadian Labour Defence League, the Labour League Choir of Toronto, and the Russian and Ukrainian Workers of Brantford protested against the embargo, not only because it was causing undue hardship for the Canadian worker, but also because it interfered with the progress of Soviet Russia.[26] 'This action,

24 J. Cupello to Bennett, 5 March 1931, ibid.
25 J.E. Masters to Bennett, 5 March 1931, ibid.
26 Canadian Labour Defence League to Bennett, 2 March 1931, ibid.

which is the broadest and most drastic yet taken by any capitalist government in the world,' wrote H. Guralnick, secretary of the Canadian Labour
Defence League, to Bennett, 'is all the more outrageous since it is taken
at a time when over 350,000 workers are unemployed in Canada to-day,
and is indicative of the sharpening war plans of the Canadian Imperialist
government, who in league with the rest of the world imperialists is getting ready to declare war upon the USSR.' The same letter branded the
accusations of Soviet dumping and forced labour as nothing more than
lies and slanders whose purpose was to disrupt the Five-Year Plan. The
Worker (6 June 1931), the official voice of the Communist party of
Canada, also maintained that the Canadian prime minister was supporting
a general armed invasion of the Soviet Union and that he was robbing the
Canadian workers of fruitful employment which would have resulted from
the proposed Canadian-Soviet commerce.

Even non-Communist newspapers remained baffled by the ban on Soviet goods. The independent *Manitoba Free Press* (9 March 1931) expressed its inability to understand the government's prohibition of Soviet
anthracite, since Canada did not produce any significant amount of her
own, and concluded that the embargo probably 'resulted from the natural
love the Government has for excluding foreign trade.' The *Financial Post*
(5 March 1931) could not envisage any immediate advantage gained by
the government legislation, and declared that 'it is seldom that any enter-
prising salesman ever had a door slammed in his face with the sharp
finality of Canada's embargo on imports of any kind from the Union of
Soviet Socialist Republics.' The *Vancouver Sun* (28 March 1931) labelled
the embargo 'a political-holy war on Russia, waged by Premier Bennett,
joined by Premier Taschereau of Quebec.' It claimed that the original
supporters of the ban, namely, Catholics, businessmen, and manufacturers,
have now realized the adverse effects of the government legislation. The
Halifax Chronicle (23 April 1931) remarked that Bennett's government,
unable to prove the use of 'convict' or 'forced' labour in Soviet Russia,
resorted to the lame excuse that Russia was not one of the signatories of
the Versailles Treaty and therefore was subject to the newly imposed
embargo.

One of the most critical analyses of the embargo came from B.K. Sandwell, the former associate editor of the Montreal *Herald*. He maintained that the ban on Soviet products could be considered a means of protecting Canadian industries from unfair competition or as an act of hostility against the Soviet regime. He failed to see this boycott as a beneficial measure for increasing trade, for it did not help to increase Canada's trade with other countries or prevent other countries from trading with the Soviet Union. At the same time he could not understand how this act of hostility could reform the Soviet government. He agreed that Canada had legitimate reasons for opposing an anti-Christian and anti-democratic regime, which the Communists attempted to impose on Canada. But he failed to comprehend how such an embargo would reform the Soviet government. Moreover, the embargo could not prevent Moscow from getting the much-needed material and experts from the capitalist countries. Finally, the conditions under which the Russian goods were produced were probably no more inhumane than they were under the Czars. 'To palter with it [the Soviet Regime] by merely telling the Russians to take their inhumanely-made goods somewhere else,' he concluded 'will do no good to the victims and much harm to ourselves.'[27]

An equal number of letters and newspapers lauded Bennett for his judicious legislation which placed a ban on Russian merchandise. Some of the letters commended Bennett for his leadership in world economic matters. As one citizen from Ottawa expressed it: 'The United Kingdom that is your support ... should indeed be proud of the leadership you have given other parts of the British Empire in this great international problem' [Soviet dumping].[28] Bishop Arseny, spiritual leader of about 600,000 Greek Russian Orthodox in Canada, approved Bennett's stand on Soviet practices.[29] Bishop Jacob Janzen of the United Mennonite churches of Ontario also agreed with the Conservatives' policy towards the Soviet Union:

The Soviet Government is the worst enemy of the Russian people and will do anything wrong or right to the people to promote her cause which is ... world revolution and the overthrow of all existing order.

27 B.K. Sandwell, 'The Russo-Canadian Holy War,' *Canadian Forum*, vol. XI, 287–9.
28 Earl Rowe to Bennett, 28 Feb. 1931, Bennett Papers.
29 Bishop Arseny to Bennett, 3 March 1931, box 253, file U-151, ibid.

Nations trading with the Russian Government ... are helping a murderer to kill his victim, and I therefore think it to be the right thing for Canada not to trade with Russia in spite of the fact that many other nations do so.[30]

Another Mennonite clergyman, Rev. David Toews, chairman of the Canadian Board of Colonization, also approved Bennett's decision. 'We think that you have done the right thing in breaking off trade relations with Russia,' he wrote to Bennett, 'and we believe, if all the countries in the world would do the same thing, Russia would soon be brought to terms.'[31]

Many newspapers followed the arguments of Mennonite church leaders and lauded Bennett for prohibiting trade with a godless government whose aim was to spread revolutionary ideas to other countries. The *Ottawa Journal* (2 March 1931) commended the Conservative administration for rejecting the attractive machinery-gold-coal deal, or as it termed it 'the mess of pottage.' It described the Communist regime as 'anti-Christian and anti-God, one that repudiated debts and reddened the records of its administration with blood.' Montreal's *La Presse* (21 April 1931) contended that it was in the highest interest of Canada that Bennett took the initiative in prohibiting certain Russian products from coming into Canada, for the profit from the sale of these goods would only provide more funds for Communist activities and propaganda. Supporting *La Presse*'s views, the Montreal *Gazette* (28 February 1931) maintained that it would be extraordinarily audacious to carry on trade with a country whose rulers deliberately enslave workers in their attempt to make the Five-Year Plan successful. The Conservative *Mail and Empire* (2 March 1931) defended the embargo on the ground that such legislation provided a means of diminishing the possibility of Communist dictatorship in various European and Asiatic countries. It furiously denounced the Soviets' anti-god policy by which 'home and family are being destroyed, and woman is being degraded.'

Scores of letters reaching Bennett's office, and some of the newspaper editorials, praised the ban placed on Russian goods because it helped the Canadian economy. 'Congratulations very Honourable Prime Minister,'

30 Bishop Jacob Janzen to Bennett, 28 May 1931, box 254, vol. 287, ibid.
31 David Toews to Bennett, 23 July 1931, ibid.

wrote P. Lacombe, secretary of the Fils Natifs du Canada, 'for taking proper means at once to put an end to the Russian dumping realizing that this so-called dumping caused considerable harm to our country.'[32] Similar types of congratulatory letters were sent by such firms as Nesbitt-Thompson & Co., and by such organizations and associations as Association Catholique des Voyageurs de Commerce, Mont-Joli, Quebec; Conseil de la Cité du Cap de la Madeleine, Le Cercle Larcoque de l'Association Catholique de la Jeunesse Canadienne Française, Sherbrooke; Le Club Ouvrier Montcalm, Montreal; Cercle Dollard des Ormeaux de l'A.C.J.C.; and from the students of Séminaire de Chicoutimi.[33]

Newspapers also expressed their appreciation of Bennett's legislation against Soviet Russia's dumping practices. The Toronto *Globe* was exceedingly pleased that the Conservative leader refused the attractive $10,000,000 worth of Russian gold and coal for Canadian manufactured farm equipment. 'Russia wants this up-to-date machinery,' commented the *Globe* (27 February 1931) 'to raise wheat with which to supply importing countries to lick the Canadian farmer still worse,' by robbing him of markets in Great Britain and elsewhere. Commenting on the same Russian offer, the Calgary *Herald* (2 March 1931), in an editorial entitled 'Canada Defies Russian Giant,' supported the *Globe*'s contention that Ottawa's refusal to accept the gold-coal-machinery barter deal helped to keep world markets open for Canadian wheat.

Early in March 1931 the discussion of the Canadian embargo on Soviet goods spread from the editorial desks of newspapers and the offices of executives to the floor of the House of Commons. Beginning the debate, Armand La Vergne (Conservative – Montmagny) announced that he was proud to be a Christian citizen of Canada, for his prime minister by his decision had defied a system that denies God, the sacredness of marriage and the inalienable rights of an individual to possess property.[34] A much longer defence of the Conservative policy came from G.B. Nicholson (Conservative – Algoma East). After quoting excerpts from the Toronto *Daily Star*, which described the plight of the Russian peasant, he rhe-

32 P. Lacombe to Bennett, 25 Feb. 1931, ibid.
33 Ibid.
34 Canada, House of Commons, *Debates*, 1931, p. 182.

torically asked whether this was the idea Canadians had of a Christian home. 'When you destroy the inviolability of womanhood, when you take from the father and mother the child which they have brought into the world, you destroy the very foundation upon which civilization rests, and I say again the civilized world cannot afford to do so.'[35] C.N. Dorion (Conservative – Quebec) added his felicitation to his chieftain, calling him 'a great Canadian statesman' who by his example was first to teach the world 'that no Christian nation should have any business relations with countries where the people are veritable outcasts among the states due to the misdeeds of their political leaders.'[36]

Besides giving religious and humanitarian reasons for discontinuing trade relations with the Soviet Union, members of Parliament alluded also to economic advantages which such a ban would bring to Canada. T. Cantley (Conservative – Pictou) favoured Bennett's policy, not because it had boycotted a Soviet regime that repudiated God, but because it had eliminated unfair competition with such basic Canadian products as coal and timber.[37] Nicholson spent a considerable part of his debating time quoting from the *Philadelphia Evening Public Ledger* to show American support for the embargo and from the London *Daily Telegraph* to uphold the allegation that slave labour was used extensively in Russia. Then he indirectly suggested the economic benefits Canada derived from the embargo by eliminating the menace of Soviet dumping: 'The lumber industry in Canada cannot live; the wheat industry in Canada cannot live; no other industry in Canada can exist and provide a standard of living, at any rate such as the people in Canada hope to have and are entitled to in competition with 150 million or 160 million slaves.'[38]

Members of Parliament from the prairies and from the far West also supported Bennett's legislation. 'Probably one of the best things that ever happened to the western farmer,' contended W.L. Loucks (Conservative – Rosetown), 'was when the government put on that embargo.'[39] C.H. Dickie (Conservative – Nanaimo) defended the policy of the Conservative government and hoped that it could be extended to salmon. He deplored the possible loss of France as a market for Canadian salmon, claiming

35 Ibid., p. 693.   36 Ibid., p. 271.   37 Ibid., p. 2635.
38 Ibid., p. 691.   39 Ibid., p. 232.

that the 'Russian representatives told the French people that no matter at what price the Canadian canners put their salmon on the market, the Russians would let them have theirs at 50 cents a case cheaper.'[40]

Members of Parliament who opposed the embargo echoed many of the arguments found in the current newspapers. The leader of the Opposition, Mackenzie King, questioned the value of the boycott, saying that because of the government's decision Russia might deliberately flood the world markets with cheap wheat just to spite Canada.[41] John Vallance (Liberal – South Battleford) was not able to see the ban on Russian goods as a solution to Canada's acute problem of a shortage of markets. On the contrary he argued that 'it would be to Canada's advantage to import a little more coal from Russia than from Pennsylvania because she might at least be able to place some wheat on a market to which Russia might otherwise sell ...'[42]

William D. Euler (Liberal – Waterloo North) termed the boycott 'inconsistent, unbusinesslike and ineffective.' He blamed the government for being inconsistent; it refused to buy Russian coal because such a purchase allegedly increased the unemployment in the Maritimes, and yet it proposed to buy the same type of coal from the United States. Then Euler alluded to the unbusinesslike methods of the government, maintaining that the Soviet embargo was not necessary to exclude such goods as lumber, furs, asbestos, and pulpwood from Canada, since they were not being imported into the country anyway. Finally, judging from the flourishing trade between Russia and the United States and a corresponding decline in Canadian trade, he was inclined to conclude that the embargo would prove to be 'ineffective.'[43]

One of the most vehement condemnations of the embargo came from Henry Bourassa (Independent – Labelle). He began his debate by objecting to the government's unparliamentary method of imposing the embargo by the use of the order-in-council, claiming that such a drastic policy should have been decided by Parliament. Then with his usual eloquence he questioned Canada's right to teach other nations moral lessons: 'And for my part I repeat, as a Christian and as a Canadian, I do not consider that we

40 Ibid., p. 2363.   41 Ibid., p. 53.   42 Ibid., p. 163.
43 Ibid., p. 2494.

have received either from Providence or from the conscience of the Canadian nation any mandate to teach lessons to other nations.' He held that if Canada refused to trade with countries governed by non-Christian principles, she would soon have few to trade with. The best service Canada could render humanity, he added, would be to introduce some of these much-vaunted Christian principles into her own business and social life.[44]

The Soviet government did not remain indifferent to the Canadian embargo. On 30 October 1930 the Sovnarkon decreed a counter embargo on Canadian goods 'forbidding all importing organizations and all trade representatives to purchase any goods whatever of Canadian origin and likewise forbidding employment of Canadian ships.'[45] Furthermore, *Izvestia* contended that the reasons given by the Canadian government for the boycott seemed illogical. 'There are,' it held, 'a number of countries who did not sign the Treaty of Versailles, such as the United States of America and others, with whom Canada has normal trade relations.' The only reason the Soviet paper could discover for such legislation was Canada's opposition to the Soviet regime.[46]

Whether the imposed embargo was illogical and ineffective, as some of the opponents of the ban held, or whether it was opportune and necessary for the boosting of the Canadian economy, as its supporters maintained, remained to be seen.

44 Ibid., p. 2031.
45 *Izvestia*, Moscow, 20 April 1931.
46 Ibid.

CHAPTER NINE

The Embargo under Strain

Early in his administration Bennett discovered that it was much easier to enact legislation prohibiting Soviet-made goods from entering Canada than to maintain this embargo in the face of urgent requests from organizations and individuals to modify it or remove it entirely. He believed that declining trade must be supported by protective tariffs. He also realized that an embargo was but a negative measure, and did not constitute a panacea for Canada's economic ills. Consequently, he attempted to foster commerce, particularly with the members of the British Commonwealth.

The embargo on furs was barely four months old when representations were made by various wholesale and retail fur manufacturers, fur dressers, and dyers and importers of furs and skins for a complete abolition of the ban on furs, or at least a modification of the boycott, so as to exclude raw furs only. The most convincing arguments brought against the existing embargo were economic. Some letters notified the prime minister that the exclusion of such good Russian furs as sable, Kolinsky, squirrel, broadtail, and Persian lamb from the Canadian market created "terrible losses" in the tourist fur trade.[1] Countless numbers of American tourists turned to such cities as New York to supply them with high quality Russian fur coats and jackets when they were not able to obtain these in Canada. But what annoyed the Canadian furriers most was the fact that many Canadians travelled South for Russian fur products. 'Anyone of our customers can go across the border,' wrote the manager of Alexander Furs Ltd. to Bennett, 'and get the article that we are unable to supply them with.' He argued that

---

1 Arthur Allan to R.B. Bennett, 31 Aug. 1931, Bennett Papers, box 254, U-151, vol. 287, 1930–1, Harriet Irving Library, University of New Brunswick, Fredericton.

Canada would not only lose trade but would also be deprived of excellent opportunities for employing skilled personnel in the fur industry.[2]

Other furriers argued that the existing ban could not be effectively enforced, since it was almost impossible to differentiate Russian fur skins from Chinese or Scandinavian skins. They pointed out that Russian Kolinsky furs could easily be sold by fur dealers as Chinese, since they look similar, and that Russian squirrel could be sold as Scandinavian.[3] Both N.F.C. Devlin, president of R.J. Devlin Co., and James Coristine, manager of Coristine Company, suggested to Bennett that a possible solution to the dilemma lay in an enforced embargo on all dressed, dyed, and manufactured fur goods or skins, while permitting entrance of Russian raw skins and furs into Canada. Such an arrangement 'would save all labour for Canadians, the public and the trade would have the variety of peltries desired and the enforcement of the thus adjusted regulations would be simplified for the government.'[4] Devlin's and Coristine's suggestion was acted upon. The government passed an order-in-council on 10 December 1931 which excluded Russian dressed, dyed, and manufactured skins and furs from Canada, but allowed raw furs to enter freely. When the embargo on furs was altered, Devlin expressed his gratitude for Bennett's 'great consideration in the matter of dealing with the Russian embargo, as it affected the Canadian fur trade and the Canadian public.'[5]

In a letter to Bennett, R.B. Hanson (Conservative – York-Sunbury, N.B.), on behalf of an industrial firm asked the prime minister if the government would remove completely its embargo on all furs. All possible arguments were marshalled to show the benefits of such legislation:

... there would be a sufficient amount of raw furs sold in Canada, which would have to be dressed and dyed here to offset anything that the dressers might lose from the importation of Russian dressed and dyed furs. In addition, the volume would be large enough to require a separate warehouse and staff of from one hundred to one hundred and fifty people consisting of office help,

2 A.J. Alexander to Bennett, 2 Sept. 1931, ibid.
3 James Coristine to Bennett, 26 June 1931, ibid.
4 W.F.C. Devlin to Breadner, 15 Oct. 1931, ibid.
5 Ibid., 15 Dec. 1931.

salesmen, fur handlers, and would be on an all year round employment basis. The volume would probably run up to about $2,000,000 per year.[6]

Bennett refused this request because he felt that lifting the ban on one item would lead to a renewed assault upon the embargo generally. In addition, he foresaw that such a move would give the British importers an excuse for increasing imports of Russians timber and wheat.[7] Thus the embargo remained unchanged until 10 September 1936, when it was lifted by Mackenzie King.[8]

The placing of an embargo on Soviet products was but the negative aspect of Bennett's program to infuse life into the Canadian economy. Trade, particularly Imperial trade, formed its constructive element. Actually, he had an exaggerated confidence in the benefits of such trade. 'The promotion of trade within the Empire together with a strong protective tariff within the Empire ...' wrote Michael Swift, 'constituted Bennett's solution for all of Canada's ills during the next few years; at least until 1933.'[9] For that reason he did his utmost to ensure the success of the Ottawa Economic Imperial Conference held in the summer of 1932.

Even prior to the convening of the conference, E.N. Rhodes, minister of finance, expressed optimism regarding its outcome. Speaking to the House of Commons on 6 April 1932, he declared: '... I do desire to record my firm conviction that we are not far removed from events which herald the dawn of better days ... and that Canada will be found in the vanguard of those nations which successfully emerged from the greatest testing time of modern history.'[10]

At its first meeting on 21 July 1932, Bennett was elected chairman of the conference. He wasted no time in specifying what he hoped would be achieved. Briefly, he wanted greater markets within the Empire, which he

---

6 R.B. Hanson to Bennett, 12 June 1931, **ibid.**
7 Bennett to Hanson, 16 July 1931, **ibid.**
8 Order-in-council, 10 Sept. 1936, Sessional Paper, no. 179, the Journal Section of the House of Commons, Ottawa.
9 Michael David Swift, 'R.B. Bennett and the Depression, 1930–1935' (unpublished MA thesis, University of New Brunswick, Fredericton, 1964), p. 71.
10 Canada, House of Commons, *Debates*, 1932, p. 1768.

said would inevitably result in greater world markets. He elaborated on the effects of this imperial trade:

When we reach an agreement by which our products pass more freely from one Empire country to another, we drive clear channels through the stagnant pools dammed up by the world upheaval, and naturally we will carry past the boundaries of the Empire and to its benefit, establish once more again throughout the world that commerce which is its very life blood. The British people in their vigour, industry, and experience have nothing to fear from foreign competition when they are united in the economic association which is now possible. When from this Conference that results, we will welcome fair and friendly competition.[11]

Obviously, Bennett regarded a flourishing Imperial trade as an effective antidote to dumping practices. In addition, the British Empire would replace such countries as Soviet Russia as potential markets for Canadian products.

Stanley Baldwin, chairman of the British delegation, openly disagreed with Bennett on Imperial preferential policy. He suggested that the members of the Empire should lower tariff barriers among themselves, but refrain from interfering with the trade between the Dominions and other countries of the world. Obviously this plan did not comply with Bennett's idea of Imperial preferential trade, since it ignored the annoying problem of Russian dumping of timber, wheat, and salmon on the British market. Bennett attempted to persuade Baldwin and his colleagues to place an economic ban on Soviet Russia, whose policies conflicted with those of the British Empire:

... When we find our orderly progress opposed, and when our social and industrial existence is threatened, it is our common duty to provide the safeguards which will leave us free to go forward on the course we have decided to be the right one. State-controlled standards of living, state-controlled labour, state-aided dumping dictated by high state policy conflict in theory and in

11 Imperial Economic Conference, 1932, *Report of the Conference* (Ottawa, 1932).

practice with the free institutions of the British Empire. The subordination of individual right and liberty to a national economic plan affronts our whole idea on national development. We must be active in defence of our institutions. We must put before all else our peace and happiness.[12]

The Canadian prime minister was not merely making generalizations. He possessed evidence to show that Canada's 'orderly progress' was opposed and her 'social and industrial existence' threatened by Russian actions. He pointed to the fact that Russia was selling her asbestos to the United States at half the price charged by Canada. Russian wheat was continuously cutting into the Canadian wheat market in Europe. Finally, Soviet Russia was undermining the Canadian lumbering industry by flooding the British market with low-priced lumber.[13] Fortunately for Bennett, other Commonwealth delegates, as well as some of the leading British newspapers, supported his views. Stanley Bruce, head of the Australian delegation, urged that effective measures be taken by the Dominions against Soviet dumping. He was supported by 'Jimmy' Thomas, the somewhat radical Labour member of the British delegation, who argued that the British workingmen suffered deeply from the unfair competition of Soviet goods. Moreover, the London *Times* (29 July 1932) and the slightly less influential *Morning Post* (29 July 1932) advocated measures to curb the dumping of Russian products.

Despite this strong support for Bennett's case, Baldwin continued to oppose a boycott of Russian goods. He held that an all-out economic war on the Soviet Union would adversely affect the existing long-term trade contracts entered into by various British firms with Moscow. He maintained that such a move would most probably interfere with the credits advanced under the Trade Facilities Act for the promotion of trade with Russia. Even if an embargo were placed on Russian products, he argued, it would be extremely difficult to enforce it in regard to lumber since Russian lumber could be sold under Swedish or Finnish labels.[14] He startled the Canadian public when he disclosed that all the Dominions charged

12 Ibid., p. 69.   13 The Toronto *Globe*, 3 Aug. 1932.
14 The *Financial Post*, 30 July 1932.

some kind of tax or duty on almost all British goods entering the Dominions, whereas the British government permitted over 90 per cent of the Dominion goods to enter free into Great Britain.[15]

Although the Canadian government denied any rift between Ottawa and London, Canadian newspapers began to elaborate on the causes of the impending failure of the conference. Several newspapers singled out Baldwin's inflexible policy towards tariffs and the issue of Russian trade as the main causes of this failure. In an editorial entitled 'Great Britain's Refusal to Bar Soviet Dumping Threatens Success of Imperial Conference,' the Windsor *Border Cities' Star* (15 August 1932) maintained that the British delegates continued to demand wide preferences for their own manufactured goods, but were most reluctant to open their markets wider to the 'primary products which Canada has to sell.' The Conservative Ottawa *Morning Journal* (18 August 1932) believed that the 'Russian bear' had 'cast a shadow' over the closing days of the conference, forcing England to prefer Russian trade to Canadian trade. The Ottawa *Le Droit* (18 August 1932) unhesitatingly placed the blame for the impending failure of the Imperial Conference on the British delegates 'who refuse to modify their attitude on the subject of the Russian dumping.'

The *Financial Post* (30 July 1932), however, attempted to play the role of a journalistic arbitrator between Ottawa and London. In its editorial, 'Russian Bear Shows Up at Ottawa,' it held that prohibitive tariffs directed by the United Kingdom against Russian products would be of tremendous importance to Canada. It argued that any moderate scale of preferential tariffs would be inadequate to cope with the problem of Soviet dumping. 'But a virtual embargo of some sort on Russian goods,' it continued, 'would give Canada an enormous opportunity in the British market in some lines, particularly if supplemented by even very moderate preferences.' The editorial ended on an optimistic note, predicting that the Soviet question which marred the Imperial Conference at Ottawa would probably be 'threshed out behind closed doors,' and that even the future of the Russian dictatorship might 'be determined under the sunny skies of Canada's capital city.'

The *Financial Post*'s prediction was partially correct; a few compro-

15 Swift, 'R.B. Bennett and the Depression,' p. 191.

mises were reached between Great Britain and the members of the Empire. The United Kingdom agreed to grant a 6 cent per bushel preference on Empire wheat in order to control foreign dumping and to make Canada and Australia the principal granaries of the British Isles. Appropriate tariff adjustments ensured that the food, clothing, fuel, and building material required by the people of the British Empire would be largely produced within the Empire. Cattle, bacon, butter, cheese, fruits, fish, minerals, and chemicals were specifically mentioned as items which would enjoy the Imperial tariff preferences.[16] Finally, an effective control of Soviet dumping was spelled out by article xxi of the Treaty signed by Great Britain and the Dominions:

This agreement is made on the express condition, that, if either Government is satisfied that any preferences hereby granted in respect of any particular class of commodities are likely to be frustrated in whole or in part by reason of the creation or maintenance directly or indirectly of prices for such class of commodities through state action on the part of any foreign country, that Government hereby declares that it will exercise the powers which it now has or will hereafter take to prohibit the entry from such foreign country or indirectly of such commodities into its country for such time as may be necessary to make effective and to maintain the preferences hereby granted by it.[17]

Several of the Canadian newspapers applauded the combined achievement of the British and Canadian delegates, regarding it as 'a confirmation of realities, a magnificent tribute to the ultimate wisdom of British leaders, a historic step in the advancement of British ideals and a world example,' as well as a triumph of the Canadian policy to check Soviet dumping.[18] The Regina *Star* (5 August 1932) chided those critics who claimed that Bennett was not interested in the farmers. It pointed out that the Imperial Conference at Ottawa showed that the Conservative leader was most anxious 'to obtain all the benefits he could for the primary industry of the country.' The Toronto *Mail and Empire* (6 August 1932) argued that,

16 Imperial Economic Conference *Report*, 1932, p. 25.
17 Imperial Economic Conference, 1932, *Report of the Conference*, suppl. volume (Ottawa, 1932), p. 52.
18 The Toronto *Globe*, 20 Aug. 1932.

although the new agreement reached at Ottawa would not dispose of all the Canadian surplus wheat, it would provide markets for the 100,000,000 bushels of Canada's annual exportable surplus.

In contrast the *Worker* (6 August 1932) was bitter in its attack on the Imperial Conference. 'Never was so much irresponsible and lying slander uttered against a state,' wrote the editor, 'at an important international gathering of state representatives as is being uttered at the Imperial Conference against the Soviet State.' This newspaper of the Communist party of Canada called the delegates attending the conference a 'howling pack of exploiters' who wish to place an embargo on the Soviet products, even though the capitalist countries continued to be their worst competitors.

Two months after Bennett had attempted to persuade England to limit her trade with the Soviet Union, the Danish oil tanker *Aase Maaersk*, carrying tons of Russian crude oil, appeared in Montreal harbour. This oil was being exchanged for Canadian aluminum, but Bennett denied giving the Aluminum Company of Canada authorization for the transaction. Several newspapers viewed the appearance of the *Aase Maaersk* with consternation. 'If the Danish tanker *Aase Maaersk* had been loaded with dynamite,' wrote the editor of the Lethbridge *Herald* (5 October 1932), 'and had exploded in the middle of the harbor, the effect could not have been more startling at the capital than the news that this blunt nosed ship had pulled into an unloading berth with nine thousand tons of Russian crude oil from Batum.' The Quebec *Chronicle-Telegraph* (27 September 1932) found the Canadian-Soviet barter deal ironical 'in the fact that trade between Canada and Russia should follow hard upon the heels of the Ottawa Conference in which Mr. Bennett insisted so strongly upon the United Kingdom putting an end to the dumpings from that source.'

Whether Bennett expressly consented to the aluminum-oil deal before the appearance of the Danish oil-tanker is debatable, but he was definitely aware of the suggested barter. During the first three months of 1932 he was asked by the municipal councils of Ste Anne, Bagotville, Herbertsville, and the Chamber of Commerce of Chicoutimi to modify the existing embargo so that the proposed $5,000,000 aluminum-coal deal could be transacted.[19] An urgent request, in the form of a memorandum of the unemployment

19 Bennett Papers, 1932.

situation in Shawinigan Falls, Almaville, and Shawinigan Bay, outlined the economic benefits to be derived from such a deal. It argued that the barter deal with Russia would help to ease the unemployment situation immeasurably, but it pointed out that such a deal would be possible only if the Canadian government lifted its embargo against the Soviet anthracite which constituted two-fifths of the Russian part of the barter. The memorandum went on to say that the $5,000,000 contract would keep the Shawinigan Falls plant running at full capacity for at least two years and provide work for over three thousand workmen.[20]

Bennett also received letters from two politicians in connection with this deal, one asking for the maintenance of the embargo on Russian anthracite and the other for its removal. J.A. Lavergne (Labour – Chicoutimi) defeated in the general election of 1930, felt obliged to notify his prime minister that the people of his constituency appreciated the value of the embargo on Soviet goods. He claimed that the resolutions requesting the lifting of the embargo on Russian anthracite came from certain 'public bodies' at the instigation of the 'City of Chicoutimi Chamber of Commerce, not so much for the sake of the Aluminum Company as for the welfare of some Liberal coal dealers who are anxious to handle Russian coal.'[21]

Charles Bourgeois (Conservative – Three Rivers-St. Maurice), on the other hand, begged Bennett to remove the ban on Russian anthracite so that the aluminum-coal barter transaction could be carried out. He disclosed that the Canada Power and Paper Corporation of Shawinigan had announced that it intended to close its factory on 28 May 1932, throwing some six hundred men out of work, and that the Shawinigan Chemicals Company was experiencing severe difficulties in its effort to operate profitably. Now if the Aluminum Company of Canada was also forced to close its plant, argued Bourgeois, Shawinigan would be ruined economically.[22]

After weighing the pros and cons for removing the coal embargo on Russian anthracite, Bennett decided to leave the ban untouched. He was not opposed to an aluminum-oil-gold barter deal, however, if the Soviet oil did not interfere with the preference given in Ottawa to fuel oil from

20 Memorandum of the unemployment situation in Shawinigan Falls, Almaville, and Shawinigan Bay, 24 March 1932, Bennett Papers.
21 J.A. Lavergne to Bennett, 24 Jan. 1932, ibid.
22 Charles Bourgeois to Bennett, 9 March 1932, ibid.

Trinidad. Consequently, on 17 September he granted the Danish tanker *Aase Maaersk* permission to unload her consignment of Batum crude oil, which was to be refined by the La Salle Petroleum Company of Montreal. Canada agreed to exchange $1,500,000 in aluminum for $750,000 in Soviet crude oil and $750,000 in gold.[23] A memorandum from R.E. Powell, vice-president of the Aluminum Company of Canada, seemed to imply that the proposed deal was strictly an exchange of aluminum and oil, with no Russian payments of gold involved.[24] Be that as it may, the second cargo of crude petroleum arrived at Montreal in mid-October.[25]

The Regina *Leader Post* (19 September 1932) refuted the arguments used against the aluminum-oil-gold barter. 'Canada is engaging in fiscal madness,' the editor declared, 'when she refuses to sell from stocks of which she has surplus to those who are willing to buy and able to pay.' The Winnipeg *Tribune* (20 September 1932) also came to the defence of the government's trade policy by reminding readers that Russian crude oil was not one of the products on the embargo list since it was a mixture of refined gasoline, fuel oil, and an adequate amount of crude oil to pass the Canadian tariff regulations.

On the other hand, some of the British newspapers and British business-men regarded the Canadian-Russian barter of aluminum and oil with grave suspicion. On 26 October the high commissioner for Canada, H. Ferguson, notified Bennett that many Britishers accused Canada of vio-lating the Imperial Trade Agreement of 1932. Five days later, the Canadian prime minister cabled the high commissioner, denying the allega-tion, but intimating that a change in the policy of future barters might be necessary if evidence showed that such deals interfered with the Trinida-dian preference.[26]

The commotion in England caused by the Canadian-Soviet barter deal was mild in comparison with the tension that resulted from the United Kingdom's importation of Russian timber. Early in 1932 the Canadian government registered an official protest against a proposed British agree-ment to buy 450,000 standards of Russian timber. Bennett considered such

23 The Lethbridge *Herald*, 5 Oct. 1932.
24 Memorandum from Powell to Gagnon, 5 Nov. 1932, Bennett Papers.
25 E.B. Ryckman to Bennett, 4 Oct. 1932, ibid.
26 Bennett to Ferguson, 31 Oct. 1932, ibid.

a purchase detrimental to the success of negotiations that were to take place at the Ottawa Imperial Economic Conference to be held in the summer. J.H. Thomas, secretary of state for Dominion Affairs, allayed the Canadian fears by dismissing the Anglo-Soviet negotiations as plain rumour. Yet despite the denial of Thomas, a contract was made in March between the Soviet government and Timber Distributors Limited.[27]

Bennett realized that very little could be done to alter the concluded agreement between Moscow and London. But he did ask Ferguson on 7 January 1933 to remind the British government of article xxi whereby the United Kingdom and the British Dominions at the Ottawa Conference agreed to prohibit entry from any foreign country of any commodity that would interfere with Imperial trade. Now here was a case where Russian timber importation unfairly competed with Canadian timber. Bennett urged Ferguson to stress the fact that in 1932 alone Canada imported 1,400,000 tons of British anthracite when she could have easily bought this type of coal elsewhere. He cautioned, however, that further purchases of British coal would be impossible if the Russians continued to flood Great Britain with their timber. To prepare the high commissioner for British objections to the Canadian-Russian barter deal involving cattle and oil, Bennett informed him that such a transaction would be insignificant compared with the enormous timber sales.[28]

Ferguson was not forced to defend Canada's barter deal with the Soviet Union. The British government fully realized that the contract made by Timber Distributors Limited, a syndicate of British timber importers organized for the purpose of securing an orderly marketing of Soviet timber, might violate article xxi of the agreement. Consequently, the British Foreign Office notified the syndicate to delete any clause in their new contract that might be contrary to this article.[29]

Instead of meekly complying with the wishes of the British government, Timber Distributors Limited reacted by preparing a memorandum showing that the Soviet methods of selling did not unduly interfere with Canada's trade. It contended that Canada was already supplanted by a

27 CAR, 1932, p. 328.
28 Bennett to Ferguson, 7 Jan. 1933, Bennett Papers.
29 Ferguson to Bennett, 25 Nov. 1933, ibid.

small country, Finland, as the chief exporter of timber to England. It further argued that the 10 per cent preference allowed Canada to sell wood in Great Britain at prices with which no other producer could compete, and that Canadian producers had scarcely made any efforts to adapt their method of manufacture to the complex and exacting requirements of Britain. The memorandum suggested the United States as the most natural outlet for Canadian timber.[30]

The arguments of Timber Distributors received support from the Soviet government which learned of the Canadian objections to the timber trade between Russia and England from the British Board of Trade. The Canadian high commissioner, Ferguson, strenuously opposed the dispatch of the Canadian memorandum containing letters from Bennett and from himself, explaining how Russian timber could be excluded under article XXI of the Ottawa agreements. Ferguson admitted that he had no objection to showing the documents to the firm representing Russia in London 'but its dispatch to Russia has not the approval of the Canadian government.'[31] The Toronto Globe (2 November 1933), commenting on this incident, claimed that it could not understand 'why official correspondence between Canada and the mother country with regard to an agreement reached between them should be submitted to Moscow for dissection ...'

The Soviet note to Ottawa indicated that the documents had indeed been 'dissected.' The Moscow note argued that the probable reasons for the decline of the Canadian timber trade were the increase of timber consumption by home industries, the exhaustion of several species of eastern Canadian softwoods, and the exceptional increase of trade between the United States and Canada. It called particular attention to the fact that Canadian exports of timber products to the United Kingdom had declined considerably even before World War I, thus dismissing Russian 'dumping' as one of the causes of this decline. It branded the Canadian allegation that slave labour was used in Soviet lumber camps as false, and defended the retention of the 'fall clause,' which provided for lowering of prices to undersell competitors, on the ground that this was one of the means of retaining markets for home industries.[32]

30 Memorandum of the general imports of softwoods into the United Kingdom, ibid.
31 The Toronto Star, 1 Nov. 1933.
32 Ferguson to Bennett, 5 Dec. 1933, Bennett Papers.

In a letter to Ferguson, Skelton disagreed with several of the statements made by the Soviet government and deplored some of its intentional omissions. He realized fully that the Soviet government was willing to accept any price for its timber in order to get foreign credits, but at the same time he was unable to understand how any country could compete with the huge sales and low prices of the Russians. Finally, he disclosed the fact that the Soviet government threatened to flood Great Britain with low-cost timber and thus deprive Canada of a valuable timber market.[33]

The unusual willingness of the British government to please Canada helped to eliminate some of the tensions created by the British importation of Russian timber. The British government asked Timber Distributors to provide Canadians ample opportunity for fair competition by reducing their original contracts for sawn softwoods to 350,000 standards and by excluding the 'fall clause' in their contracts. To prevent any possible leakage of Soviet timber products through such countries as Finland, Sweden, and Poland, the British government requested that her representatives in these countries report any unusual consignments of Soviet timber 'which may appear destined to the United Kingdom market and which may have undergone further processing of sawing and dressing.'[34]

On behalf of the Canadian government, Bennett expressed his appreciation for the earnest efforts of the British government to arrive at a reasonable solution of problems that had arisen as a result of the importation of Russian timber into the United Kingdom and for the evident desire of the United Kingdom Government 'to maintain alike the intent and spirit of Article xxi of the United Kingdom-Canada Agreement.' The Canadian prime minister mentioned the elimination of the 'fall clause' and the decrease of importation of Russian softwoods, particularly Siberian pine, as specific items for which Canada was grateful to Great Britain.[35]

Although the new arrangements negotiated between London and Moscow pleased Canada, they did not obtain the same warm reception in all quarters of the British Isles. The Manchester Guardian (23 January 1934) blamed Bennett for the unsatisfactory terms of the agreement made at the Ottawa Conference in 1932. It accused the prime minister of forcing the United Kingdom to help him recover from the economic chaos for

33 Skelton to Ferguson, 12 Dec. 1933, ibid. 34 Ferguson to Bennett, 24 Jan. 1934, ibid.
35 Bennett to Ferguson, 28 Jan. 1934, ibid.

which he was responsible: 'After losing the American market for Canadian softwoods, he [Bennett] tries – and in some degree succeeds – to force the British Government to help him out of his mess.'

Bennett's problems were far from being solved. On 12 May 1934, Ferguson informed the Conservative leader that there was evidence of importation of Russian lumber through Narva and Riga, and suggested that H.H. Stevens, minister of trade and commerce, contact Trade Commissioner McGillivray at Narva to secure all the details.[36] Bennett allayed his high commissioner's apprehensions by reminding him that the British representatives in Finland, Poland, Norway, Sweden, and Latvia were instructed by the Foreign Office to report any irregular shipments of Soviet timber.[37] Canada did not pursue the matter any further.

What caused Bennett grave concern was the contract being negotiated between British Timber Distributors and the Soviet Union in January 1935. Reportedly the new agreement revived the controversial 'fall clause' which permitted Russian low-priced timber to flood the British market. Despite the protest of the Canadian high commissioner, British Timber Distributors insisted on buying some 400,000 standards of timber and on retaining, at least in spirit, the 'fall clause.' W. Runciman, president of the British Board of Trade, came to the rescue of the Canadian high commissioner by warning the timber syndicate that any new contract containing the 'fall clause' would be considered by the government to be null and void.[38]

British Timber Distributors again modified their demands and indicated a readiness to compromise. At the suggestion of Canada the timber company agreed to limit its import of Russian timber to 300,000 standards. It also agreed to regulate the importation of planed lumber in order to avoid the repetition of the 1934 situation when planed lumber was allowed to flood the British market.[39] Thus the problem of importation of Soviet timber, which strained the relations between Canada and England during the years 1932–5, resulted in a compromise.

Another proposed deal that tested the flexibility and the stability of the

36 Ferguson to Bennett, 13 May 1934, ibid.
37 Bennett to Ferguson, 12 May 1934, ibid.
38 Ferguson to Bennett, 15 March 1935, ibid.
39 Ferguson to Runciman, 1 April 1935, ibid.

embargo was the Canadian-Soviet cattle deal. Presumably encouraged by the relative success of the aluminum-oil deal, the Russian trade delegation in New York, called Amtorg, suggested that a cattle-oil barter arrangement be made between Canada and Russia. Since the Soviet Union had no trade delegation in Canada, the transaction had to be carried out through private agents. George Serkau agreed to represent the western Canadian syndicate interested in arranging this barter. Serkau, a Canadian citizen, posed as a lawyer, though according to the records of the Law Society of Manitoba, he had never articled as a law student. For several years he worked with Monteith, Fletcher and David, a law firm in Altona, Manitoba. Despite a complaint lodged against him by the Manitoba Law Society for practising without proper authorization, he did manage to succeed Fletcher as head of the firm.[40]

The first intimation of Serkau's barter plan appeared in his letter to Robert Weir, the minister of agriculture.[41] The minister's aid was sought in overcoming some of the technical problems that had arisen. First of all, there was the necessity of providing the essential rolling stock and facilities for handling livestock from the seaports into the interior of Russia. Then there was the difficult task of ascertaining the breeds of cattle, the localities to which the various breeds might best adapt, and the best methods for purchasing and inspecting them. The difficulty of proper selection was further increased by the fact that Amtorg possessed only one agronomist and he had no special training in animal husbandry. Finally, the approach of the cold Canadian winter would necessitate the construction of suitable winter shelters to accommodate the animals before their shipment to Russia.[42]

Although the federal minister of agriculture did not promise government aid in providing rolling stock and the facilities for handling these cattle, he did make clear the suitability and the high quality of Canadian cattle. He informed Serkau that he could quite easily obtain 100,000 head of cattle which could adapt to the Russian weather and vegetation. He held that the English, Scottish, and American importers could attest to the

40 W. Kennedy to Bennett, 9 Jan. 1932, ibid.
41 George Serkau to Weir, 28 Oct. 1932, Sessional Paper 114 (a).
42 Ibid.

hardiness of Canadian cattle breeds. As to the grading of the cattle, he assured Serkau that the Canadian system of grading was one of the best in the world. The Canadian Record of Performance and the Advanced Registry for dairy cattle unequivocally testified to the high milk-producing qualities of Canadian cattle. Even the non-pure-bred cattle could be evaluated by the provincial and federal cow-testing schemes. Finally, he reminded Serkau that no cattle were as free from tuberculosis as the western Canadian breeds.[43]

Encouraged by Weir's detailed information, Serkau immediately contacted the secretaries of various breeders' associations representing the principal breeds in Canada, asking them for photographs, catalogues, show records, and other literature pertaining to registered cattle.[44] In another letter to the minister of agriculture, Serkau asked for 'the number of cattle and horses in Canada according to the last census, and any other statistical information pertaining to these live stocks.'[45] Four days later Serkau received from the Department of Agriculture data covering the number of purebred livestock registered in Canada during the past five years as recorded in the Canadian National Live Stock Records Report of 1931. According to this report, the total livestock population of the Dominion during 1931 ran as follows: 3,128,966 horses, 3,512,000 milch cows, and 4,478,000 other types of cattle.[46]

The only apparent hurdle confronting Serkau in the proposed barter deal was the means of transporting the cattle to Russia and bringing thousands of tons of low-priced petroleum from Black Sea ports to Canada within a year's time. If the shipment of petroleum could be carried out, the Canadian refineries would be taxed unduly. On the other hand, if the time for the exchange of cattle and oil were lengthened to two or two and a half years, the livestock producers would be extremely annoyed by the delay.

In a two-page memorandum to Weir, Serkau elaborated on his problems, and on their possible solutions. He suggested, as one of the solutions, a diversification of the Russian part of the barter, consisting of kerosene, lubricating oil, and anthracite, since these products could be transported

43 Weir to Serkau, 2 Nov. 1932, ibid.   44 Serkau to Weir, 6 Nov. 1932, ibid.
45 Serkau to Bennett, 6 Nov. 1932, ibid.   46 Burgess to Serkau, 10 Nov. 1932, ibid.

to Canada and disposed of here within a year. But the difficulty posed by the existing embargo on Soviet coal had to be faced. A more acceptable solution, argued Serkau, would be to stipulate the immediate shipment of cattle to Russia in exchange for a gradual importation of Russian petroleum. But, since it would take considerable time to convert the petroleum into circulating currency as payment for the cattle, he urged the Canadian government to guarantee Russian 7 per cent bonds on a $4,000,000 loan payable 1 June 1935. To support his case he cited two examples of governments backing exporters, namely, the British government's guaranteeing to the extent of 60 per cent the British exporters' bonds, and the German government's establishment of a fund of $75,000,000 to back Russian bonds. He emphasized the fact that the increased price of livestock from the present two and one-quarter cents to five cents would more than compensate the government's investment.[47]

Weir, who initially supported the barter scheme with some enthusiasm, now frowned upon the plan since it included the importation of anthracite which was on the embargo list.[48] A former minister of agriculture in King's cabinet, W.R. Motherwell, accused Bennett of forcing Weir to cancel the deal. '... his [Weir's] lord and master [Bennett] came along from mid ocean on his way home [from England] and snuffed out the proposition like a candle, after which the minister [Weir] had to get into line.'[49]

In a report to the House of Commons on trade relations with Russia on 31 January 1933, Bennett outlined the reasons for his opposition to Serkau's suggestions. 'No Canadian government,' he stressed, 'would seriously consider a proposal to provide credit facilities for a syndicate of vendors and at the same time to guarantee that the alleged purchaser, the Soviet Government, would discharge its obligations to the vendors.'[50] He also mentioned that Weir asked Serkau for evidence to show that the Soviet government supported such a transaction, but did not receive any.

The subject of Serkau's barter deal came up again on 3 February, when the House was discussing the vote for the Commercial Intelligence Service of the Department of Trade and Commerce. W. Irvine (U.F.A. –

47 Serkau to Weir, 21 Dec. 1932, ibid.
48 CAR, 1933, p. 90.
49 Canada, House of Commons, Debates, 1933, p. 3476.
50 Ibid., p. 1671.

Wetaskiwin) asked H.H. Stevens, the minister of trade and commerce, why the cattle-oil transaction failed to be realized. Stevens argued that Serkau's barter deal was indefinite as to the amount of money necessary for his overhead expenses. At one time Serkau claimed that he needed $8,000,000, whereas at another time he estimated that $1,000,000 was all that was required. Then Stevens referred to the fact that Serkau did not prove that Soviet Russia was cognizant of this deal. But his strongest argument against Serkau's proposal for government guarantees lay in his moral inability to use the taxpayers' money to guarantee a group of promoters against the government of Russia's breach of contract. He also considered the removal of the embargo on anthracite, which was to form part of the barter products, to be inadvisable because the ban provided a market for British coal.[51]

David Spence (Conservative – Parkdale) supported Stevens's stand on the cattle-oil barter, suggesting that the entire deal might be political propaganda to get the farmers dissatisfied: 'Who knows that Serkau ever had official instructions from Russia to go into a deal of this kind? Who knows that it is not simply propaganda of two or three yellow journals in this country, to create strife in this country between the party in opposition and the government.'[52]

Some of the members of the Opposition did not consider the barter proposal a species of propaganda, but rather a possible means of helping the distressed farmers. Agnes Macphail (U.F.O. – Grey, S.E.) reminded the House that not only were the farmers suffering from a lack of markets but the non-agricultural people also were affected by the 'lack of purchasing power on the part of the farmers.' Then she pleaded with the government to help execute the barter: '... if there is a possibility that Russia will take cattle and hides from us at prices as good as or better than they can now be sold for or exchanged for oil or any other product then I think it is the business of the government to do what they can to promote such a bargain.'[53] W. Irvine asked if the government had taken steps to ascertain whether the proposals of Serkau were sanctioned by the Soviet government. Stevens replied that his government did not enter into negotiations with Russia or for that matter, with any other country.[54] W.R. Motherwell

51 Ibid., pp. 1793–6.   52 Ibid., p. 1804.   53 Ibid., p. 1795.
54 Ibid., p. 1796.

accused the government of 'idling away, fiddling and diddling' instead of helping the farmers.[55]

Many cattle breeders' associations also asked the government to help Serkau to carry out the barter deal. The British Columbia Beef Cattle Growers Association, the United Farmers of Ontario and Community, and the Farmers of Thunder Bay District urged Bennett to remove the embargo on coal and execute the exchange.[56] The Canadian Aberdeen Angus Association informed him that the association did have a sufficient number of cattle for the proposed transaction.[57] In a detailed resolution, the Saskatchewan Cattle Breeders' Association pleaded with the government to support the barter, since there were some 520,000 surplus cattle which could not be sold because of a lack of markets.[58]

At the same time Bennett received letters advocating the continuation of the existing ban on Soviet goods. A resident of Winnipeg warned the prime minister against the resumption of trade relations with Bolshevik Russia, because such a policy would only impoverish Canada by encouraging the production of such Russian goods as wheat, lumber, and pulpwood which would interfere with Canadian markets.[59] H.P. Kennedy, president of Edmonton Stock Yards Limited, doubted whether Canada possessed the requested number of cattle, and objected to aiding a state which was bent on the destruction of Christian religion and institutions.[60] A medical doctor from the University of Toronto opposed the cattle-oil deal because it would only entail more deficit spending, without benefiting the farmers.[61]

Despite the objections presented by members of Parliament and by a number of citizens, Serkau was determined to conclude the barter agreement. In his modified plans, mailed to Bennett on 23 February 1933, he suggested that he could easily arrange the exchange of 100,000 cattle and 10,000 tons of salted hides for 720,000 tons of Soviet anthracite and an

55 Ibid., p. 1803.
56 The British Columbia Beef Cattle Growers Association to Bennett, 31 Jan. 1933; United Farmers of Ontario and Community to Bennett, 11 Jan. 1933; the Farmers of Thunder Bay District to Bennett, 30 March 1933: Bennett Papers.
57 The Canadian Aberdeen Angus Association to Bennett, 30 Jan. 1933, ibid.
58 Saskatchewan Cattle Breeders' Association to Bennett, 16 Feb. 1933, ibid.
59 Ralph H. Webb to Bennett, 3 Jan. 1933, ibid.
60 H.P. Kennedy to Bennett, 7 Feb. 1933, ibid.
61 A.C. Evans to Bennett, 3 Jan. 1933, ibid.

undetermined number of tons of petroleum. No mention was made of any government guarantees on loans. But anticipating strong opposition to the importation of anthracite, Serkau assured the prime minister that such a relatively small amount of coal could not possibly affect the existing commerce with Wales and the United States. He argued, furthermore, that the cumulated profits gained through the barter would also affect favourably the prices on dairy products, hogs, sheep and poultry.[62]

Presumably annoyed by the interminable correspondence of Serkau, Bennett invited him to a meeting on 28 February, presided over by the minister of trade and commerce, H.H. Stevens, and attended by E.B. Ryckman, minister of internal revenue, D. Wilgress, former trade representative to Russia, and two other minor officials. The meeting proved to be a gruelling one for Serkau as Stevens and Ryckman took turns at cross-examining him. Beginning the inquiry, Stevens reiterated the persistent stand of the government, which had claimed time and again that it was not opposed to trade with Moscow, provided the goods exchanged or bought were not on the embargo list. He harped on the fact that the government had no evidence that Soviet Russia agreed to the barter, and he suggested that Serkau should begin his business deal by bartering a modest number of 1,000 head of cattle first before attempting to handle one hundred times that number.

Serkau's reply seemingly contradicted some of his earlier requests made in letters to Weir. He claimed that his syndicate could get along without government guarantees. He denied the allegation that he was asking for the removal of an embargo on Soviet products, and further denied that he was an agent of the Soviet government. In response to Stevens's request he was prepared to submit a contract between the Russian government and his syndicate to the Canadian government for ratification.[63]

No doubt the rebuff he received at the hands of the two cabinet ministers irked Serkau, but it did not prevent him from persisting in his demands. He notified Stevens that the Soviet government was now willing to accept frozen beef, provided that Ottawa accepted anthracite coal and petroleum

---

62 Serkau to Bennett, 23 Feb. 1933, ibid.
63 Memorandum of the conversation in the office of the Hon. H.H. Stevens, 1 March 1933, ibid.

in exchange.[64] Stevens invited Serkau to his office again on 26 May and reiterated the government's policy on the coal embargo. Disappointed, but not visibly upset, Serkau thanked Stevens for being so frank before leaving his office.[65]

Serkau seemed to fade from the barter scene and Benjamin Ginsberg replaced him as head of the syndicate wishing to arrange the cattle-oil deal. In a telegram to Sir George Perley, the acting prime minister, Ginsberg insisted that he needed no financial assistance from the government, but he did ask for the removal of the embargo on Soviet anthracite.[66]

Apparently his first letter prompted no action, for he again appealed to the acting prime minister:

The cattle situation is getting worse each day and it is a shame to see such daily sacrifices. You can readily understand that unless something is done very shortly that it will be impossible for a deal to be carried through. MacMillan, a large rancher in the High River district said that the cattle industry was in danger of extinction and I may say that I have spoken to a great many others who are interested in the industry and tell me that it must collapse if something is not done very soon.[67]

Perley reassured Ginsberg that his government was fully aware of the importance of the cattle industry to the country, and was naturally most anxious to co-operate in any way that would effectively improve the agricultural markets. He added that it was precisely for this reason that the government interviewed Serkau on 28 February. Unhesitatingly he blamed Serkau for the failure of the barter deal because he did not arrange any definite plans for the transaction.[68]

Ginsberg's cause was supported by R. Gardner (U.F.A. – Calgary), who claimed that he was not concerned with whether Canada could or could not import certain products from the Soviet Union. What he was interested in was what could be done for the farmers of the southern part of Alberta.

64 Serkau to Stevens, 22 March 1933, ibid.
65 Stevens to Bennett, 26 May 1933, ibid.
66 Benjamin Ginsberg to Bennett, 12 July 1933, ibid.
67 Ginsberg to George Perley, 23 Aug. 1933, ibid.
68 Perley to Ginsberg, 26 Aug. 1933, ibid.

According to his estimate, some 85 per cent of the cattle would die during the winter from lack of food.[69]

Perley's reply was similar to that given to Ginsberg. He told Gardner that his government was fully aware of the conditions in southern parts of the prairies, and that it was anxious to help the farmers. But he refused to be convinced that the lifting of the ban on Russian coal would solve the economic problems, contending that Great Britain was Canada's best customer for agricultural products, including cattle.[70]

Ginsberg's effort to have the embargo on Russian anthracite removed proved as futile as Serkau's. The government continued to repeat that there was nothing to prevent anyone who wished to buy goods from Russia or to sell goods to her from doing so. But there was a conditional clause attached to the government's trade policy. None of these goods could be on the embargo list. With this inflexible stand on the importation of Soviet anthracite, the huge cattle-oil-coal barter deal failed to become a reality.

69 R. Gardner to Perley, 21 Aug. 1933, ibid.
70 Perley to Gardner, 26 Aug. 1933, ibid.

CHAPTER TEN

The Comintern and the Communist Party of Canada

Previous chapters have demonstrated the Canadian government's concern over the rise of radicalism in Canada prior to 1919. This concern developed into an almost irrational fear of any labour and social unrest, which was frequently identified by prominent government officials and by editors of Canadian daily newspapers as fruits of Bolshevism. Some of this fear stemmed from the revolutionary proclamations of the Third International and some from the activities of the Communist party of Canada. To many people of Canada Russia was intimately linked with the Third International and with the Communist party of Canada.

In December 1918, Prime Minister Borden informed the acting prime minister, Sir Thomas White, that Communist propaganda was being vigorously pushed in Germany, Switzerland, and the Scandinavian countries. In his opinion the Communist agents would be extending their efforts to Canada and to the United States.[1] Three months later, he notified White that the existing unrest in Holland, Belgium, France, and Italy was initiated by Bolshevik agents who should be carefully watched in case they created agitation in Canada.[2]

In March 1919 many Bolshevik agents were stimulated to greater efforts in their mission by the institution of the Third International. The objectives of these agents were enunciated clearly by the Comintern, a term synonymous with the Third International. In simple language their goal was

1 Sir Robert Borden to Sir Thomas White, 2 Dec. 1918, Borden Papers, OC, MG, 26, H I(a) vol. 112, PAC, Ottawa.
2 Borden to White, 27 March 1919, ibid.

the overthrow of capitalism and the establishment of 'the dictatorship of the proletariat and of an international soviet republic.'[3] To facilitate the achievement of these aims, national Communist parties were organized into wholly subordinate sections of the Comintern.[4] The seven congresses of the Comintern reiterated the original revolutionary aims of the organization, but shifted its tactics according to the changing policies of the Communist party of the Soviet Union.

In view of the declared revolutionary objectives of the Comintern, practically every country that signed a treaty with the Soviet Union insisted on a clause by which each party promised to refrain from hostile actions and inimicable propaganda. The conclusion of formal treaties, however, did not completely eliminate Communist propaganda and interference in the internal affairs of the countries concerned. When Canada expressed a wish to adhere to the Anglo-Soviet Trade Agreement of March 1921, the Comintern headquarters began forging Canadian passports for the use of Soviet agents who were attempting to enter Canada.[5] The work of reproducing foreign passports was done in a Russian government office on Lubianka Street, Moscow, by five experts.[6] Three Canadian passports bearing number 2728 were issued to three different individuals under three different Governors General, the Duke of Connaught in 1916, the Duke of Devonshire in 1917, and Lord Byng of Vimy in 1921.[7] The detection of this forgery did not eliminate future forgeries or illegal entrance of undesirables into Canada.

However, the Canadian government was in a position to refuse questionable personnel to the Soviet trade delegation located in Montreal. Among the individuals barred from Canada were Peter Voikov, Gregory Weinstein, Santori Neuorteva, and Madame Alexandra Kollantai. Voikov was an active revolutionary in Switzerland and a member of the Executive

3 Library of the Communist International, vol. 22, 602, quoted in Gunther Nollau, *International Communism and World Revolution* (London, 1961), p. 53.

4 Thesis of the Communist International as adopted by the Second World Congress held in Moscow, Aug. 1920. The Communist party of Great Britain, London, 1920.

5 R.M. Hodgson, British chargé d'affaires in Moscow to Earl of Balfour, 24 June 1922, Public Record Office, London, co 42/1043.

6 R.M. Hodgson to Lord Curzon of Kedleston, 5 June 1922, ibid.

7 B.E.W. Childs, commissioner of police of the metropolis, New Scotland Yard to the British Foreign Office, 3 Aug. 1922, ibid.

Committee of the Regional Ural-Soviet, which sentenced the Imperial family to death. Weinstein was implicated in subversive activities as an organizer of the Bolshevik secret service not only in the United States but also in Canada and in Australia.[8] Madame Alexandra Kollantai corresponded with the members of the Canadian Communist party, particularly with those interested in the women's movement.[9]

When the Canadian government refused admission to Peter Voikov, the head of the Soviet trade delegation to Canada, the Soviet government then presented Yakov Davidovich Janson, generally spelled Jansen, as his replacement. Although the Canadian government did grant Jansen permission to come to Canada, it was, nevertheless, uneasy, for the new head was a prominent member of the Comintern and a professional revolutionary. Moreover, his brother Carl, better known in Communist and police circles as Charles Edward Scott, contributed to the formation of the Communist party of Canada and the maintenance of a link between the Comintern and the Party. The Department of External Affairs was warned of the possible collusion of these two fanatically dedicated brothers.[10] The Canadian government was, indeed, relieved when it learned that A.A. Yazikov had been appointed the official agent of the Soviet trade delegation and that Y.D. Jansen had been dropped from this delegation.

When the members of the Soviet trade delegation did arrive in the spring of 1924 they gave the Canadian government the impression that they were not only interested in trade but also in disseminating Communist literature among the various ethnic groups of Canada. Four of the twenty boxes directed to the trade delegation were found objectionable. They contained literature dealing with the overthrow of the capitalist system and the establishment of a Soviet republic in Canada. Prime Minister King expressed his disapproval of such a procedure, arguing that it was a violation of the Anglo-Soviet Trade Agreement dealing with the item of propaganda.[11] A number of interviews with the official Soviet agent, A.A.

8 British Foreign Office to the under-secretary of state for the Colonial Office, 9 Oct. 1922, Department of External Affairs, file 1110, box 265183, PAC Record Centre, Ottawa.
9 Cortlandt Starnes, Commissioner of RCMP to Sir Joseph Pope, 4 Dec. 1922, ibid.
10 Cortlandt Starnes to Pope, 16 Jan. 1924, ibid.
11 F.H. Clergue to A. Yazikov, July 1924, file 555, box 265346, ibid.

Yazikov, restored some of King's confidence in the objectives of the trade delegation. His trust reached a record low with the discovery of the wholesale forgery of one-hundred-dollar Imperial Bank notes, a discovery in which the trade mission was implicated. The Canadian prime minister considered the forgeries exceedingly serious and contemplated asking the mission to return home.[12]

Probably, while King was consulting the Colonial Office as to the best procedure in dealing with this problem, he reviewed the contents of the minutes of a meeting of the Colonial Commission of the Third International held in Moscow on 3 December 1922. This secret report confirmed the existing suspicion of the revolutionary intention of the Third International as far as the British Dominions and colonies were concerned. One of the members of the commission emphasized the importance of creating unrest in such British Dominions as Canada, Australia, and the Union of South Africa, in order to encourage the independence movement of the colonies and a complete 'severance from the metropolis.' To make this unrest effective, the same member suggested that the national Communist parties infiltrate the army, trade unions, and various levels of government. Moreover, it suggested that a vigorous campaign be fought against the Church since this institution was allegedly a faithful branch of the bourgeoisie.

Canada was considered ripe for revolution, but unfortunately it possessed one of the weakest Communist parties in the British Empire. To strengthen the Canadian Communist party it was agreed by a majority of 15 to 1 to have the Canadian organization direct 'its activities in accordance with the premises laid down in the programme of the Australian Party.' The latter party stressed the policy of rallying of the factory and agricultural proletariat around the party; it encouraged the use of the most aggressive members in labour unions and in various levels of government.[13]

In the light of the instance of the importation of Communist literature and of the forgery of the Canadian bank notes and cognizant of the revolutionary objectives of the Comintern, the Canadian government kept

12 See chapter v, 118–22.
13 Joseph Pope to W.L.M. King, 20 March 1923, W.L.M. King Papers, Memoranda and Notes, King Papers, MG 26, J. 4, vol. 63, PAC, Ottawa.

a discreet vigilance on the activities of the Soviet trade delegation. Prime Minister King reminded the chief Soviet trade agent that he and his colleagues must confine themselves to legitimate activities and refrain from all Communist propaganda.[14] This the agent agreed to do.

By and large the members of the trade delegation did keep their promise. Admittedly, some of the members, including the chief agent, A. Yazikov, and his successor, L. Gerus, did take part in a number of patriotic ventures quite consistent with the practices of most diplomatic corps. For instance, Ivan Kulik, accompanied by his wife, travelled to Winnipeg where he delivered a lecture, 'Proletarian Writers and Proletarian Literature,' to the Ukrainian Labour Farmer Temple Association.[15] In another gathering, this time at the trade delegation residence at 212 Drummond Street, Kulik promised the French Canadian Communists a French-speaking organizer. The French-Canadian organizer, C. Paquette, was lauded by another Soviet trade representative, M. Divilkovsky, who agreed with his colleague that the Comintern would come to the aid of the Quebecers.[16]

When the trade delegate, L. Gerus, arrived in Montreal he did take part in advertising the economic progress of his country. In an interview with Gerus, Skelton reminded the chief trade agent that he and his colleagues must refrain from propaganda, particularly among the Ukrainians and Russians of Montreal.[17] Gerus took exception to this demand and felt that is was unjust to deprive the members of his delegation from recreational and cultural contacts with the Canadian people.[18]

One of the best examples of a cultural enterprise supported by the Soviet trade delegation was the Cultural Relation League organized by Jack Counsell of Hamilton, who was also the legal adviser of the delegation. This league aimed to break down some of the prejudice and anti-Soviet feeling in Canada.[19] Counsell was not only interested in publicizing the economic

---

14 Memorandum of an Interview between the prime minister and A. Yazikov, 7 Aug. 1924, file 1110, box 265183, DEA, ibid.
15 Report of the RCMP on Ivan Kulik, sent to O.D. Skelton, 31 March 1925, ibid.
16 Det. Corp. A.W. Appleby, RCMP in charge of Montreal District, to the RCMP commissioner, C. Starnes, 4 May 1925, ibid.
17 From J.W. Phillips, RCMP officer, commanding Quebec Division to the commissioner, C. Starnes, Montreal, 18 Jan. 1927, ibid.
18 Gerus to O.D. Skelton, 21 Feb. 1927, ibid.
19 C. Starnes to O.D. Skelton, 2 Oct. 1925, ibid.

and cultural successes of Russia but also in encouraging further contacts between the Communist party of Canada and the Comintern.[20]

Although the Department of External Affairs was not unduly alarmed by the police reports of the activities of the Soviet trade delegates and of the establishment of the Cultural Relation League, it was perturbed by the rumour that Moscow had sent $75,000 to the Soviet trade delegation to be used in Canada for propaganda purposes.[21] The same report informed Skelton that the Drummond headquarters received great numbers of toys which were to be sold in parcels containing Communist propaganda. Skelton gave little credence to the subsidy rumour but at the same time he welcomed further news on it. He again reiterated the policy of the Canadian government with regard to the spread of any propaganda, saying that 'if any public evidence of such propaganda were obtainable, the position of the Delegation would become untenable.'[22]

Since no action was taken against the Soviet delegation, the rumour was probably false. However, the Canadian government was aware of the fact that the Drummond headquarters was the receiving station for secret messages that came from the Comintern to the Central Executive of the Communist party of Canada.[23] Moreover, the headquarters was actively engaged in sending confidential reports to Moscow on the revolutionary movement in Canada, as well as on events and policies of political and economic significance.

If the members of the Soviet trade delegation were rather careful where they went and what they said, the same was not true about the Canadian Communist party members. They openly supported the Soviet Union, advocated the eradication of the capitalist system of government and the creation of a Soviet republic in Canada. Their advocacy of force to change society and their participation in strikes, riots, and demonstrations created a distaste for and a suspicion of Soviet Russia and everything it stood for. A criticism of the Canadian Communist party was regarded as a criticism of the Communist party of the Soviet Union; a trial and arrest of Canadian Communists implied a condemnation of Soviet Russia and its system. To

20 H. Miller of New Scotland Yard to C. Starnes, 23 April 1925, ibid.
21 C. Starnes to O.D. Skelton, 27 May 1925, ibid.
22 O.D. Skelton to C. Starnes, 2 June 1925, ibid.
23 C. Starnes to O.D. Skelton, 3 Oct. 1925, ibid.

the Canadian government and to the Canadian people the Communist party of Canada was a division of the Comintern, directed from Moscow and supported by the Soviet leaders.

From its origin in May 1921 the Communist party of Canada received its directives from the Comintern. It was the Comintern that urged the various Communist groups, particularly the Ukrainian Labour Temple Association and the Finnish Social Democratic party to unite to form one party. In 1924 the Comintern recommended that the overt Workers' party join the Communist party of Canada. The resolution of the members of the convention reflects the complete subservience of the branch to Moscow: 'The Communist Party of Canada, Section of the Third International assembled in its constituents convention in May, 1921, endorses and adopts unanimously, on roll-call vote, the 21 points for affiliation with the Communist International as binding upon all delegates present and for its entire membership, without any reservation.'[24]

Because it was subservient to a foreign power and took its direction from the Comintern, the Communist party of Canada was unlike any other Canadian political party. The Comintern made it abundantly clear that each elected member of the Communist party must consider himself not a legislator but 'an instigator' who was answerable to the Communist party alone.[25] In turn the Communist party was responsible to the Comintern in Moscow.

Some of the direction and inspiration from the Comintern to its divisions came through correspondence. Most of it, however, came from the representatives who attended the congresses and the plenums of the Comintern and of the Profintern, Red International of Labour Unions. The first Canadian and prominent member of the One Big Union, Joseph Knight, attended the Third Congress of the Third International and of the Profintern. In response to the recommendations of the Comintern he attempted to persuade the OBU to join the Red International Labour Union.[26] At the Fourth Congress of the Comintern held in 1922, the Canadian delegates, Florence Custance, John MacDonald, and Maurice

24 The *Communist*, vol. I, no. 1, Toronto, 1921.
25 Rex *v.* Buck *et al.*: Transcript of Evidence Heard Before the Supreme Court of Ontario, 2–12, Nov. 1931, Toronto, 1931, p. 386.
26 William Rodney, *Soldiers of the International* (Toronto, 1968), p. 45.

Spector were urged by the Third International to establish 'a fully open and legal Communist party whose policies are to be based upon co-operation with the trade unions.'[27] At the Fifth Congress held from 17 June to 8 July 1924, the Canadian Communist delegates, Malcolm Bruce, Tim Buck, and A.T. Hill agreed to follow the policy of the Comintern and initiate the 'bolshevization' of the Canadian workers.[28]

At the Sixth Congress considerable attention was paid to Canada, although some of the problems discussed here were mentioned at the Seventh Plenum of the Fifth Congress held during the last two months of 1926. The representatives at the Sixth Congress held in 1928 were John MacDonald, Maurice Spector, A.G. Neal, editor of *Vapaus*, and John Navis representing Finnish and Ukrainian members of the Canadian Communist party. At this gathering MacDonald attempted to rectify the notion of Nikolai Bukharin, the new Comintern chairman, who maintained that Canada was entirely within the economic sphere of the United States. He did not minimize the influence of the United States, but at the same time he referred to Great Britain's investment of three billion dollars in Canadian industry as an indication that Canada continued to depend on London. He emphasized that the main work of the Canadian Communist party lay in the organization of the non-union worker. To carry out this vital role the Party intended to send a number of workers to Moscow for special courses on Communist ideology, strategy, and tactics.[29] Spector, like MacDonald, stressed the importance of making Canada economically independent of Great Britain. He promised that the Communist party of Canada would work towards gaining the support of the Canadian people in case the Soviet Union was attacked by a foreign power. Finally, he requested financial as well as moral support for the progress of the Party.

He did not have to wait long for detailed instructions from Moscow. In 1929 the Comintern informed the Canadian Communist party that it placed too much emphasis on unity from the top and minimized the importance of the 'grass-roots movement.' It urged the organization of French Canadian workers into an active section of the Party. Above all it

27 Ibid., p. 63.   28 Ibid., p. 83.
29 *Pravda*, Moscow, 24 Aug. 1928.

suggested that an entirely new approach be taken with regard to the 'class struggle,' in view of the new autonomy accorded Canada by the Balfour Declaration of 1926. The Canadian Communist members were advised to centre their strategy around the oppressive nature of the Canadian 'middle class' rather than on the theme of complete independence from Britain.[30] But to achieve this independence, revolutionary struggle was necessary.[31]

The clear directives from Moscow were transmitted to its party members by means of conventions, letters, and newspapers. The principle of democratic centralization was evident in the organization of Canada into nine districts, each supervised by the Executive Council of the Communist party of Canada. Among many other duties, the members of each district were responsible for the dissemination of Bolshevik propaganda and for the infiltration of labour unions. The *Report of the Royal Commission* on Soviet espionage in Canada revealed that each Communist member was urged to get control 'through the election of secret members to the directing committee of as many types of functional organizations as possible, including trade unions, professional associations and broad non-party organizations such as youth movements and civil liberties unions.'[32]

The Communist party of Canada (CPC) used not only labour unions but other organizations and newspapers through which to exert its influence. The Friends of the Soviet Union and the Maxim Gorky clubs, two front organizations controlled by the Party, tried to spread Bolshevik doctrine among professional groups. The Workers' Ex-Service Men's League was primarily interested in organizing street demonstrations. To influence the

30 John Porter, 'The Struggle Against the Right Danger in C.P. of Canada – the Dominion Problem,' *Communist International*, London, vol. II, no. 23, 1929, 944.
31 Letter from the Executive Committee of the Communist International to the Communist Party of Canada, 1928, ibid.
   Another directive from the ECCI to the Central Committee of the Communist Party of Canada, 3 Oct. 1929, urged the formation of the Ukrainian and Finnish groups in the Communist party. Moreover, it asked the CPC to extend the organization of Red Unions into other organized industries.
   From the Politsecretariat of the ECCI to the Central Committee of the CPC, 3 Oct. 1929, 'The Communist Party of Canada,' box 9, envelope 15, Department of Public Records and Archives, Toronto.
32 *Report of the Royal Commission* (to investigate the facts relating to and the circumstances surrounding the communication of secret and confidential information to agents of a foreign power), Ottawa, 1946, p. 69.

youth of Canada, the extremely enthusiastic Young Communist League initiated anti-war and anti-fascist movements in high schools, colleges, and universities.

Almost every ethnic group was provided with a Communist-orientated newspaper. Among the more important were the *Worker*, the official organ of the Party, the Russian paper, *Bor'ba*, the Polish *Glos Pracy*, the Finnish *Vapaus*, and the Ukrainian *Ukrayinski Robitnychi Visty*. These newspapers continuously glorified the achievements of the Soviet Union, condemned any publicity or movement which criticized Russia, and supported unions and groups which found fault with the existing Canadian capitalist economy. During federal, provincial, and municipal elections many of these newspapers launched a vigorous campaign in favour of the local communist candidates.

Canadian Communists were particularly active during the depression years. Many an unemployed labourer was kindly disposed towards the Communists if for no other reason than that they were interested in the relief of his plight. Scores of workers participated in anti-government demonstrations in Winnipeg, Sudbury, and Montreal. These demonstrations, as well as some of the strikes, were organized by committees in which the Communists played a significant role.

Not all Canadians regarded the Communists with benevolence and tolerance. On the contrary, they expressed opposition to their aims and their tactics. One medical doctor suggested that these 'paid agents of Russia' who were creating disturbances among the illiterate farmers from south eastern Europe should be deported.[33] The premier of Alberta, J.E. Brownlee, was alarmed by the growth of Communist activities in the Ukrainian districts of his province and suggested that the RCMP investigate the causes of these disturbances with a view to prosecuting the worst offenders.[34] Both the Loyal Orange Association of British America and the Employers Association of Manitoba asked Prime Minister Bennett to enlarge the authority of the courts for 'the purpose of investigating and keeping in touch with the revolutionary propaganda and activities of the

33 C.B. Lawford, Smokey Lake, Alberta, to R.B. Bennett, 16 Dec. 1930. Bennett Papers, University of New Brunswick, file c-650, vol. 141.
34 J.E. Brownlee to R.B. Bennett, 14 Jan. 1931, ibid.

Communists in Canada.' They urged the government to declare the CPC illegal since it was 'affiliated with the Communist International at Moscow' and advocated the overthrow of the Canadian government by force and violence.[35] The mayor of Winnipeg too was painfully aware of the results of Communist activities in his own city and urged Bennett to pass legislation whereby the disturbers could be 'sent back to Russia, the country of their dreams.'[36]

Perhaps the most dramatic gesture to deal with the Communists came from the mayor of Sudbury, who experienced considerable difficulty in suppressing radicalism in his city. Under his inspiration the Sudbury City Council went on record asking the Dominion government 'to deport all undesirables and Communists' and to have this resolution forwarded to the government of Ottawa, and to all municipalities in the Dominion asking them to endorse Sudbury's action.[37] The response was most favourable as dozens of municipalities, towns, and cities across Canada endorsed the resolution.

In reply to the many requests for action to restrict the activities of the Communists, Bennett expressed his concern but indicated the difficulty of deporting some of the undesirables to the country of their origin, namely Russia, which refused to accept them. Many of the petitioners must have breathed easier when they heard that the Communist leaders were arrested. On 11 August 1931 the Toronto city police aided by the RCMP raided the Communist party headquarters and arrested its leaders: Tim Buck, the political secretary of the Party; John Boychuk, the organizer of the Ukrainians in Canada; Thomas A. Ewen, the chief secretary of the Workers' Unity League; M.L. Bruce, the editor of the *Worker*; Sam Carr, the chief assistant to Tim Buck; T. Hill, the main Finnish Communist organizer; T. Cacic, the Yugoslav organizer; Matthew Popovitch, leader of the Ukrainian branch of the Party, and Mike Golinsky. The arrests were made under section 98 of the Criminal Code, which forbade the establishment of and the association with any organization that advocated violence.

35 C.B. McCready, grand secretary of the provincial Grand Lodge of Manitoba, to Bennett, March 1931; C.F. Roland, managing secretary of the Employers Association to R.B. Bennett, 21 April 1931, ibid.
36 R.H. Webb, mayor of Winnipeg to Bennett, 25 Feb. 1931, ibid.
37 H.B. McKeown, city clerk of Sudbury, to Bennett, 23 April 1931, ibid.

Each of the nine men was charged with supporting sedition and conspiracy and each was released on $15,000 bail.

The key witness of this ten-day trial was an RCMP sergeant, John Leopold, who for five years, from 1922 to 1927, disguised under the name of Esselwein, served as a secretary of the Regina branch of the Canadian Communist party and the secretary of the International Union of Painters, Paperhangers and Decorators.[38] Armed with important documentary evidence which he copied from official Party policy statements, he disclosed that the prime aim of the Communist party was to organize the working classes in order to overthrow by force the current government and other democratic institutions. He confirmed the growing suspicion that there existed a close link between the Comintern and the Communist party of Canada. He told the jury that the convention of the Party held in Toronto in 1927 advocated the abolition of the BNA Act because of its subservient character and promised to work towards a boycott of goods to any country fighting the Soviet Union.[39]

On 12 November 1931 Justice Wright sentenced Tim Buck, Ewen, Hill, Bruce, Boychuk, Carr (alias Cohen), and Popovitch to five years for conspiring with a foreign power to overthrow existing institutions. Cacic was given a two-year term and Golinsky was acquitted. All of the sentenced Communists except Bruce, who was Canadian born, were to be deported after serving their terms. The Communists appealed their cases. On 13 January 1932 the Ontario Court of Appeal, consisting of Sir William Mulock, W.E. Middleton, D.R. Grant, J.E. Orde, and C.A. Masten unanimously dismissed the appeal except for the third count of indictment, which was concerned with the accused being parties to a seditious conspiracy.[40]

Communist newspapers were infuriated by the trial and the subsequent imprisonment of the leaders. The Russian Communist party organ, *Pravda* (26 November 1931), considered the 'mock trial' in Toronto as 'a further link in the policy of terror applied by the Canadian bourgeoise against the revolutionary labour organizations.' 'We have another striking illustration,' stated the Soviet paper, 'of transaction of bourgeois "democ-

38 Tim Buck to A. Balawyder (unpublished letter, 31 Jan. 1968).
39 CAR, 1931, p. 426.
40 The King *v.* Buck *et al.* (published by direction of Honourable W.H. Price, attorney general for Ontario 1931).

racy" to methods of open Fascism ... in the form of constitutional guarantees and legality.' The *Worker* (24 June 1931), the mouthpiece of the Communist party of Canada, added some of its own local colour to *Pravda*'s allegation by maintaining that Attorney General Price was an agent of Bennett's fascist government. The editor appeared completely bewildered by the decision of the Canadian courts, in light of the work done by the Communist leaders to help better the economic conditions of Canada.

On the other hand, the Montreal *Gazette* (14 November 1931) concurred with the sentences arguing that the 'aims of Communism are wholly and utterly inconsistent with established principles of government and the organization of society in Canada ...' The *Halifax Chronicle* (10 November 1931) also agreed with the decision of Justice Wright, reminding the readers that one of these organizers, Tom Ewen, received instructions from Moscow's International Committee for Revolutionary Miners to organize the Revolutionary Mine Workers Union both in Alberta and in Nova Scotia.[41]

The topic of the trial of the Communist leaders was introduced in the House of Commons by John R. MacNicol (Conservative – Toronto–Northwest). He claimed that the concluded trial disclosed the dangerous character of the Communists and demanded an investigation of such leftist or Communist organizations as the Workers' Unity League, the National Unemployed Workers' Association, the Friends of the Soviet Union, and the Mine Workers' Union.[42] A.A. Heaps (Labour – Winnipeg North) retorted that MacNicol was exaggerating the dangers of Communist infiltra-

41 It is significant to note the militancy of the directives:
'In view of the distinct radicalism of the workers of Canada indicated by the events of the Red Day in Nova Scotia, these measures are rendered all the more necessary for the purpose of giving a revolutionary leadership to these growing class battles.
'Both in the unorganized industries and among the organized workers you should initiate strike movements, set up councils of action and strike committees composed of organized as well as unorganized workers.
'The latest development in Canada, the final and complete transformation of the Canadian Congress into a mere tool of capitalism forces us to take up the question of establishing a revolutionary trade union centre.'
From the Executive Committee of the Communist International to the Central Committee of the Communist party of Canada, 'The Communist Party of Canada,' Box 9, envelope 15, Department of Public Records and Archives.
42 Canada, House of Commons, *Debates*, 1933, p. 2192.

tion. He held that the most effective means of checking Communism was the solution of the economic problems of the country, particularly the increasing unemployment.[43]

Immediately after the trial of the Communists, Bennett was deluged with thousands of petitions for their release. These petitions came primarily from such Communist affiliated associations as the Canadian Labor Defence League, the Unemployed Married Men's Association, the Friends of the Soviet Union, Women's Labour League, and the Workers Benevolent Associations. By the spring of 1933 the Canadian Labor Defence League, which obtained the support of thousands of non-Communist Canadians, had some 196,000 names on petitions for the release of the Communists.[44]

The repeal of section 98 of the Criminal Code, under which the Communists were tried, was advocated by such MPs as J.S. Woodsworth, A.A. Heaps, and Angus MacInnis of the CCF, Ernest Lapointe of the Liberals, Agnes Macphail of the UFO, on the grounds that the legislation was contrary to British law, which protected individuals holding unorthodox views. On the other hand, Conservatives led by J.R. MacNicol, W.J. Loucks, G.B. Nicholson, and Armand R. Lavergne stressed the serious nature of the Communist menace and the close connection between the Communist party of Canada and that of Moscow.[45] Although Tim Buck was released from the penitentiary in 1934, section 98 was not repealed until 1936.

While Tim Buck and his colleagues were serving their sentences, a number of Communists were deported for acts of sedition. Aaroo Vaaro, editor of the Finnish Communist paper, *Vapaus*, was deported on 17 December 1932 and Dymitr Chomicki (Dan Holmes) in January 1933. Konrad Cessinger, the under-secretary of the German Workers and Farmers Union, and seven other radicals were deported also. Woodsworth bitterly criticized the government for allowing innocent people to be deported, without being given the chance of a fair trial. On the other hand, the minister of justice, H. Guthrie, stated that he was convinced of

43 Ibid.
44 Signatures and endorsations demanding the release of the eight Communist leaders, 18 Feb. 1933, Bennett Papers, University of New Brunswick.
45 Canada, House of Commons, *Debates*, 1933, pp. 2186–203.

the legality of the steps taken by the RCMP in arresting the suspects.[46] The decision of the Board of Inquiry at Halifax to deport the undesirables was upheld by the Supreme Court of Nova Scotia and the Supreme Court of Canada.

Although the petitions of the Canadian Labor Defence League did not stop the deportation of the ten Communists detained in Halifax, they did aid in the release of Tim Buck. On the night of his first public appearance he received a hero's welcome at Maple Leaf Gardens. On 28 December 1934 another welcome was accorded him by some 10,000 people in Montreal. Upon rising to speak Buck was greeted with tremendous applause and cheering followed by the singing of 'The International.' In his preliminary remarks he stated that he had been requested by the Executive of the Communist International to convey their best wishes and greetings to the Quebec workers. Then in broken French he told the audience that his party refused to go underground and defied the government to do anything about it. Finally, he made it clear that he and his colleagues were released from prison not because of any change of heart on the part of Bennett, but rather because of the mass pressure brought upon him by the working class of Canada.[47]

Even after the release of Tim Buck the Communist party of Canada continued to be an unlawful association. Therefore, the Communists used numerous legitimate fronts among which the Canadian Labor Defence League and the Workers Unity League were the most effective. The former consisting of prominent humanitarians who had no sympathy for Communist ideology as such worked for the release of the Communist leaders. The latter, including many non-Communists, organized the 1935 abortive march on Ottawa from the western relief camps.

Encouraged by such important Communist leaders as Arthur Evans, some 900 men broke the relief camps in British Columbia and started a march on Ottawa. By the time the campers reached Regina the number had increased to 2,000. On 12 June the government issued an order to stop the march and forbade the men to leave Regina. Bennett, who was

46 Ibid., 1932, pp. 2658–9.
47 J.H. MacBrien, commissioner of RCMP, to Hugh Guthrie, 9 Jan. 1935, Bennett Papers.

convinced that the organized effort of the Communists was aimed at the 'overthrow of constituted authority' did, however, agree to meet Evans and seven of his lieutenants.[48]

Among the demands presented by the eight-man delegation were a six-hour day, a five-day week, and a minimum wage of fifty cents an hour. Although the government was not able to meet these demands at that time it was willing to take care of the unemployed campers at the newly erected camp at Lumsden. The two-hour discussion between the delegation and Bennett proved fruitless, as far as immediate results were concerned.

Back in Regina the RCMP officer in charge of the campers ordered the local population to stop giving the marchers money or handouts and had already banned further public meetings. In addition, the marchers were forbidden to go farther east. Some of the campers attempted to defy the government order and board the train for their trip to Ottawa. Five were arrested and charged under section 98 of the Criminal Code.

Evans and his colleagues called a mass meeting on 1 July to protest the arrest of the five men. The RCMP, and Regina city police surrounded the platform and arrested the leaders. Suddenly some of the campers turned on the police with sticks and stones, and shots were fired by city police. The results were tragic; one city policeman was beaten to death and a camper was fatally wounded. About one hundred persons, including RCMP and city police, were injured, several seriously. Extensive property damage also ensued. Out of 130 persons arrested, 24 were brought to trial. Nine of these were convicted of creating disturbances and sentenced to terms of from five to fourteen months.

The subject of relief campers and the Regina incident was brought up in the House of Commons by J.S. Woodsworth. Most of the members of Parliament who took part in the debate believed that the majority of the campers were not Communists, but were convinced that some of the leaders were inspired by Communist ideology. 'I frankly admit,' asserted Woodsworth, 'that as far as I can ascertain, the men in control of the trekkers are Communists or belong to the subsidiary Communist organizations.'[49] A.A. Heaps held the same view as Woodsworth when he said that 'it is indeed unfortunate that the young men from the camps came under

48 CAR, 1935, p. 428.
49 Canada, House of Commons, *Debates*, 1935, p. 4048.

the control of leaders who are part and parcel of the Communist movement of Canada.'[50] H. Guthrie, minister of justice, declared that he was
convinced that 'the disruption of the camps ... was the result of the communist propaganda.'[51]

Many of the members of the Opposition, however, argued that the Communists took advantage of the existing economic conditions which the
government had failed to remedy. They pointed to the irritation caused
by inadequate facilities found in the unemployment camps, and singled
out the arrogant fashion in which both city police and the RCMP disrupted
a peaceful meeting at Regina. Opposition leader Mackenzie King and
H.H. Stevens, who sat as an independent member of Parliament following
his disagreement with Bennett over price spread, questioned the right of
the federal government to interfere with the maintenance of order in a
province.[52]

Despite the opposition of the federal government, Premier Gardiner of
Saskatchewan decided to appoint a commission to investigate the riot. The
commission, consisting of Chief Justice J.T. Brown, Justice W.M. Brown,
and Judge A.E. Doak of the District Court, held a series of enquiries for
sixty days, during which time 359 witnesses were heard.[53] The commission
supported the federal government's decision to stop the marchers from
proceeding farther than Regina on the grounds that the number would
have increased to over 5,000 before they reached Ottawa. Such a large
group of dissatisfied workers would have created an embarrassing situation
in the nation's capital. The report of the commission referred to the Communists as the organizers of the march and dismissed poor food and inadequate facilities as the fundamental causes of the riot.[54]

Although it would be incorrect to place all the blame for the strikes,
riots, and mass demonstrations on the Communists, many of the disturbances were Communist led or Communist inspired. The unemployed
and disheartened workers were an easy prey to leaders who promised their
followers an earthly paradise where justice and prosperity would prevail.
Unfortunately, many of the workers did not discover in Bennett that crea-
tivity and initiative usually associated with great leaders. His inability to

50 Ibid., p. 4151.
52 Ibid., p. 4144.
54 Ibid., p. 314.

51 Ibid., p. 4053.
53 CAR, 1935, p. 313.

achieve any rapport with the working class alienated many labourers, driving them towards the Communist movement. In addition, such members of Bennett's cabinet as G.D. Robertson, minister of labour, C.H. Cahan, secretary of state, and R.J. Manion, minister of railways and canals, were permeated with the fears of the 'red scare' so common in 1919–20, which frequently identified legitimate protest with Communism.

Bennett, as well as many businessmen, associated the activities of the Communists with the revolutionary objectives of the Comintern. Naturally, Russia, the home of the Comintern, was looked upon with suspicion and distrust. One of the reasons for the imposition of the embargo on Russian coal, woodpulp, pulpwood, lumber, asbestos, and furs on 27 February 1931 was the flood of petitions from Canadian citizens for some type of restraint on the activities of the Canadian Communist party and on its parent the Third International. Some of the petitioners argued that trade with Russia would only provide the Bolshevik agents with funds to stir up trouble in Canada, undermine democratic institutions, and destroy Christianity. Others maintained that the Soviet Union deliberately flooded Canadian markets in order to create economic chaos which the local Communists exploited.[55] These arguments not only influenced Bennett's decision to impose an embargo on Soviet goods but also steeled his determination against the lifting of the embargo despite a considerable amount of pressure from commercial concerns, left-wing organizations, and individuals.

The new shift in Soviet foreign policy announced by Stalin in 1935 helped to reconcile the antagonism between the Soviet Union and Western powers, including Canada. Stalin asked his diplomats to secure military alliances with the major powers against Nazi Germany. He also directed the Comintern to reverse its aggressive attitude towards the socialist and radical parties of the capitalist countries and to combine with these groups to form 'a united front' against the emerging fascist threat. The 'united front' policy was elaborated at the Seventh Congress of the Comintern held in Moscow during the summer of 1935. Here national Communist parties were urged to form an electoral alliance with other anti-fascist parties, whether socialist or merely reformist, and if at all possible to merge

55 See chap. 8, pp. 136–7.

their respective trade unions or youth groups with those found in the bourgeois countries. The various Communist parties were encouraged 'to apply the united front tactics in a new manner ...' by participating in 'election campaigns of a common platform ... with a common ticket of the anti-fascist front ...' At the same time the delegates were warned that the 'united front' policy did not mean the abdication of the Communist right 'to political agitation and criticism.'[56]

Significantly, a number of 'united front' organizations appeared in Canada under the inspiration of the Communist party. Among these were the Free Bread League, the National Unemployment Workers' Association, and the League Against War and Fascism. Admittedly, many of the members of these groups were not Communists but supporters of movements advocating the alleviation of the economic plight of the Canadian people or opposing the totalitarian regimes of Germany and Italy.

Several 'united front' groups attempted to boycott Canada's participation in the Winter Olympic Games held in Berlin in 1936, on the grounds that such participation openly sanctioned the dictatorial policies of nazism. During the exhibition games played with western and eastern Canadian senior hockey teams, the Canadian Olympic team was encouraged to refrain from participating in the games in Berlin by the use of banners hoisted during the exhibition contests and through parades staged in various large Canadian cities. At the same time the German consulate in Montreal was showered with protests and resolutions from 'united-front' organizations condemning Hitler's persecution of Protestants, Catholics, Jews, and Communists.[57] The parades and resolutions, however, did not affect Canada's decision to take part in the Winter Olympic Games.

In accordance with the directives of the Seventh Comintern Congress, the Canadian Communists expressed their willingness to support the policies of the Canadian Socialist party and the Co-operative Commonwealth Federation, commonly known as the CCF, much to the annoyance of the latter. During the federal election campaign of 1935 handbills printed

56 Jane Degras (ed.), *The Communist International ... Documents 1919–1943*, vol. III (Toronto, 1965), 361–5.
57 From the German consul in Montreal to the German Foreign Office, 17 Jan. 1936, no. 530, *Das Deutsche General Consulat für Kanada*, Library of Congress, Washington, DC.

by the East Hamilton Communist Association urged the voters to support CCF candidates in the East Hamilton constituency, using the slogan: 'Boost a CCF and Communist Government.'[58] At a provincial election rally the Canadian Communist leader, Tim Buck, asked the voters to support the CCF election program.[59] Furthermore, the CPC paper, the *Worker*, appeared with such slogans as: 'For a united labour slate of CCF and Communists.'[60]

Understandably, Woodsworth, leader of the CCF, was irked by the Communists' alleged support of CCF policies. He expressed his displeasure at the Communist tactics during a debate in the House of Commons: 'I do not like the Communist Party. They have given our Co-operative Commonwealth Federation Party more trouble than any other party ... I have been opposed by the Communist party and so have my colleagues.'[61]

Despite the CCF's public announcements of their desire to dissociate themselves from the Communist party of Canada, the latter continued to seek closer collaboration with them. One of the organizations which sought to bring this about was the Friends of the Soviet Union (FSU), which was sponsored by the CPC. According to a handbill published by the FSU, the objectives of this organization included the dissemination of truthful information about the Soviet Union, helping to re-establish normal relations between Canada and the USSR, and preventing war against Russia.[62]

Louis Kon, one of the secretaries of the FSU and a staunch friend of the members of the Soviet trade delegation located in Montreal from 1924 to 1927, asked J.S. Woodsworth whether the item of friendlier relations be-

58 Toronto *Daily Star*, 31 Sept. 1935.
59 *Winnipeg Free Press*, 13 March 1935.
60 The *Worker*, Toronto, 19 Dec. 1935.
61 Canada, House of Common, *Debates*, 1939, p. 2256. The CCF attitude towards the Communist party and the United Front which it sponsored is clearly demonstrated in a discussion between a number of CCF members of Parliament and members of the League of Social Reconstruction, which was founded in 1932 for the purpose of advocating economic and social policies destined to serve the common good of Canadians. In the discussion on the United Front both Woodsworth and David Lewis opposed any affiliation with the Communist party of Canada. Frank McInnis felt that change in the economic and social structure of Canada should come about through peaceful means and not by violence as advocated by the Communist party.
   Summary of Discussion between the CCF parliamentary group and the League for Social Reconstruction, CCF Records, MG 28, IV-I, vol. 168, PAC, Ottawa.
62 Louis Kon to J.S. Woodsworth, 5 Nov. 1935, 'Friends of the Soviet Union, 1935–38,' CCF Records, MG 28, IV-I, vol. 157, ibid.

tween his party and the FSU could be placed on the agenda of the forth-coming CCF convention.[63] After receiving an unsatisfactory reply to his request, Kon pleaded with M.J. Coldwell, then the secretary of the CCF, to permit him ten minutes of the convention time to present his group's desire for co-operation with the CCF.[64]

In the absence of Coldwell, his assistant notified Kon that his request would be placed before the National Council when it met in Toronto towards the end of July. At the same time he was rather positive that it would not be possible 'to allow a non-member of the CCF to submit any resolutions to the CCF Annual Convention or, similarly, to give the floor to any such non-members.'[65]

The refusal of permission to speak at the convention did not, however, deter Kon from making another request. He invited the CCF to join the FSU in the celebration of the twentieth anniversary of the Bolshevik Revolution. He detailed the nature of the participation. In the first place he asked the co-operation of various groups, including the CCF, in sending President M. Kalinin of the Soviet Union an acknowledgment of the social, economic, and political progress made by the Soviet regime during the past two decades. Secondly, the FSU hoped to mail a specimen of a Canadian painting and a Canadian handicraft to the Soviet people. Finally, the association planned to arrange, in large centres of Canada, twentieth anniversary mass meetings where 'comparative pictures of the Russia of the past and of the Soviet Union in its many aspects would be given by appropriate speakers.'[66]

The National Council of the CCF, which met in Winnipeg on 24, 25, and 26 July, felt that it was not in a position to take an active part in the twentieth anniversary of the Soviet Union in view of the fact that it had considerable work of its own to do. At the same time, the country as well as CCF members of Parliament had frequently paid tribute to Russia's accomplishments since the Russian Revolution, and had sought the friendliest relations with Moscow at all times.[67]

The FSU received another setback in its attempt to foster friendlier

63 Ibid.
64 Louis Kon to M.J. Coldwell, 21 June 1936, ibid.
65 Assistant to M.J. Coldwell to Louis Kon, 24 June 1936, ibid.
66 Claire Roche to J.S. Woodsworth, 15 July 1937, ibid.
67 David Lewis to C. Roche, 18 Aug. 1937, ibid.

relations with the CCF when the editor of the *New Commonwealth*, the official organ of the CCF, refused to provide space for news on Soviet Russia and on the activities of the FSU in Canada and elsewhere.[68] In addition, the newspapers declined to publish several letters to the editor submitted by the National Office of the FSU. Evidently annoyed by the policy of the *New Commonwealth*, Louis Kon compared the CCF organ with the Montreal newspaper *Le Devoir*, which he alleged was controlled by the Jesuits. He could not understand why a socialist newspaper such as *New Commonwealth* refused to publish material which most capitalist newspapers agreed to publish.[69] Obviously, the CCF refused to support the policies of the Communist party of Canada because its ideology was incompatible with the democratic ideals of the CCF.

However, the CCF was drawn into 'a united front' against fascism. To many Canadians fascism was more dangerous to world peace and to democratic institutions than was communism. By 1936 the Canadian press was engaged in a devastating editorial war on Mussolini and Hitler, depicting them as enemies of democracy and creators of totalitarian systems of government. Francisco Franco, general of the Spanish legion which fought against the Republican government, was lumped with the two Fascist dictators as another enemy of democracy.

In response to the directives of the Comintern, the Canadian Communist party formed 'a united front' against fascism. The formation of an international brigade to fight on the side of the Loyalists against the forces of Franco constituted an important aspect of this 'united front' policy.[70] The concept of international brigades was initially introduced to the Comintern by the French Communist leader, Maurice Thorez. Within a relatively short period of time national Communist parties engendered surprising amounts of support for this policy among Communist and non-Communist Canadians.

The Canadian international unit, organized by the CPC was the Mackenzie-Papineau Battalion named after two outstanding leaders of the 1837 Rebellion in Upper and Lower Canada. Altogether some 1,200

68 Louis Kon to the editor of the *New Commonwealth*, 18 July 1937, ibid.
69 Louis Kon to David Lewis, 10 Aug. 1937, ibid.
70 Hugh Thomas, *The Spanish Civil War* (London, 1961), p. 296.

Canadians went overseas to fight on the side of the Republican or Loyalist governments. Many of these volunteers were not inspired by Communist ideology, although their leaders were. Some enlisted in order to fight fascism; others, disillusioned and disheartened by the Canadian scene created by depression longed for a better world ... a world where economic and social security would be matched by political liberty; still others went for the sake of adventure.[71]

Regardless of the motivation of the rank and file of the volunteers, the leaders of the CPC were determined to organize the raw inexperienced recruits into a successful fighting unit. To help achieve this aim, Tim Buck, the national secretary of the CPC, and Allan Dowd, a dedicated organizer of the battalion, visited Spain and conferred with the Republican leaders on the best deployment of Canadians in the struggle. Both Buck and Dowd made this side trip to Spain following the Universal Peace Conference held in Brussels in September 1936. At this conference some five thousand representatives from 32 countries discussed means of limiting the civil war by agreeing on a policy of non-intervention. The resolutions of this meeting were presented by its organizer, Viscount Cecil Chelwood to the League of Nations, only to be shelved by the league because of its inability to apply sanctions against the aggressor. Therefore, both sides in the conflict continued to obtain aid in the form of men and material. Upon his return to Canada, Dowd was determined to provide the Loyalists with the help they needed.[72]

It is difficult to determine the number of volunteers who belonged to the Communist party of Canada. One can only conjecture that a fair number of the volunteers from the Ukrainian and Finnish ethnic groups were card-carrying party members. Several veterans of the war demonstrated their political allegiance when they promised to use the skills and techniques of guerrilla warfare and barricade-building learned in Spain in a revolution which they hoped would take place in Canada.[73]

The Communist party of Canada made use of the general pro-Loyalist

71 Victor Hoar and M. Reynolds, *The Mackenzie-Papineau Battalion* (Toronto, 1969), p. 26.
72 Ibid., p. 8.
73 From S.T. Wood, commissioner of the RCMP, to O.D. Skelton, 1 Dec. 1938, Department of External Affairs, file 291-E, box 26550.

feeling in the organization of the Committee to Aid Spanish Democracy, commonly known as the Spanish Aid Committee, comprised of many non-partisan humanitarians. The chairman was the Reverend B.H. Spence, the honorary chairman was the Reverend Dr Salem C. Bland, and the vice-chairmen were Tim Buck, Allan Dowd, Dr Rose Henderson, and Graham Spry.[74] In this array of prominent Canadians, Buck and Dowd were the only card-carrying Communist party members.

The main aim of this committee was to secure moral and financial support for the Spanish Republic. It did not recruit combatants; this was the task of the CPC. However, it attempted to procure the financial aid necessary for the material care of the volunteers while in Spain and for their rehabilitation upon their return to Canada. Operating from head-quarters in Toronto and from branches in Windsor, Montreal, Vancouver, and Winnipeg, this committee with its hundreds of dedicated volunteers prepared speeches, organized rallies, and distributed pamphlets with the aim of winning the public to its cause.[75]

Nine months after the formation of the Spanish Aid Committee, another organization, the Friends of the Mackenzie-Papineau Battalion, was formed with the expressed purpose of alerting Canadians to the struggle in Spain so that they might become involved morally, financially, and politically.[76] In line with the 'united front' policy of the Comintern, the executive of this organization consisted of Communist and CCF party members. The latter party was primarily concerned with the humanitarian aspects, providing personnel and medical care for the wounded. Despite the Communist attempts to involve the CCF in the political aspects of the war, the party under the leadership of Graham Spry, one of the members of the Friends and the chairman of the Ontario CCF provincial organization, refused to help in the recruitment of volunteers.[77] However, many CCF members helped in the repatriation of the survivors and in the rescinding of the Foreign Enlistment Act of 31 July 1937.

The government legislation prohibiting the dispatch of aid in the form of men and material involved an intricate legislative procedure. On 18 February Minister of Justice Ernest Lapointe moved that certain aspects

74 Victor Hoar and Reynolds, *The Mackenzie-Papineau Battalion*, pp. 9–10.
75 Ibid., p. 9.   76 Ibid., p. 100.   77 Ibid., p. 100.

of the Imperial Foreign Enlistment Act of 1870 be amended in order to make it relevant to the times which were characterized by rapid means of communication and transportation. The bill received its second reading in late February and the assent of Parliament on 10 April. It was then applied to the Spanish Civil War on 31 July by an order-in-council placing an embargo on arms and ammunition to Spain and making it unlawful for a Canadian to enlist or to induce others to enlist to fight in the Spanish Civil War.[78]

In the debate on Canada's foreign policy Prime Minister King defended the amended Foreign Enlistment Act. He emphasized that the act was aimed at keeping Canada neutral by preventing her 'from being drawn into foreign conflicts by the actions either of manufacturers of munitions or of organizers of recruiting.'[79] He admitted that a substantial number of Canadians and foreigners had already left Canada to go to Spain. Since August, however, no passports had been issued to nationals, although some volunteers did make their way by indirect routes. As far as the embargo was concerned, it did not apply to clothing, food, and medicine.

Several members of Parliament disagreed with the terms of the act. The CCF leader, J.S. Woodsworth, a dedicated pacifist, deplored the limited neutrality expressed by Justice Minister Lapointe. 'If it is to be made illegal,' argued Woodsworth, 'as I think it should be, to enlist in the armed forces of any foreign state at war with a friendly state, I do not see why there should be a permit to do otherwise.'[80] In his reply to the CCF leader, Lapointe maintained that, though Canada did not wish to become involved in any conflict, it did wish to help the sufferers on both sides of the conflict through such humanitarian agencies as the International Red Cross.[81]

The CCF member for Vancouver Centre, Angus MacInnis, differed with his leader, insisting that the embargo on the shipment of arms and ammunition to Spain be lifted so that the Loyalists could defend themselves against the 'gangsterism' of Franco and his supporters, Hitler and Mussolini. He deplored the attitude of some of the democratic countries who considered

78 Governor general-in-council, 31 July 1937, PC 1837 (Queen's Printer).
79 Canada, House of Commons, *Debates*, 1938, p. 3187.
80 Ibid., 1937, p. 1945–6.   81 Ibid., 1937, p. 1947.

Republican Spain 'the criminal in this affair.'[82] He reminded the members of Parliament that the Popular Front government of Spain was democratically elected in February 1936 and that Spain continued to be a respectable member of the League of Nations whereas both Germany and Italy were no longer members.

As expected, Communist and united-front organizations objected to the imposition of the embargo. The Canadian League for Peace and Democracy petitioned the Canadian government to remove 'the embargo on loyalist Spain and supply her with the needed goods and credits ... and instead place an immediate embargo on exports to Japan.'[83] A Hamilton district trades and labour council also urged the removal of the embargo, calling the attention of the government to the fact that such a restriction against the democratically elected Republican government of Spain demonstrates Canada's opposition to the Canadian ideals of freedom and democracy.[84] Similarly a resolution from the Regina branch of the Communist party of Canada asked Ottawa to remove the ban on arms, ammunitions, and food so that the Loyalists could defend their 'democracy and preserve world peace.'[85] One of the most comprehensive requests came from a Winnipeg branch of the Friends of the Mackenzie-Papineau Battalion. Members of this branch petitioned the Canadian government to remove the ban on all goods going to Spain; they condemned the Italian and German intervention in the Civil War and requested the rehabilitation of the Canadian volunteers who 'fought as soldiers of democracy on the Loyalist side.'[86]

The CCF party branches also expressed their disapproval of Canada's policy towards Spain. 'We ask that Canada's foreign policy not be linked with such betrayal of Democracy, Liberty and Justice,' wrote the secretary of one branch, 'but that Canada instead lift its embargo on Loyalist Spain

82 Ibid., 1938, p. 3249.
83 Canadian League for Peace and Democracy to King, 23 Feb. 1939, King Papers, vol. 263, PAC, Ottawa.
84 H.W. Wilson, secretary of the Hamilton District Trades and Labour Council to King, 13 Feb. 1939, King Papers, vol. 282, ibid.
85 J. Sawekyse, secretary of the Stokes Branch of the Communist party of Canada, 16 Feb. 1939, vol. 279, ibid.
86 Marshall G. Gauvin, chairman of the Resolution Committee of the Winnipeg Committee to Aid Spanish Democracy, to King, 30 Jan. 1939, vol. 267, ibid.

and give aid to those Heroes of Democracy.'[87] Another branch passed a resolution asking for the revision of the government's legislation on the ground that the Spanish government was democratically elected, was, like Canada, a member of the League of Nations, and was fighting against an unprovoked aggressor.[88]

While considerable heat was engendered in the discussion of removing the embargo, little was said by the members of Parliament on the problem of repatriation. A reference was made to communism and to the Spanish volunteers in a debate on national defence by Maxime Raymond, Conservative member for Beauharnois-Laprairie. He maintained that the real threat to freedom was not from without but from within, that is from the Communist agitators. He alluded to the volunteers who entered the 'red army of Spain.' 'This I admit,' he added, 'does not give me sorrow; it will rid us of these undesirables provided they do not return here.'[89]

The disposal of the undesirables was not that simple for, as Canadians, the Spanish volunteers did expect to be repatriated. In order to ascertain the legal rights of these volunteers to re-enter Canada, officers of the RCMP and representatives of the departments of Immigration and of External Affairs met on 1 March 1938. The RCMP official was of the opinion that these volunteers should be denied entrance to Canada 'upon the ground that they had either committed a breach of the Foreign Enlistment Act or were engaged contrary to the policy of the Government in the Spanish War.' On the other hand, the immigration official held that 'in most, if not all instances, the nature of the absence from Canada would be inconsistent with an intention of settlement abroad.'[90] The policy of the Immigration Department prevailed.

This general policy was of considerable importance in the light of future international developments. On 5 July 1938 the Non-intervention Committee of 27 European countries adopted a resolution re-affirming its

87 Vernon J. Grainger, secretary of the CCF Branch of Fort William, to King, 14 March 1939, ibid.
88 An enclosure of a letter from J. Guthrie, secretary of the Ladysmith CCF Club, 8 June 1938 to J.S. Taylor, MP for Nanaimo, BC, forwarded to King, 14 June 1938, vol. 260, ibid.
89 Canada, House of Commons, *Debates*, 1937, pp. 910–11.
90 Memorandum on the return of volunteers from Spain, King Papers, 19 Oct. 1938, MG 26, J4, vol. 212.

previous commitment of non-intervention, and provided among other measures for the withdrawal of foreign volunteers from Spain. An international committee appointed by the League of Nations was to verify the evacuation of the non-Spanish combatants. Although Canada was not a member of the committee, she did express through the British Foreign Office her desire to co-operate in the repatriation of her nationals.

Unlike Great Britain and France, Canada refused to pay for the transportation of the volunteers to and across Canada for the simple reason that these Canadians went to Spain without the consent and in some cases contrary to the wishes of the government. However, the Canadian government was willing to provide an immigration officer to screen the volunteers, readmitting or refusing them according to the provision of the Immigration Act. Accordingly, the assistant immigration commissioner, R.N. Munroe, was dispatched to Barcelona. The government felt that sending an experienced officer to Spain would facilitate matters by eliminating the usual difficulties encountered at Canadian ports.[91]

Munroe was alerted to the possibility that some undesirables who fought on the side of the Loyalists might attempt to use passports taken from Canadian volunteers killed in the war.[92] After a careful scrutiny by the immigration officer some nine volunteers were refused admission into Canada, but their cases were appealed to Ottawa for reconsideration. Most of the nine volunteers were members of the Communist party of Canada. As far as ethnic origin was concerned four were Bulgarian, two Hungarian, two Romanian, and one Jewish. The RCMP commissioner felt that none of these nine should be admitted into Canada unless they furnished definite proof that they were Canadian citizens.[93]

Those who were readmitted into Canada by the Immigration Officials were faced with a major problem. Since the Canadian government refused to pay for the transportation of these volunteers, money had to be obtained from other sources. According to CPR officials, the Friends of the Mackenzie-Papineau Battalion assured the company that they would provide the necessary funds. For some reason or other the Friends refused to get involved in raising money to defray the expenses of volunteers' trips

91 From O.D. Skelton to V. Massey, 9 Dec. 1938, Department of External Affairs, box 265550, file 291-E, PAC Record Centre, Ottawa.
92 S.T. Wood, commissioner of the RCMP, to O.D. Skelton, 1 Dec. 1938, ibid.
93 S.T. Wood to O.D. Skelton, 11 Aug. 1939, ibid.

to Canada. They maintained that it was the policy of the organization to send cigarettes, tobacco, and food to the volunteers as well as to aid in the rehabilitation of the veterans rather than in providing money for their transportation to and from Spain.[94]

Evidently, some of the CCF members were aware of the Friends' policy and were not too happy about it. Two of them, M.J. Coldwell, MP, and David Lewis, the national secretary of the CCF, felt that it was not just for some of the Canadian volunteers to suffer because of the 'incompetence and unbusinesslike methods' of the Friends who reportedly promised financial aid for the transportation of the volunteers. In their interview with O.D. Skelton, the under-secretary of state, the CCF party members argued that 'in the interest of avoiding controversy' some means should be devised for the repatriation of the volunteers. Skelton replied 'that the people who would doubtless wish to avoid controversy were those who had raised the funds for sending the men over and who were now trying to raise the funds to bring them back.'[95] The problem of finance was finally resolved when the Spanish Republican government supplied $20,000 for the conveyance of these Canadians.[96]

The 'united front' policy against fascism did help to give the Communist party of Canada a more respectable image. While many prominent Canadians, among them Justice Minister Lapointe and Paul Martin, shared the communist fear of fascism, others associated freely with the leading Communists in their anti-fascist campaign. Somehow the fear of the Bolshevik agents in Canada decreased as Canadian businessmen, university professors, and politicians worked side by side with the Communists in the Spanish Aid Committee, Canadian Labor Defence League, and the League Against War and Fascism. Among these were J.S. MacLean, president of Canada Packers, Professor Eugene Forsey, and Graham Spry. No doubt, the tolerant attitude towards communism helped in the lifting of the embargo on Russian goods and the signing of a new trade agreement with Moscow in September 1936.

While many Canadians were more favourably disposed towards the

94 From J. Taylor, executive secretary of the Friends of the Mackenzie-Papineau
   Battalion to M.J. Coldwell and D. Lewis, 24 Dec. 1938, ibid.
95 O.D. Skelton, Memorandum, 'Spanish Volunteers,' 23 Dec. 1938, W.L.M.
   King Papers, MG 26, J4, vol. 212, PAC, Ottawa.
96 V. Hoar and M. Reynolds, *Mackenzie-Papineau Battalion*, p. 228.

Communists, Premier Maurice Duplessis and his Union Nationale party considered communism a threat to national security and personal liberty. In order to stop the growth of radicalism and communism in his province, Duplessis passed the Padlock Law of 1937. Two of its sections are particularly significant. Section 3 of the law made it 'illegal for any person who possesses or occupies a house within the province to use it, or allow any person to make use of it to propagate communism or bolshevism by any means whatsoever ...' and Section 12 made it 'unlawful to print or publish in any manner whatsoever or to distribute in the province any newspaper, periodical, pamphlet, circular, document ... propagating or tending to propagate communism or bolshevism.'[97]

Woodsworth urged the federal government to repeal the Padlock Law, arguing that it came within the area of federal jurisdiction and consequently was *ultra vires*.[98] In reply to the CCF leader, Minister of Justice Lapointe suggested that the elimination of economic and social injustice was a better means of fighting communism than the repeal of the Padlock Law, which interfered with provincial rights.[99] Joseph Jean (Liberal – Mercier) supported the non-intervention policy of Lapointe, maintaining that it was up to the people of Quebec to decide what types of legislation served them best.[100] Understandably, both Woodsworth and his colleague, A.A. Heaps, disagreed with Jean's reasoning, arguing that it was indeed the duty of the federal government to protect the freedom of all Canadians, including the people of Quebec.[101]

Many Canadian newspapers, associations, and individuals disapproved of the enactment of the Padlock Law and urged the federal government to have it repealed. In its editorial of 27 March 1937 the *Winnipeg Free Press* called the Quebec legislation 'the most oppressive law against radicals ever directed and passed in this country.' It referred to the absence of any definition of the term 'communism' or 'bolshevism' as an open invitation to arbitrary arrests. The editorial concluded with a hopeful prophecy that no one would follow Quebec, for 'elsewhere in Canada ... there is a healthy belief that ideas are not things to be afraid of.' Equally vehement in its

97 Canada, the *Labour Gazette,* vol. XXXVIII, no. 10, 1938.
98 Canada, House of Commons, *Debates,* 1937, pp. 2290–1.
99 Ibid., pp. 2293–4.   100 Ibid., 1938, p. 3420.   101 Ibid., p. 3369.

attack against the terms of the Padlock Law was the *Ottawa Journal* which, on 24 March 1937 argued that the Quebec legislation was not aimed against lawlessness but against the basic freedoms of the press and of speech.

On the other hand, Montreal's *Gazette* (25 March 1937) agreed with the Padlock Law, maintaining that its purpose was to protect the people of Quebec against communism, which had increased considerably since the repeal of section 98 of the Criminal Code in 1936: 'If this province does not want Communism, and cannot depend upon the Federal Parliament and Federal legislation for the protection which it considers necessary, the only alternative is provincial legislation.' Montreal's *La Presse* (18 March 1937) was also sympathetic towards Duplessis' legislation, observing that this law was in the spirit of the Catholic church which had continuously denounced the teachings of communism. But it went on to remind the people of Quebec that no new society can be built on legislation alone; it must be based upon Christian justice and Christian charity.

Petitions from groups and individuals reflected the growing concern of the Canadian people with the effects of the Padlock Law. The St. Lambert Women's Club considered the law a violation of the Constitution of Canada and an interference with the individual's right to freedom of speech, press, and assembly.[102] Another group, the Women's Labour League, demanded that the Padlock Law be disallowed because, besides interfering with the basic rights of man, it was being used to break up trade unions.[103] Similarly, the Grand Orange Lodge of Manitoba asked the minister of justice to disallow the Act because it 'infringes most seriously upon the liberty of the individual and strikes at the very root of democracy and rights as free citizens of a British Dominion.'[104] A resolution from a Young Women's Hebrew Association asked for the nullification of the Padlock Law because it denied civil liberties and property rights to Canadian citizens.[105] One petition signed by scores of citizens from Campbells

102 Amine F. de Mille, corresponding secretary of the St. Lambert Women's Club, St. Lambert, P.Q., to Lapointe, 8 June 1938, Ernest Lapointe Papers, Memoirs, Notes and Petitions, 1935–41, MG 27, III, B 10, vol. 42, PAC, Ottawa.
103 M. Gavin, secretary of Women's Labour League to Lapointe, 8 June 1938, ibid.
104 T.W. Pentland, grand master of the Grand Orange Lodge of Manitoba to Lapointe, 30 May 1938, ibid.
105 Resolution from the Young Women's Hebrew Association, Toronto, to W.L.M. King, 2 May 1938, ibid.

Bay, Quebec, demanded that the Padlock Law either be proclaimed *ultra vires* or be submitted to the Supreme Court of Canada in order to determine its legality.[106]

Not all petitions to the minister of justice asked for the disallowance of the Padlock Law. Many urged the minister not only to keep the law intact, but also to enact federal legislation similar to that passed by the Quebec government. One hundred and thirty-eight signatures from Cartierville endorsed a recommendation which requested the federal government to refrain from tampering with the Padlock Act and urged Ottawa to introduce legislation that would prohibit the importation and distribution of Communist literature.[107] About a dozen French Catholic parishes petitioned Lapointe to outlaw the Communist party of Canada, whose policy is to destroy religion, interfere with family life, and abolish private property.[108]

Premier Duplessis himself defended the enactment of the Padlock Law on 9 January 1939 during an address to the Montreal Canadian Club. 'Let other provinces do what each province wishes to do. Let Canada do what Canada wishes to do, but in the province of Quebec there is no room for Communism and if there is no room there is no house and if the room is bad the house should be padlocked.' He called communism the 'worst murderer in the world,' for it not only brought about physical misery but it also poisoned the minds and the hearts of the people. He compared communism to such diseases as smallpox and tuberculosis by punning on the abbreviation 'T.B.,' saying that it stood for Tim Buck. He felt that the best means of dealing with the disease of communism was to prevent its spread. He denied that the Padlock Law violated the liberty of man, for, according to him, Quebec police did not arrest the guilty individual but padlocked his house. Finally, he referred to the repeal of section 98 of the Criminal Code by the federal government as one of the main causes for the growth of the Communist party, pointing out that if the Canadian government refused to combat communism, then Quebec would 'be the

106 Campbells Bay, Quebec, to W.L.M. King, 14 June 1938, ibid., vol. 42.
107 The citizens of Cartierville to Lapointe, 7 March 1938, ibid., vol. 40.
108 The parishes of St. Arsène, St. Eusebius, etc. to Lapointe, 6 April 1937, ibid., vol. 16.

one to show the light and be the bulwark of law and order and common sense.'[109]

During the House of Commons debate on the validity of the Padlock Law, J.A. Bradette (Independent – Cochrane) criticized Soviet Russia and communism. He held that the Communists 'were not content to apply their ideas to Russia; they wanted to spread them all over the white and coloured world.' To substantiate this statement he referred to a strike in Cochrane in 1935, which according to him 'was instigated by Communist leaders ... in the pay of Soviet Russia.'[110]

One of the most bitter critics of Soviet Russia and of the Comintern was Wilfred Lacroix (Liberal – Quebec-Montmorency). He argued that the Comintern supported the Communists in Canada. In his opinion, communism was anti-Christian since it favoured divorce and abortion. He maintained that the Comintern or the Third International was organized to carry on revolutionary activities throughout the world. He then summarized the relationship between the Commissariat for Foreign Affairs and the Third International: 'While the Commissariat for Foreign Affairs officially represents the Soviet Government and maintains contact with the Foreign Offices of other countries in all official relations between states, the Third International deals in its capacity of special organization of the Russian Communist party and of the Soviet State ... for the purpose of world revolution.' He concluded his speech by stating that the twenty years of Communist rule in Russia had resulted in 'bondage, slavery, terrorism, persecution, and barbarity,' results against which many Canadians were preparing themselves to struggle.[111]

Several members of Parliament disagreed with Lacroix's condemnation of Russia. William Hayhurst (Social Credit – Vegreville) felt that Russia was 'not that vile a hotbed of the Third International' that some claimed it to be. Malcolm McLean (Liberal – Melfort) spoke in favour of the Russian people. 'I do not believe any white people,' he argued, 'are more democratic at heart than the people of Russia and I am quite satisfied that they

109 Quoted in E.A. Forsey, 'The Padlock – New Style,' *Canadian Forum*, March 1939, vol. XVIII, no. 218, p. 363.
110 Canada, House of Commons, *Debates*, 1938, p. 3415.
111 Ibid., 1939, pp. 1179–80.

do not enter upon that revolution deliberately desiring to inflict pain, hardship and death of millions of their people.'[112]

Quebec members of Parliament were supported by groups and individuals who requested the government to take drastic measures against the Communists and the Soviet Union. One association, called the Constitutional League of Canada, formed to combat communism, informed the prime minister that the Communist party of Canada was 'part and parcel of the Soviet Union.' 'The whole wealth of ideas of the party, their whole agitation and propaganda, all their organization and actions, are directed against the interest of Canada and calculated to promote the interest of the Soviet Union.'[113]

Scores of petitions from French-Canadian parishes requested the minister of justice to pass legislation which would outlaw the Communist party of Canada because it was supported by the Comintern – a branch of the Soviet government.[114] Furthermore, the Confederation of Catholic Workers of Canada, in its resolutions of 1936 and 1937, recommended that the federal government should not only 'prevent the Communist Party from enjoying a legal existence in Canada,' but also sever all diplomatic relations with the Soviet Union if it continued 'to disseminate Communist propaganda ...'[115]

A step towards federal legislation to curb communism was taken by Wilfred Lacroix when he introduced into the House of Commons on 16 January 1939 a bill to amend section 7 (d) of the Post Office Act which would prohibit the dissemination of Communist doctrine through second-class mail.[116] Lacroix argued that communism was so harmful to Canadians that a federal law should be passed to prevent the spread of this pernicious philosophy.[117] Wilfred Gariepy (Liberal – Three Rivers) supported Lacroix's motion, citing the beneficial results of the Padlock Law. 'This communistic doctrine,' he concluded, 'has no right to exist under the

112 Ibid., pp. 2259, 4432–3.
113 J.H. Zachary, secretary of the Constitutional League of Canada, to W.L.M. King, 28 May 1936, E. Lapointe Papers, MG 27, III, B 10, vol. 40, PAC, Ottawa.
114 Parishes of St. Eusebius and St. Arsène to Ernest Lapointe, 6 April 1937, ibid.
115 Canada, the Labour Gazette, vol. XXXVII, 43, and vol. XXXIX, 46, Ottawa, 1937–9.
116 Bill no. 4: An Act to Amend the Post Office Act ... introduced on 16 Jan. 1939, by W. Lacroix, E. Lapointe Papers, vol. 16.
117 Canada, House of Commons, Debates, 1939, p. 1176.

Canadian flag; it has no right to be protected by the institutions of our country.'[118]

One of the staunch supporters of civil liberties, J.S. Woodsworth, expressed his opposition to the proposed bill on the ground that it violated the basic freedoms of speech and press. 'I believe,' he maintained, 'that in the long run the doctrines of the communists will be shown to be false and ill-founded and that the truer doctrines, the better founded doctrines, will prevail.'[119] Angus MacInnis also opposed the bill because it placed the legislators on the level of the Communists themselves: '... after all, when I advocate the suppression of ideas which I do not like I come down to the level of those groups who suppress ideas with which they do not agree.'[120]

Minister of Justice Ernest Lapointe felt that the bill would prove ineffective in that it did not provide means of checking first-class mail, through which, in his opinion, plenty of Communist propaganda infiltrated into Canadian homes. In addition, he observed that the proposed legislation would also include all literature dealing with nazism and fascism. Paul Martin (Liberal – Essex West) agreed with Lapointe's argument that such an act would be most difficult to enforce and therefore would 'lend itself to all sorts of abuses' which in the long run would outweigh the advantages.[121] In line with the same type of reasoning, Malcolm McLean (Liberal – Melfort) maintained that anyone who was clever enough to devise a brand of propaganda that interferes with democracy 'will be clever enough to get propaganda through the mails without a great deal of difficulty.'[122] Because of the stubborn opposition of many members of Parliament from all political parties to the amendment of section 7 (d) of the Post Office Act, the bill failed to reach third reading.

Although King was aware of the importance of French-Canadian support in federal elections, he was not greatly worried about the accounts of alleged subversive activities of the Canadian Communists in Quebec. Some of the Quebec federal Liberal members objected to the passing of the Padlock Law by Premier Duplessis and blocked the Lacroix bill which attempted to prevent the dissemination of Communist literature by mail. King, unlike Bennett, felt that the people of Canada would reject the

118 Ibid., p. 2255.   119 Ibid., p. 2256.   120 Ibid., p. 4429.
121 Ibid., pp. 1184, 4435–6. 122 Ibid., p. 4433.

Canadian Communist movement as they had rejected other radical movements. As far as Russia was concerned, he, like Bennett, did consider Russia an alien power. However, he did not agree with the imposition of an embargo on Soviet-made goods, for in his opinion such a measure would only deprive Canada of a market for her products at a time when other countries protected themselves by high tariff walls. Consequently, the Liberal government under King lost no time in negotiating a trade treaty with the Soviet Union in 1936, a year after they came to power.

The era of 'good-feeling' initiated by the Canadian-Soviet trade agreement was stifled by the signing of a ten-year non-aggression pact on 23 August 1939 by Hitler and Stalin. The newspapers showed their displeasure at this agreement. The *Ottawa Citizen* (23 August 1939) called the new German-Russian agreement a conspiracy against peace negotiated by two nations which were as incompatible as fire and water. The *Winnipeg Free Press* (22 August 1939) also found the news of the agreement bewildering. It argued that one of the central themes of *Mein Kampf* was its hatred of bolshevism. The Winnipeg paper held that the pact would be of short duration because Hitler was known not to keep his word. The Toronto *Globe and Mail* (23 August 1939) viewed the agreement as 'Soviet trickery' and 'a Nazi bribery.' According to this daily, Stalin was anxiously waiting for the capitalist countries to tear one another apart so that he could come in and take advantage of the shambles.

The Canadian Communist newspaper, the *Clarion* (26 August 1939) took an unexpected attitude towards the agreement. It maintained that the pact did not alter Soviet foreign policy: Russia continued to fight for the preservation of peace and for the destruction of fascism. It singled out Chamberlain as the architect of much of the world's misfortunes; his appeasement policy had enabled the Germans to overrun Poland, thus threatening the Soviet Union. Hitler, too, was attacked. He was pictured as a warmonger who, under 'the mask of saving the world from Bolshevism,' menaced the peace-loving democracies of the world. Towards the end of 1939 the *Clarion* began to support Nazi Germany as well as the Soviet Union.

Prime Minister King was notified by Tim Buck of the Canadian Communist party's stand on the Nazi-Soviet Pact. Writing on behalf of the

Communist party of Canada he informed King that his party stood for 'the independence of Poland and for the restoration of the national freedom of Czechoslovakia and Austria.' He urged the Canadian government to take the initiative in calling a world conference of all countries including the USSR and the USA in order 'to obtain the fullest co-operation in the war against fascism and to pave the way for a democratic peace without indemnities or annexation.' He denounced the appeasement policy of Great Britain to which Canada had subscribed. Finally, he called on the prime minister to create a union government with labour and Communist members in it so that this anti-fascist struggle might be more effective.[123]

The independent line of the Canadian Communist party was altered towards the end of 1939 to conform with the foreign policy of the Soviet Union. The Canadian Communists became extremely vocal in supporting the Soviet Union and Nazi Germany at the cost of attempting to disrupt the Canadian war effort. Consequently, any support the CPC received in their campaign against the Fascists during the years 1935–9 were, to a large extent lost by the Molotov-Ribbentrop Pact and by the activities of the Communists. In May 1940 the Communist party of Canada was banned under the Defence Regulations. With the invasion of the Soviet Union by Hitler in 1941 the CPC made another round about turn and advocated the support of the Allies in their effort to defeat Nazi Germany.

123 Tim Buck to W.L.M. King, 8 Sept. 1939, King Papers, MG 26, J., vol. 264.

CHAPTER ELEVEN

Towards a
Better Understanding

The year 1934 witnessed a more tolerant attitude towards the Communist party of Canada and towards the Soviet Union. In 1934 the seven Communist leaders who were imprisoned for conspiring with foreign powers to overthrow the Canadian system of government were paroled as a result of continued protests by some of the members of Parliament and by a flood of petitions from individuals and groups. The CCF party, in particular, objected to the imprisonment of individuals whose ideas the government did not share. One of the largest assemblies of signatures, 200,000 in number, obtained through the ceaseless efforts of the communist-inspired Canadian Labour Defence League, urged the prime minister to release the Communists.

During 1934, Canada, along with thirty-four other countries, invited the Soviet Union to join the League of Nations. Most of the countries who encouraged Russia to join the league hoped that this world organization might influence her to become more law-abiding and pressure her into refraining from fomenting revolutions in other countries. It was also argued that Russia's participation in the work of the league would help in the preservation of world peace. Canada was interested in the effectiveness of this world body since she regarded the league 'with all its limitations, as an indispensable and continuing agency of international understanding ...'[1]

Canada took an active part in the various organs and committees of the league. Prime Minister King was chosen chairman of the Sixth Committee which dealt with the problems of mandates, minorities, and slavery. Another member of Parliament, Hubert B. Ames, was one of the advisers on the Saar Basin. In 1925, Senator Raoul Dandurand was elected presi-

1 R.A. MacKay and E.B. Rogers, *Canada Looks Abroad* (Toronto, 1938), pp. 93–101.

dent of the Sixth Assembly of the League and two years later, partly because of the prestige of the new president, Canada was admitted into the enviable circle of the League Council. King attributed his country's new position to her 'ideas of toleration and goodwill' which she demonstrated in both her domestic and foreign affairs.[2]

Two factors seemed to influence Canada's policies in the league. Perhaps the most important was the awareness that as a North American country she represented the non-intervention policy of the United States, who was not a member of the league.[3] It was primarily for this reason that she opposed article x of the Constitution, which committed league members to a policy of resorting to economic and military sanctions against aggressors. The second fact which determined Canada's role in the league was the attitude of French-Canadians towards such controversial topics as participation in European wars.

At the very time when Canada favoured the league because it helped to maintain peace by promoting co-operation in economic and social areas, the Soviet Union dubbed it a tool of the imperialist powers. In the words of *Izvestia*, the league was 'an essentially capitalist coalition.'[4] Trotsky denounced it as 'the shadow of the mailed fist of the Allied Supreme Council,'[5] and Bukharin considered it a monstrous worldwide trust that tended to crush the working-class movement. Lenin looked upon the league with distrust and viewed the newly formed Comintern as an antidote to the imperialistic and anti-working-class league.[6]

Some of the Soviet's unfavourable attitudes towards the league were altered after the substantial assistance given by it to victims of the Russian famine of 1921–3. The league's representative, Dr Nansen, was lauded by Lenin and his government for his outstanding contribution in alleviating the sufferings of the Russian people.

Although Soviet Russia was accorded *de jure* recognition by most European nations in the 1920s, her associations with the revolutionary

---

2 CAR, 1927–8 (Toronto), p. 140.
3 Robert B. Farrell, 'Planning and Control of Canadian Foreign Policy' (unpublished PH D thesis, Harvard University, 1952), p. 584.
4 *Izvestia*, Moscow, 13 May 1919.
5 'Why the U.S.S.R. Joined the League,' the *New Fabian Research Bureau*, 1934, p. 8.
6 Lenin, *Sochineniia* (Leningrad), vol. xxv, 597.

policies of the Comintern continued to alienate the goodwill of these nations. Relations between Russia and the Western nations were severely strained during the 1930s when Moscow was forced to resort to dumping her products in order to obtain the necessary credits to finance industrialization. Western nations imposed embargoes on Soviet products to protect their own industries.

The aggressive foreign policy of Hitler helped to bring Soviet Russia and many Western countries together. In 1932 Stalin negotiated non-aggression pacts with Poland, Latvia, and Estonia. He was most anxious to negotiate a similar type of treaty with France, an implacable enemy of Germany, but discovered that such an agreement would be impossible without Russia's becoming a member of the league. The Soviet leader then attempted to join with the Baltic States, France, Finland, Czechoslovakia, Poland, and even Germany to form an East European Locarno. When it became evident that neither Germany nor Poland favoured such a plan for Europe, the Soviet Union decided to enter the League of Nations. Nazi Germany was interested, however, in an alliance between herself and Russia aimed against the combined forces of England, France, and the United States. 'Herein,' exclaimed the German General von Seeckt, 'lies the point of Russia's closest rapprochement with Germany.'[7]

Hitler drove Stalin further towards the League of Nations by his crusade against the Communists. Along with the Jews, Communists were blamed for many of the evils afflicting Germany. But it was the belligerent nature of Hitler's speeches that worried Stalin: 'The German Government has shown that its only hope is military adventure. We must say to these Fascist buffoons that there is a limit to every kind of quixotism. We will not put up with these bad jokes any more.'[8] With a growing rift between Berlin and Moscow, Russia softened its attitude towards the 'imperialist League.' In a rather unusual move Soviet Foreign Commissar Litvinov supported the league's disarmament program: 'Never will we reject an organized international collaboration for strengthening peace. And we do not repudiate union with any existing or future organizations, if we have reason to believe them faithful to the cause of peace.'[9]

7 Christopher C. Robinson, 'Why the Soviets Look to the League,' *Saturday Night*, 25 Aug. 1934.
8 Ibid.   9 Ibid.

The Allies were pleased with Moscow's changed attitude towards the league. The sentiments of most Western nations could be summarized in the words of Winston Churchill, who asked the leaders of Europe to sacrifice their prejudices for the sake of world peace. 'Unless she [Soviet Russia],' he observed, 'formed a living part of Europe, unless she became a living partner of the League of Nations, there could be neither peace nor victory.'[10]

A more formal invitation, signed by thirty-five nations including Canada, asked the Soviet Union to enter the league. This request, dated 15 September 1934 and forwarded to the People's Commissariat for Foreign Affairs, suggested that in the interest of universal peace Russia join the league, 'bearing in mind that the mission of maintaining and organizing peace, which is the fundamental task of the League of Nations, demands the co-operation of all the countries of the world.'[11]

Despite the generous invitation of the thirty-five nations, Communist Russia could not be legally admitted into the world organization without a two-thirds supporting vote from the General Assembly. Such a vote could not be taken for granted, for such countries as Poland, Switzerland, Belgium, and Holland opposed Russia's entrance on the grounds that she continued to be the centre of subversive activities and world revolution. According to the Swiss delegate, Motta, Russia would, if she were admitted, use the league for subversive activities. Then he went on to state the reasons for his country's objection to Russia's entry into the league: '... in every sphere – religious, moral, social, political, economic ... this form of Communism is the most radical negation of the ideas by which we breathe and have our being. Today the common feeling of all patriotically and nationally minded Swiss is that the League is embarking on a hazardous undertaking. As we see it, it is venturing to wed water and fire.'[12]

France's foreign minister, Louis Barthou, was the spokesman for the pro-Russian group. He argued that his countrymen suffered greater financial losses from their Russian investments than any other group of nationals.

---

10 Winston Churchill quoted in the article: 'Why the u.s.s.r. Joined the League.'
11 Sessional Paper, no. 161, 15 Feb. 1934, Journal Section of the House of Commons, Ottawa.
12 Motta of Switzerland on the question of the entry of the ussr into the league, 17 Sept. 1934, *League of Nations*, Official Journal, Records of the Fifteenth Ordinary Session of the Assembly, Minutes of the Sixth Committee (Geneva, 1934), p. 19.

He, too, was opposed to religious persecution, but at the same time he maintained that the problems of the world could not be solved by reciprocating intolerance by more intolerance or by a policy of isolating Soviet Russia. His arguments were shared by the representatives of Great Britain, Poland, Czechoslovakia, Turkey, and Canada.[13]

O.D. Skelton, Canada's under-secretary of state for External Affairs, agreed that freedom was necessary for the success of the league, but at the same time argued that even a country which does not subscribe to democratic ideals could do much towards lessening the tensions between nations. He informed the assembly that Canada, too, had suffered from the subversive activities of the Third International. But he was quick to point out that 'the unreserved acceptance by the Soviet Union ... of the undertaking to observe all the international obligations of the covenant must necessarily involve a satisfactory attitude on this point in the future.' Finally he alluded to the fact that many Canadians had relatives or friends in Russia who continued to suffer. Through what better organization could these people be helped than through the League of Nations. Russia's entrance into this league would inevitably facilitate this aid.[14] Arguments similar to those used by Skelton helped to dispel some of the prejudice against the Soviet Union and aided her entry into the league on 18 September 1934.

The Soviet press hailed Russia's entry into the world organization as a definite step towards the preservation of peace. *Izvestia* (20 September 1934) prided itself that neither frenzied campaigns of such diehards as Hitler and Mussolini nor the sustained hostility of the Vatican was able to hinder her admittance. Re-emphasizing the original purpose of the league, the newspaper stated that 'the Soviet Union has entered the League of Nations precisely in order to support the powers who strive to maintain and consolidate peace.' *Pravda* (20 September 1934) considered the event of Soviet Russia's entry into the league a decisive victory for the proletariat whose representatives could work for the peace of mankind without, however, 'renouncing any feature whatever of this State, ... [but] remaining true to its aims and ideals.' A similar view was reiterated on 18 September by Litvinov in his address to the assembly when he stated that the Soviet

13 F.D. Walters, *A History of the League of Nations* (London, 1960), vol. 1, 584.
14 Skelton on the question of Russian entry into the league, *League of Nations*, p. 25.

Union did not intend to alter its ideology on becoming a member of the league. 'The Soviet Union,' declared Litvinov, 'is entering the League to-day as a representative of a new-social-economic system, not renouncing any of its special features and like the other states here represented, pre-serving intact its personality.'[15]

Many Canadian newspapers applauded Russia's entry into the League of Nations as a means of preserving peace in the world. The *Montreal Daily Star* (18 September 1934) dismissed the usual economic, political, and social objections to Russia's admission as groundless. Then it praised the British position with which Canada heartily agreed: 'The British Government to-day is actively in favour of Russia's admission to the League. This is not because the present Government has turned Com-munist or will welcome any more cordially the propaganda of the Third Internationale. It is because British statesmanship believes that under present conditions it is better to have Russia inside the League than outside of it. Canada clearly takes the same view.' The Montreal *Gazette* (18 Sep-tember 1934) also supported Russia's admission into the world organiza-tion, but on the ground that she would be in a position to exert 'great influence' in the 'East and in the West.' Similarly, the Hamilton *Herald* (20 September 1934) saw Russia's entry into the league as a means of controlling the belligerent Japanese in the Far East. On the other hand, the *Ottawa Citizen* (17 September 1934) held that Russia needed the league more than the league needed Russia. It emphasized the danger of Nazi aggression as one of the main reasons for the Soviet Union's desire to enter the league.

A rather cautious position was taken by the Regina *Leader Post* (17 September 1934) and the Montreal *La Presse* (20 September 1934). The Saskatchewan daily argued that Russia might have 'a greater peaceful intent than some nations that have been associated with the League, but now are no longer members of it.' Obviously Germany and Japan were the countries alluded to by the newspaper. Montreal's *La Presse* expressed scepticism concerning the role Russia would play in world affairs. It feared that European people would most likely be 'disenchanted' and 'disappointed' with Russia.

15 Litvinov's address to the assembly, 18 Sept. 1934, ibid., pp. 66–7.

In the Canadian House of Commons Russia's entry into the League of Nations was hailed as a move in the proper direction by some members of Parliament and criticized by others. Minister of Justice H. Guthrie voiced the opinion that it was 'far better for the peace of the world that countries like Russia ... should belong to the League and come under its influence than they should remain outside it.'[16] J.S. Woodsworth congratulated the government for its decision. Although he agreed with Bourassa's arguments for an autonomous foreign policy, he disagreed with his reasons for opposing Russia's entrance into the league.[17]

Henri Bourassa was critical of the government's policy towards Russia. After quoting copiously from addresses given at the General Assembly by such opponents of Soviet admittance to the international organization as Motta of Switzerland and De Valera of Ireland, he detailed the atrocities and the un-Christian behaviour for which Moscow was responsible. Then he went on to say: 'This is the nation we [Canada] have kissed on both cheeks, we, a Christian nation, we a nation whose government and policy repose on old traditions, on the liberty of conscience, on respect for the dignity of men and the divinity of God.'[18] Ian Mackenzie (Liberal – Vancouver Centre) also disagreed with Bennett's conciliatory attitude towards the Soviet Union, calling his change of policy towards Russia a species of hypocrisy.

Besides supporting the admission of Russia into the League of Nations, Canada, in 1936, fostered better understanding between herself and the Soviet Union by removing the embargo against Soviet-made goods and by signing a new trade agreement with Moscow. A Canadian industrialist who played a prominent role in promoting trade with Russia was F.H. Clergue, chairman of the Export Committee of the Canadian Car and Foundry Company. Urged by I. Boyeff, president of the Amtorg Trade Corporation, a Russian trade agency in New York, he insisted that the Canadian government remove the existing embargo on Soviet goods and that it exchange consular representatives with Moscow.[19] Such a move by

16 Canada, House of Commons, *Debates*, 1935, pp. 2302–3.
17 Ibid., pp. 2292, 2297.
18 Ibid., pp. 1184, 2290.
19 From F.H. Clergue to O.D. Skelton, 26 April 1935, Department of External Affairs, Public Records Centre, Ottawa, box 265346, file 555-29c.

the Canadian government would enable Canadian industrialists, particularly those associated with railway equipment, to secure a share of the commercial business.[20] Among the companies interested in this promising trade were Dominion Steel and Coal Corporation, Dominion Bridge Company, and Dominion Engineering Works.[21] If these firms did not take advantage of the promising market, then the United States would continue her trade with Moscow which had already reached the sum of $100,000,000 during each of the previous two years.[22]

But there were other advantages accruing from such a trade. Besides industrial products, Canada would be able to sell her surplus supplies of grain, cattle, and horses since the Soviet Union had a desperate need of livestock and grain. In turn, such trade could boost the Canadian economy, providing work for the unemployed and income for their families.[23]

The Canadian government took the position that there was nothing to prevent the Soviet government from entering into a trade agreement with Ottawa. The withdrawal of the Russian trade mission from Montreal in 1927 had no bearing on Canada's trade relations with Russia since it did not place any barrier on the extension of trade with Moscow.[24] If Moscow did want an exchange of diplomatic representatives then it was up to the Soviet government to initiate the procedure to bring this about.[25]

Such assurances from Ottawa did not please the Soviet trade and financial representatives. Both I. Boyeff and M. Sherover, president of the Soviet American Securities Corporation, wanted the Canadian government to remove the embargo on Soviet products and establish normal relations with Russia before embarking upon commercial negotiations.[26] The latter warned Clergue that any delay in establishing normal ties with Moscow would militate against the possibility of a flourishing trade. Clergue relayed this message to the government, adding other arguments of his own. He felt that the shipment of goods to Russia could be done during the spring, summer, and autumn seasons and even be extended to

20 Ibid., 31 May 1935.
21 Ibid., 26 April 1935.
22 Ibid., 23 Nov. 1935.
23 Ibid., 5 Dec. 1935.
24 Memorandum of Skelton, 1 May 1935, ibid.
25 From Skelton to Clergue, 6 June 1935, ibid.
26 Telegram from M. Sherover to Clergue, 9 Dec. 1935, ibid.

the winter if the Black and Baltic seas were used.[27] Moreover, the dispute between Russia and the United States over war loans,[28] as well as the restrictions placed by the Soviet government on German trade, could boost Canada's chances for increased commerce.[29] Clergue emphasized the importance of immediate action on the part of Canada if she wanted to take advantage of the given opportunities.

Prime Minister King was aware of these advantages, but he was preoccupied with other matters of government, particularly those associated with the Federal-Provincial Conference. However, in May 1936 he did ask Vincent Massey, Canada's high commissioner in London, to inform the Soviet ambassador to the United Kingdom that his government was willing to normalize trade relations with the Soviet Union by removing the embargo on Soviet goods. He also intimated that Ottawa would send one of the cabinet ministers to discuss trade with Russian representatives. While King was anxious to foster trade with the Soviet Union, he did not wish to conclude any trade agreement which would interfere with Canada's commerce with Great Britain.[30]

Massey discussed King's proposal with the Soviet ambassador, M. Maisky, on 8 June. During the course of the conversation Maisky enquired if Canada wished to exchange trade missions as she had done in 1925 and if these commercial relations would be followed shortly by an exchange of ambassadors. Massey pointed out that Canada had diplomatic relations with but three countries and did not see why trade agreements could not be negotiated without the exchange of ambassadors, trade missions, or consuls. Maisky agreed to communicate the Canadian government's views to Moscow and to notify Massey as soon as he received word from his government.[31]

27 From Clergue to Skelton, 16 Dec. 1935, ibid.
28 Ibid., 18 Dec. 1935.
29 From Colonel H.J. Mackie to King, 26 Dec. 1935, ibid.
30 W.L. Mackenzie King to Vincent Massey, 29 May 1936, King Papers, MG 26 J, PAC, Ottawa.
31 Massey to King, 10 June 1936, ibid.
    Following the lifting of the embargo by both Russia and Canada there was a sincere attempt made to increase trade. In December 1936, Stanislaus J. Sourvillo, assistant manager of the Department of the People's Commissariat for Foreign Trade of the USSR paid a visit to Ottawa where he discussed trade with W.E. Euler, minister of trade and commerce. Although these talks were frank, they failed to

On 18 June 1936 Maisky visited Vincent Massey, informing him that he had received word from his government 'to the effect that they would accept in principle the proposals that trade relations should be resumed between Canada and the USSR ... ,' and that Moscow welcomed a visit from a Canadian cabinet minister. Maisky, however, was quick to point out that since the Canadian government initiated the embargoes it was up to her to remove them first. Massey disagreed with this suggestion, arguing that the cancellation of the embargoes should be carried out simultaneously and preceded by discussion, possibly between a Canadian cabinet minister and the Soviet government. The matter was left in abeyance, awaiting informal talks between the Canadian minister and Soviet officials.[32]

During the summer of 1936, W.D. Euler, minister of trade and commerce, visited Russia, where he discussed with the Soviet government the restoration of normal conditions of international trade between his country and the Soviet Union. Upon his return to Canada, the Canadian government on 12 September 1936 cancelled the order-in-council of 27 February 1931, which placed an embargo on such Russian goods as coal, pulpwood, pulp, furs, timber, and asbestos.[33] The Soviet government reciprocated Canada's move by rescinding its decrees of 20 April 1931, which prohibited 'all importing organizations and trade representatives of the USSR to make any purchases of goods of Canadian origin as well as the chartering of vessels under the Canadian flag.'[34]

The official Russian news agency, *Tass*, on 14 September 1936 discussed the nature of the new trade agreement between Ottawa and Moscow. It

resolve many technical problems. For instance, Sourvillo was puzzled by the fact that it was necessary to buy Canadian metals in London or in New York rather than in Canada.

Another difficulty lay in the fact that foreign trade was the monopoly of the Soviet government which carried out commercial transactions through various importing organizations. Orders for merchandise obtainable on the North American continent were usually placed with the Amtorg Trading Corporation located in New York. Douglas S. Cole and his successors as Canadian trade commissioners at New York negotiated trade transactions for Canadian firms who wished to trade with Russia. D.S. Cole to L.D. Wilgress, 2 Dec. 1937, Department of Trade and Commerce, file no. 22320, Ottawa.

32 Massey to King, 19 June 1936, King Papers, MG 26J, PAC, Ottawa.
33 Sessional Paper, no. 179, 12 Sept. 1936, Order-in-Council PC 2354, Votes and Proceedings, Second Session of Parliament, Ottawa, 1937.
34 Acting People's commissar for foreign trade, ibid.

noted that Rhakhovski, chairman of the All-Union Coal Export and Import Corporation, commonly known as the *Soyuzugleexport*, intended to export some 250,000 metric tons of anthracite coal to Canada. It drew special attention to the fact that Russia would refrain from shipping coal to the Maritime provinces and would distribute its sales among as many exporters as could handle coal effectively.[35]

Generally speaking, the news of the recently negotiated trade agreement between Canada and Russia was welcomed by most members of Parliament, heads of firms, and newspapers. Prime Minister King considered the removal of the embargo on Russian goods as a positive measure taken by his government towards economic recovery.[36] This view was not shared by R.B. Bennett, the leader of the Opposition, who held that the increase of trade between Canada and the Soviet Union was but an inevitable feature of a general world economic recovery.[37] The former Conservative minister of trade and commerce, H.B. Hanson, maintained that the new Canadian-Russian trade agreement was a direct violation of the terms of the treaties signed by Canada at the Ottawa Imperial Economic Conference in 1932.[38]

In the opinion of M.W. Wilson, president and managing director of the Royal Bank of Canada, the reopened Russian markets would provide a stimulus to agriculture and manufacturing industries.[39] C.C. Thompson, assistant manager of the Prince Edward Island Potato Growers' Association, could not see any immediate result of the trade agreement.[40] However, the South Wales Coal Owners' Association estimated that some 6,000 to 7,000 miners would be seriously affected by Canada's decision to buy Russian rather than Welsh anthracite.[41]

Most Canadian newspapers favoured the lifting of the embargo on Soviet goods. In its editorial of 15 September 1936 the *Winnipeg Free Press* praised the Liberal party's policy of extending trade in all directions

35 Statement for the Press issued by W.D. Euler on 12 Sept. 1936.
36 Canada, House of Commons, *Debates*, 1937, p. 46.
37 Ibid., p. 29.
38 Montreal *Daily Star*, 14 Sept. 1936.
39 Ibid.
40 Ibid.
41 The Montreal *Gazette*, 1 Oct. 1936.

and of enlarging markets for such export products as dairy cows, horses, metals, and seed grain. Both the Montreal *Gazette* (14 September 1936) and the *Ottawa Journal* (14 September 1936) commended the minister of trade and commerce for negotiating a treaty which encouraged trade without discriminating against any group of people. The practice of 'dumping' was controlled by the terms of the agreement which limited the importation of coal to 250,000 metric tons a year, forbade the sale of coal to the Maritime provinces, and required that the sale price of coal be equal to that charged by other coal dealers.

The removal of the embargo on Soviet goods did not substantially increase the total import–export trade between Canada and Russia during the years 1936–9. The total imports in 1936 were valued at $279,441, those in 1935 at $265,039; exports for 1936 reached a low of $1,201 compared with $21,712 in 1935. However, by 1938 the import–export figures were $627,419 and $516,715 respectively.[42] Significantly, the imports for 1939 dropped to $412,339 whereas the exports increased to $699,285.[43]

The Canadian-Russian trade agreement had little effect on the attitude of many Canadians towards the Soviet system of government or towards the policies of the Comintern. Canadian businessmen and members of Parliament welcomed any increase of trade, be it with Communist or non-Communist states. Assuredly, it was not their purpose to encourage the spread of communism by finalizing a trade agreement with the Soviet Union.

42 *Canada Year Book* (Ottawa, 1939), p. 553.
43 Ibid., 1940, p. 507.

CHAPTER TWELVE

Conclusion

Canadian-Soviet relations can only be understood in the broad context of Canadian foreign policy during the period between World Wars I and II. Canada's participation in World War I created in Canadians a new sense of national identity. They became conscious of the fact that they belonged to a separate nation which had full powers to negotiate with foreign countries without being restricted by Great Britain. At the same time the majority of Canadians argued that Canada's independence in foreign affairs could be worked out within the framework of the British Commonwealth.

Even as a member of the British Commonwealth, Canada refused to become unduly involved in policies which might commit her to responsibilities in international affairs. This isolationist outlook was encouraged by the French-Canadian dread of foreign entanglements and by the desire of Canada to avoid any act which might offend the non-commitment policy of the United States. It was in this spirit of North American continentalism that Canada strove to amend article x of the Covenant of the League of Nations, which called for economic and military sanctions against any aggressor. Again, it was to support the United States that Prime Minister Meighen argued in 1921 against the renewal of the Anglo-Japanese alliance. To Meighen such a renewal would only create tensions between the Commonwealth and the United States.

The movement towards an independent foreign policy, commenced by Borden and Meighen, was continued by the Liberals under Mackenzie King. In 1922 King refused to heed the appeal of Lloyd George to come to the aid of Great Britain in the Chanak crisis because Canada was not consulted before the request was made. A year later, Canada for the first time signed an international treaty without the presence of British representatives when Ernest Lapointe, minister of justice in King's cabinet, signed the Halibut Treaty with the United States.

Further steps towards complete independence in foreign affairs were taken by the Dominions at the Imperial conferences of 1923 and 1926. The conference of 1923 stated that with respect to the negotiation, signature, and ratification of treaties in which only a part of the Empire was affected, each Dominion was given the right to negotiate these treaties itself and to arrange for their signature and ratification. Significantly, the Locarno Treaty in 1925 was negotiated by the United Kingdom government which secured the insertion of a clause that it was not binding upon any Dominion unless that Dominion agreed to its terms.

At the Imperial Conference of 1926, Great Britain and the Dominions agreed to the 'equal status' right whereby all of the Dominions and the United Kingdom were to be treated as 'autonomous communities within the British Empire equal in status and in no way subordinate one to another in any respect of their domestic or external affairs ...'[1] This conference also decided that in the future the governor general should represent the monarch only and that a high commissioner could represent the British government in commonwealth countries. A committee under the chairmanship of Ernest Lapointe studied the legal aspects of the 'equality status.' The recommendations of the committee were approved by the Imperial Conference of 1930 and a year later became the basis of the Statute of Westminster.

Despite the movement for an independent foreign policy, the Canadian government continued to use the diplomatic services of the British Foreign Office and to follow many of the suggestions of the British government. Canada decided to comply with the recommendation of the British government and delayed the restoration of trade with the Soviet Union until London regularized her relations with Moscow. Ottawa agreed to send some of the Canadian contributions to the victims of the Russian famine through the Russian Famine Fund administered by the British Red Cross. In 1924 Canada accorded *de jure* recognition to the Soviet Union after Great Britain had done so. Three years later she seemingly followed Great

1 CAR, 1926–7, p. 125.

Britain in severing relations with Soviet Russia. King, however, continued to insist that Canada's diplomatic recognition of the Soviet Union and Canada's break with her were carried out independently of Great Britain.

To a casual observer, it does appear that Canada continued to act like a colony in following the behests of Britain. But because she was a relatively small nation, Canada did not see the necessity of establishing new embassies, particularly when the British Foreign Office was willing to serve her needs. Even by 1929 Canada had ambassadors or high-ranking diplomatic representatives only in the United Kingdom, the United States, France, and Japan. One of the problems encountered by Canada in establishing new embassies was the recruitment of competent personnel. As a general rule, most of the members for her legations came from the staffs of Canadian universities.

From 1928 to 1935 Canada appeared to follow an almost completely autonomous course in her relations with the Soviet Union. In 1929 she refused to restore her quasi-diplomatic ties with Moscow even though Great Britain did so. Two years later Bennett placed an embargo on Russian commodities, some of which found ready markets in Britain. The Canadian prime minister even took the initiative of urging the British government to restrict her trade with the Soviet Union and to foster commerce with the members of the British Commonwealth instead.

The United States had only an indirect influence on Canadian-Soviet relations. In 1927 King singled out the United States as an example of a country which carried on flourishing trade with the Soviet Union even though diplomatic relations between Moscow and Washington were not regularized formally. Before placing an embargo on Russian goods Bennett ordered the study of the reasons for and the consequences of the American ban on Russian timber.

A decidedly disturbing influence on Canadian-Soviet relations was the policy of the Comintern and the activity of the Communist party of Canada. In the post-war years many Canadians viewed communism with horror and the Soviet Union with distrust. Doubtless the revolutionary directives sent to the Communist party of Canada encouraged Canadians to link riots, strikes, and disturbances in Canada with communism. Although the 'Red Scare' tended to be somewhat exaggerated, it did affect Canada's attitude towards the Russian famine of 1921–3, the resumption of trade in 1922, the *de jure* recognition, the diplomatic rupture, the failure to restore ties in 1929, and the imposition of the embargo in 1931.

Disturbing as the activities of the Comintern and the Canadian Communist party proved to be, Canada did enjoy a period of relatively successful commercial relations with the Soviet Union. As the sixth largest trading nation in the world, Canada welcomed every opportunity of finding new markets for her surplus agricultural and manufactured products. Even when King severed diplomatic ties with Moscow in 1927, he hoped that the action would not discourage trade through unofficial channels.

These relations were influenced also by labour, ethnic, and political pressure groups. In the early 1920s the Canadian government was urged by labour unions, business firms, and industrialists to renew trade with the Soviet Union. Similarly the deluge of letters reaching Bennett's desk from labour groups influenced him to impose an embargo on Russian merchandise.

Of the many ethnic groups, French Canadians more than any other group appeared to affect Canada's attitude towards the Soviet Union. They seemed to be consistently opposed to the Soviet regime, even to the extent of encouraging an embargo on Russian products on the grounds that the Soviet government aimed to destroy Christianity and democratic institutions. Surprisingly enough, few requests for a ban on Russian products or for a complete rupture with Moscow came from such ethnic groups as the Ukrainians whose home land was annexed by Soviet Russia during the civil war. Some of the ethnic groups voiced their opinions on foreign affairs through their members of Parliament.

Relatively few members of Parliament were vitally interested in Canadian-Soviet relations during the interwar period. Some Maritime and Prairie members of Parliament objected to Russia's dumping of anthracite in Canada and to flooding European wheat markets. Such Labour members as J.S. Woodsworth, W. Irvine, and A.A. Heaps were intrigued with the novelty of the socialist planning initiated in Soviet Russia and saw in her a vast market for Canadian products. Henri Bourassa frequently participated in parliamentary debates on the Soviet Union, not because he approved of communism, but because he objected to the Canadian government's 'slavish imitation' of Great Britain in dealing with Russia.

Thorough study of the interwar period does not reveal a clearly defined Canadian policy towards the Soviet Union. Many of Canada's decisions appeared to be made without any thought to a consistent, long-range policy. Sporadic pressure from economic or ethnic groups or the desire to placate the electorate of certain districts seemed to dictate the policy of the government at any given time. The only consistent characteristic trait of Canada's foreign policy was the attempt by Ottawa to avoid at all costs any issue that might disrupt national unity.

Bibliography

I / PRIMARY SOURCES

1 Manuscript Documents

Borden Papers, oc and RLB Series, MG 26, H I (a) Public Archives of Canada [PAC], Ottawa

CCF Records, MG 28 IV–1, vol. 157, PAC, Ottawa

Collected Papers of R.B. Bennett, U-150, box 252, U-151, box 254, Harriet Irving Library, University of New Brunswick, Fredericton, NB

Colonial Office, Dominion Office and Foreign Office Papers 371, Public Record Office, Chancerylane, London, England

Das Deutsche General Konsulat für Kanada, Library of Congress, Washington, DC

Department of Public Records and Archives, Toronto, Ontario, box 9, envelope 15, 'The Communist Party of Canada'

Department of External Affairs, PAC Record Centre, Ottawa

Department of Trade and Commerce, file no. 22320, Ottawa

Foster Papers, MG 27 II, D 7, vol. 44, PAC, Ottawa

Governor-General's Numerated Files, G 21, file no. 34691, vols. I (a) (b) 1911–24; 2 (a) (b) 1925–9; 1 (a) (b) 1910–39; PAC, Ottawa

E. Lapointe Papers, MG, 27, III, B, 10, vols. 16, 40, 42 (Notes, Memoranda, Petitions), PAC, Ottawa

Loring Christie Papers, MG 30, E 15, vol. B, PAC, Ottawa

Meighen Papers, MG 26, Series II, PAC, Ottawa

RCMP Records, HQ 761. Q.1, PAC, Ottawa

Rowell Papers, MG 27, II, D. 13, vol. 17, PAC, Ottawa

Sessional Papers, nos. 161, 179, 180, 442 (a) Journal Section of the House of Commons, Ottawa

Siberian Expeditionary Force, Army Records, folder 17, PAC Record Centre, Ottawa

W.L.M. King Papers, MG 26 (Memoranda and Correspondence), PAC, Ottawa

2 Printed Documents

Canadian Annual Review, Toronto, 1918–39.

Canada, House of Commons, *Debates*, 1923–39, Ottawa

– *Canada Yearbook*, 1939 and 1940, Ottawa

– *Labour Gazette*, 1937–9, Ottawa

– *Law Reports of the Supreme Court of Canada*, Ottawa, 1933

– *Votes and Proceedings*, Second Session of Parliament, Ottawa, 1937

Degras, Jane (ed.), *Soviet Documents on Foreign Affairs*, vol. 1 (Toronto, 1951)

– *The Communist International, 1919– 1943, Documents*, 2 vols. (Toronto, 1956–60)

Dokumenty Vneshnei Politiki, SSSR (Moscow, 1957–66)

Great Britain, House of Commons, *Debates*, 1927, London

– House of Lords, *Debates*, 1927, London

– *His Majesty's Stationery Office, Accounts and Parliamentary Papers*, cmd. papers, 1869, 1890, 3418, 3467

League of Nations, *Official Journal, Records of the Fifteenth Ordinary Session of the Assembly, Minutes of*

the Sixth Committee, Geneva, 1934
– *Records of the Third Assembly Plenary Meetings*, 2 vols., Geneva, 1922
Report of the Royal Commission (to investigate the facts relating to and the circumstances surrounding the communication, by public officials and other persons in positions of trust, of secret and confidential information to agents of a foreign power), Ottawa, 1946
Resolutions of the Sixteenth Congress of the Communist Party of Russia, June 1930. *Kommunisticheskaia Partiia Sovetskogo Soiuza* (Moscow, vol. III [7th ed.]) 1954
Statutes of Canada, 1919, 2 vols., Ottawa
'Trade Agreement between His Britannic Majesty's Government and the Government of the Russian Socialist Federal Soviet Republic,' *League of Nations Treaty Series*, 6 vols., Geneva
Woodward, E.L. (ed.), *Documents in British Foreign Policy, 1919–1934* (first, second and third series), London, 1946

II / SECONDARY SOURCES

Anderson, Violet (ed.), *World Currents and Canadian Course* (Toronto, 1937)
Armstrong, William E., *Canada and the League of Nations* (Geneva, 1930)
Balawyder, A., *The Winnipeg General Strike* (Toronto, 1967)
Baykov, Alexander, *The Development of the Soviet Economic System* (Cambridge, 1950)
Beloff, Max, *The Foreign Policy of Soviet Russia*, 2 vols. (New York, 1947–9)
Borden, Henry (ed.), *Robert Laird Borden: His Memoirs* (Toronto, 1938)
Borkenau, Franz, *World Communism: History of the Communist International* (New York, 1939)
Bradley, John, *Allied Intervention in Russia 1917–20* (London, 1968)
Brand, Carl F., *British Labour's Rise to Power: Eight Studies* (Stanford, 1941)
Browder, Robert Paul, *The Origins of*

Soviet-American Diplomacy (Princeton, 1953)
Buck, Tim, *30 Years, 1922–1952: The Story of the Communist Movement in Canada* (Toronto, 1952)
Budish, J.J. and Shipman, Samuel S., *Soviet Foreign Trade, Menace or Promise* (New York, 1931)
Carr, E.H., *A History of Soviet Russia: The Bolshevik Revolution, 1917–1923*, 3 vols. (London, 1950–53)
– *Socialism in One Country, 1924–1926*, 2 vols. (London, 1954)
Chamberlain, William H., *The Russian Revolution, 1917–1921* (New York, 1960)
Coates, W.P. and Zelda, R., *A History of Anglo-Soviet Relations* (London, 1943)
Cudahy, John, *Archangel: The American War with Russia* (Chicago, 1924)
Davies, Arthur, *Canada and Russia, Neighbours and Friends* (Toronto, 1944)
Davis, Kathryn W., *The Soviets at Geneva* (Geneva, 1934)
Dawson, Robert MacGregor, *The Development of Dominion Status* (Toronto, 1937)
– *William Lyon Mackenzie King: A Political Biography*, vol. 1: 1874–1923 (Toronto, 1958)
Eastman, S.M., *Canada at Geneva* (Toronto, 1946)
Eayrs, James, *The Art of the Possible: Government and Foreign Policy in Canada* (Toronto, 1961)
– *In Defence of Canada, from the Great War to the Great Depression* (Toronto, 1964)
– *Northern Approaches* (Toronto, 1961)
Epp, Frank, *Mennonite Exodus* (Altona, Manitoba, 1962)
Eudin, A.J. and Fisher, H.H., *Soviet Russia and the West* (Stanford, 1957)
Fisher, H.H., *The Famine in Soviet Russia, 1919–1923* (New York, 1927)
Fisher, Louis, *The Soviets in World Affairs, 1917–1929*, 2 vols. (Princeton, 1951)
Florinsky, Michael T., *World Revolution*

and the U.S.S.R. (New York, 1933)
George, David Lloyd, *War Memoirs of David Lloyd George* (Boston, 1933–7)
Glazebrook, G. de T., *A History of Canadian External Relations* (Toronto, 1950)
Goodman, Elliott R., *The Soviet Design for World State* (Columbia University Press, 1960)
Graham, Roger, *Arthur Meighen: And Fortune Fled*, vol. II (Toronto, 1963)
Havighurst, Alfred F., *Twentieth Century Britain* (Evanston, 1962)
Hoar, Victor and Reynolds, M., *The Mackenzie-Papineau Battalion* (Toronto, 1969)
Imperial Economic Conference, 1932, Report of the Conference (Ottawa, 1932)
Imperial Economic Conference, 1932, Report of the Conference, suppl. vol. (Ottawa, 1932)
Jasny, Naum, *Soviet Industrialization, 1928–1952* (Chicago, 1961)
Keenleyside, H., Eayrs, James, *et al.*, *The Growth of Canadian Policies in External Affairs* (Toronto, 1960)
Keith, Arthur Berriedale, *The Sovereignty of the British Dominions* (London, 1929)
Kirkconnell, Watson, *Seven Pillars of Freedom* (Toronto, 1944)
Lederer, I.J. (ed.), *Russian Foreign Policy* (New Haven, 1962)
Lenin, V.I., *Sochineniia*, 35 vols. (Leningrad, 1949)
Logan, H.A., *Trade Unions in Canada* (Toronto, 1948)
Lokshin, E.I., *Ocherki Istorii Promyshlennosti, SSSR, 1917–1940* (Moscow, 1952)
Lovestone, Jay, *Soviet Foreign Policy and the World Revolution* (New York, 1935)
Lower, A.R., *Colony to Nation* (Toronto, 1946)
Ludendorff, Erich von, *Ludendorff's Own Story*, vol. II (New York, 1929)
Lyman, R.W., *The First Labour Government 1924* (London, 1957)

MacKay, R.A. and Rogers, E.B., *Canada Looks Abroad* (Toronto, 1938)
Manning, C.A., *The Siberian Fiasco* (New York, 1952)
Mansergh, Nicholas, *Survey of British Commonwealth Affairs: Problems of External Policy, 1931–1939* (London, 1952)
Masters, D.C., *The Winnipeg General Strike* (Toronto, 1950)
McInnis, F., *Canada, A Political and Social History* (Toronto, 1963)
McNaught, K., *A Prophet in Politics* (Toronto, 1963)
Mourin, Maxime, *Histoire des Grandes Puissances, 1919–1947* (Paris, 1947)
Nollau, Günther, *International Communism and World Revolution* (London, 1961)
Neatby, H. Blair, *William Lyon Mackenzie King* (Toronto, 1963)
Nicolson, Harold, *King George VI: His Life and Reign* (London, 1953)
North, Robert P., *Soviet Russia in World Politics* (New York, 1963)
Palmer, E.H., *Consultation and Co-operation in the British Commonwealth* (Oxford, 1934)
Popov, V.I., *Diplomaticheskie Otnosheniia Mezhdu SSSR i Anglii, 1929–1939* (Moscow, 1965)
Potemkin, Vladimir G., *Istoriia Diplomatii*, 2 vols. (Moscow, 1941–5)
Randall, Francis B., *Stalin's Russia* (Toronto, 1965)
Rodney, William, *Soldiers of the International – A History of the Communist Party of Canada, 1919–1929* (Toronto, 1968)
Rubenstein, Alvin Z., *The Foreign Policy of the Soviet Union* (New York, 1960)
Schapiro, Leonard, *The Communist Party of the Soviet Union* (New York, 1959)
Schwartz, Harry, *Russia's Soviet Economy*, 2nd ed. (New York, 1954)
A Short History of the U.S.S.R., vol. II (Moscow, Academy of Sciences of the USSR, 1965)
Skilling, H.G., *Canadian Representation*

Abroad: From Agency to Embassy
(Toronto, 1946)

Soward, F.H., Parkinson, J.F., Mackenzie,
N.A.M., and MacDermot, T.W.L.,
*Canada in World Affairs – The Pre-
War Years* (Toronto, 1941)

Stalin, Joseph, *Problems of Leninism*, 32
vols. (New York, 1934)

Stefansson, V., *The Adventure of Wrangel
Island* (New York, 1925)

Strakhovsky, Leonid I., *The Origins of
American Intervention in North Russia
(1918)* (Princeton, 1932)

Swettenham, John, *Allied Intervention in
Russia, 1918–1919, and Part Played by
Canada* (Toronto, 1967)

Thomas, Hugh, *The Spanish Civil War*
(London, 1961)

Thompson, John M., *Russia, Bolshevism,
and the Versailles Peace* (Princeton,
1966)

Toynbee, Arnold J., *Survey of International Affairs, 1927* (London, 1929)

Trukhanovskii, Vladimir G., *Istoria
Mezhdunarodnykh Otnoshenii i
Vneshnei Politiki SSSR*, 3 vols.
(Moscow, 1963)

Ulam, Adam, *The New Face of Soviet
Totalitarianism* (Cambridge, 1963)

Ullman, Richard H., *Anglo–Soviet
Relations, 1917–21* (Princeton, 1961)

Underhill, Frank H., *The British Commonwealth* (Durham, 1956)

Unterberger, Betty M., *America's
Siberian Expedition, 1918–1920*
(Durham, 1956)

*Vneshnaia Politika Anglii Na Peruom
Etapem Obshchego Krizisa Kapi-
talisma, 1918–1939* (Moscow, 1962)

Vygodskii, Semenivlevich, *Vneshniaia
Politika SSSR, 1924–1929* (Moscow,
1963)

Walters, F.P., *A History of the League of
Nations*, 2 vols. (London, 1960)

Wilgress, Dana, *Dana Wilgress Memoirs*
(Toronto, 1967)

Yuzyk, P., *The Ukrainians in Manitoba*
(Toronto, 1953)

III / ARTICLES,
MONOGRAPHS AND THESES

Adams R., 'Mackenzie King and the
Soviet Trade Mission to Canada
1924–27' (unpublished MA thesis,
Ottawa University, 1971)

Allan, W.B., 'The Shadow of Russia,'
*Journal of the Canadian Bankers'
Association*, vol. XXXVIII, 1930–1

Baker, White J., 'The Soviet Five Year
Plan,' *National Review*, vol. 96, 1931

Balawyder, A., 'Canada and the Famine
in Soviet Russia and the Ukraine
(1921–1928),' *New Review*, vol. IV,
no. 4, 1964

Barnes, Samuel Henry, 'The Ideologies
and Policies of Canadian Labor
Organization' (unpublished PH D thesis,
Duke University, 1951)

Beattie, Steuart, 'Canadian Intervention
in Russia, 1918–1919' (unpublished
MA thesis, McGill University, 1957)

Bechofer, C.E., 'Starving Russia and the
Nansen Scheme,' *New Statesman*, vol.
XVIII, 1921

'The C.C.F. and the Communists,'
Canadian Forum, vol. XXIII, 1943–44

Chamberlain, William Henry, 'Communist
Basic Tactics: Rule or Ruin,' *Russian
Review*, vol. 20, 1961

Chernomurskii, M.N., 'Sovetskaia
Promyshelnnost v peruye gody NEPA,'
Voprosy Istorii, no. 2, 1965

Chicherin, G., 'Lenin i Vneshnaia
Politika,' *Voprosy Istorii*, no. 3, 1967

'Counterfeit Canadian Bank Notes,'
Russian Review, vol. III, 1925

Dewar, George A.B., 'Britain's Recognition of Soviet Russia,' *Foreign Affairs*,
vol. III, 1924

Diubaldo, Richard J., 'Wrangling over
Wrangel Island,' *Canadian Historical
Review*, vol. XLVII, 1967

'The Duel at Geneva,' *New Statesman*,
vol. 17, 1922

Farley, Miriam S., 'Russia Warms to the
League,' *Current History*, vol. 40, 1934

Farrell, Robert B., 'Planning and Control of Canadian Foreign Policy' (unpublished PH D thesis, Harvard University, 1952)

Fisher, H.A.L., 'Mr. Lloyd George's Foreign Policy,' Foreign Affairs, vol. I, 1923

Fisher, Ruth, 'Background of the New Economic Policy,' Russian Review, vol. 7, 1948

Florinsky, Michael, 'Soviet Foreign Policy,' Slavonic Review, vol. XII, 1934

Forsey, E.A., 'The Padlock – New Style,' Canadian Forum, vol. XVIII, no. 28, March 1939

Fry, Michael, 'Britain, the Allies and the Problem of Russia, 1918–1919,' Canadian Journal of History, vol. II, no. 2, 1968

'Great Britain: Economy and Unemployment,' Round Table, vol. XXI, London, 1931

Historicus, 'Stalin on Revolution,' Foreign Affairs, vol. 27, 1929

Hopper, Bruce C., 'Narkomindel and Comintern: Instruments of World Revolution,' Foreign Affairs, vol. XIX, 1941

Houghton, N.D. 'Policy of the U.S.A. and other Nations with Respect to the Recognition of the Russian Soviet Government, 1917–1929,' Documents of the American Association for International Conciliation, New York, 1929

'Insurgent Labour in Canada,' New Statesman, vol. 13, 1919

Jebb, Richard, 'Imperial Aspects of Foreign Policy,' Empire Review, 1924

Joynt, Carey B., 'Canadian Foreign Policy 1919–1939' (unpublished PH D thesis, Clark University, 1957)

Kaneva, O.D., 'Disposal of Russian Famine Funds,' Russian Review, vol. I, 1923

Keith, A.B., 'Notes on Imperial Constitutional Law,' Journal of Comparative Legislation, vol. VII, 1925

Krasilnikov, A.N. 'Iz Istorii Antisovetskoi Politiki Praviashchikh Kru-ov Anglii (1929–32),' Voprosy Istorii, no. 4, 1958

'Labour Organizations in Canada,' Department of Labour, Ottawa, 1926

Lashchenko, P.I., 'Narodnoe Khoziaistvo SSSR v Vostanovitel'ny Period (1921–5),' Voprosy Istorii, no. 7, 1953

Lefeaux, W.W., Winnipeg, London, Moscow – A Study of Bolshevism, Winnipeg, 1921

Lobonov-Rostovsky, A., 'Anglo-Russian Relations through the Centuries,' Russian Review, vol. 7, 1948

Mackenzie, Norman, 'Canadian Policy in the Far East,' Queen's Quarterly, vol. 40, 1933

Maisky, I.M., 'Anglo–Sovetskoe turgovoe Soglashenie, 1921,' Voprosy Istorii, no. 5, 1957

Mead, F.J., 'Communism in Canada,' Royal Canadian Mounted Police Quarterly, July 1935

Molotov's Address to the Sixth Congress of Soviets, Soviet Union Review, vol. IX, 1931

Morrison, A.E., 'R.B. Bennett and the Imperial Preferential Trade Agreement 1932' (unpublished MA thesis, University of New Brunswick, 1966)

'The New Europe,' Round Table, vol. 25, 1934–5

Osiakovski, S.F., 'Some Aspects of Soviet Foreign Trade,' Political Quarterly, vol. 11, 1940

Oudendyka, William J., 'Stalin's New Policy,' Fortnightly Review, vol. 152, 1939

Pendle, George, 'Commonsense about Russia,' Review of the River Plate, reprinted in International Digest, Nov. 1931

Porter, John, 'The Struggle Against the Right Danger in the Communist Party of Canada – The Dominion Problem,' Communist International, vol. VI, no. 23, London, 1929

Radek, Karl, 'The Bases of Soviet Foreign

Policy,' *Foreign Affairs*, vol. 12, Jan. 1934

Reid, Escott, 'Canada and the Threat of War: A Discussion of Mr. Mackenzie King's Foreign Policy,' *Toronto Quarterly*, vol. vi, Jan. 1937

– 'Mr. Mackenzie King's Foreign Policy, 1935–6,' *Canadian Journal of Economics and Political Science*, vol. iii, Feb. 1937

'The Recognition of the Soviet Government,' *Spectator*, vol. 132, 1924

Report of Albert Thomas, *Canadian Congress Journal*, Ottawa, 1931

Robin, M., 'Radical Politics and Organized Labour in Canada, 1880–1930 (unpublished ph d thesis, University of Toronto)

Robinson, Christopher C., 'Why the Soviets Look to the League,' *Saturday Night*, Aug. 25, 1934

Sandwell, B.K. 'The Russo-Canadian Holy War,' *Canadian Forum*, vol. xi, 1930–1

Scheffer, Paul, 'American Recognition of Russia: What it would mean to Europe,' *Foreign Affairs*, vol. ix, 1930

Schlieper, H.C., 'The Historical Background of the Soviet Constitution' (unpublished ma thesis, McGill University, 1963)

Scott, F.R. 'The Communists, Senators, and All That,' *Canadian Forum*, vol. xii, Jan. 1932

– 'The Permanent Bases of Canadian Foreign Policy,' *Foreign Affairs*, vol. x, July 1932

– 'The Trial of the Toronto Communists,' *Queen's Quarterly*, vol. 37, 1932

Scroggs, W.O., 'Russia and World Trade,' *Foreign Affairs*, vol. xii, 1933

Sellen, Robert W., 'The British Intervention in Russia, 1917–1920,' *Dalhousie Review*, vol. 40, 1960–1

Shane, Theodore K., 'British Reaction to the Soviet Union, 1924–1929 – A Study of Policy and Public Opinion' (unpublished ph d thesis, Indiana University, 1952)

Siegfried, André, 'Canada's Foreign Policy,' *Fortnightly*, vol. 146, 1936

Smith, Gaddis, 'Canada and the Siberian Intervention, 1918–1919,' *American Historical Review*, vol. lxiv, 1959

'The Sources of Soviet Conduct,' *Foreign Affairs*, vol. 25, 1947

Soward, F.H., 'Sir Robert Borden and Canada's External Policy, 1911–1920,' *Report of the Canadian Historical Association*, 1941

Stefansson, V., 'The History and Importance of Wrangel Island,' *Spectator*, 9 June 1923

Stevenson, J.A. 'Sectional Factors in Canadian Foreign Policy,' *Foreign Affairs*, vol. 16, 1938

Swift, Michael David, 'R.B. Bennett and the Depression, 1930–1935' (unpublished ma thesis, University of New Brunswick, Fredericton, 1964)

Triska, Jan F., 'A Model for Study of Soviet Foreign Policy,' *American Political Science Review*, vol. lii, 1958

Trukhanovskii, V.G., 'K Voproso ob Osobennostiakh Ekonomicheskogo Razvitiia v 1924–1929 godakh,' *Voprosy Istorii*, no. 3, 1962

Tucker, Robert C., 'Stalin and the Uses of Psychology,' *World Politics*, vol. viii, July 1956

Ulam, Adam B., 'Soviet Ideology and Soviet Foreign Policy,' *World Politics*, vol. ii, 1959

Underhill, Frank H., 'Parliament and Foreign Policy,' *Canadian Forum*, vol. xvi, June 1936

U.S. House of Representatives, Committee on Foreign Affairs, *The Strategy and Tactics of World Communism*, 80th Congress, 2nd session, Washington, 1948

Wasserman, W.S., 'Russia as a World Factor,' *L'Europe Nouvelle*, reprinted in *International Digest*, May 1931

Why the U.S.S.R. Joined the League, New Fabian Research Bureau, New York, 1934

Wilgress, Dana, 'From Siberia to Kuibyshev: Reflections on Russia, 1919–1943,' *International Journal*,

vol. XXII, no. 3, 364–75
'The Winnipeg Strike,' *Labour Gazette,*
vol. 19, 1919

Zinner, Paul E., 'Ideological Bases of
Soviet Foreign Policy,' *World Politics,*
vol. IV, July 1952

IV / NEWSPAPERS

Affiliation

Border Cities' Star, Windsor	Independent
Catholic Register, Toronto	Catholic
Calgary Daily Herald	Independent
Chronicle-Telegraph, Quebec	Independent Liberal
Citizen, Winnipeg	Business
Clarion, Toronto	Communist
Communist 1921, vol. 1, no. 1, Toronto	Communist
Le Droit, Ottawa	Independent
Financial Post, Toronto	Financial
Gazette, Montreal	Independent Conservative
Globe, Toronto	Independent Liberal
Halifax Chronicle	Liberal
Hamilton Spectator	Independent Conservative
Herald, Lethbridge	Independent
Herald, Halifax	Independent Conservative
Izvestia, Moscow	Communist
Labor Leader, Toronto	Labour
Leader Post, Regina	Liberal
Mail and Empire, Toronto	Conservative
Manchester Guardian	Independent
Manitoba Free Press, Winnipeg	Independent Liberal
Montreal Daily Star	Independent
Morning Chronicle, Halifax	Independent
New York Times	Independent
Ottawa Citizen	Independent
Ottawa Morning Journal	Independent Conservative
Ottawa Journal	Independent Conservative
Payroll, Winnipeg	Commercial
Pravda, Moscow	Communist
La Presse, Montreal	Independent
Standard, Montreal	Independent
Star, Regina	Independent
Star, Toronto	Independent
Times, London	National and Independent
Tribune, Winnipeg	Independent
Vancouver Sunday Province	Independent
Victoria Daily Times	Independent Liberal
Western Labour News, Winnipeg	Labour
Worker, Toronto	Communist

Index

Adshead, H.B.: independence of Canada and rupture with Russia 102

Aird, Sir John: Soviet forgeries of Canadian bank notes 89

Alexander Furs Ltd.: annoyed by practice of some Canadians travelling south for furs 149–50

aluminum–oil barter deal: Bennett denies giving Aluminum Company of Canada authorization for 156; Danish tanker and 156; Bennett permits tanker to unload oil 158; influence on Canadian-Soviet cattle deal 163

American Relief Administration and Russian famine 48–9

Amery, L.S.: on forgeries of Canadian notes 90; on General Strike in Great Britain 93

Amtorg (the Russian trade delegation in New York) 163; and Canadian-Soviet cattle deal 163; difficulties encountered by 163

Anglo-Soviet Trade Agreement: preliminary discussions 36; difficulties encountered 37; signing of 37; pressure on Canada to adhere to 38; favoured by Meighen 38; obstacles to trade and postal and telegraphic correspondence 40; terms special to Canada 41; extent of immunity 42; recognition of claims 42–3; violation of 42, 59, 60, 92, 98, 101; and forging of passports 172

anti-Christian: literature destined for Russian agency in Montreal 83; Aaroo Vaaro, committed to jail for spreading seditious, anti-Christian propaganda 115; embargo on Russia because her government is 143; aiding the sale of cattle would encourage Russia to be 188

Archangel: British strengthen port of 7; Canadian forces at 7; to be withdrawn from 19–20; convict labour at 134

Arcos raid: search of Arcos building 93–4; names of high ranking Communists found as result of the 94; views of British members of parliament on the finding in 94–5; Canadian Government views on findings of 96; Gerus' explanation of 96; the effect on Canadian trade of 99–100; Sinn Fein Club's view of 101; rupture of relations between London and Moscow because of 94

Article XXI of Ottawa Agreement 1932: terms of 155; violation of 158–9; maintenance of 161

Atkinson, M.: representative of the British Appeal for Russian Famine Relief 53

Baldwin, Stanley: expresses thanks to Canada for her decision to sever relations with Russia 98; disagrees with Bennett on Imperial preferential policy 152

Balfour, Lord, A.J.: and Russian famine aid 48

Barnard, Sir Frank: describes the unrest in British Columbia to Borden 28; suggests appearance of cruiser in Vancouver 28

Bennett, R.B.: election promises of 118–19; prepared to invoke dumping clauses of Customs Act 130; asks officials of Department of External Affairs to investigate Soviet dumping practices 131; basis of the embargo on Soviet products 135; requested to place ban on Soviet products 136; ban for political reasons 136; ban would be